LANGUAGE and THEME

LANGUAGE
and
THEME

Essays on African Literature

Emmanuel N. Obiechina

HOWARD UNIVERSITY PRESS
Washington, D.C.
1990

Printed in the United States of America
This book is printed on acid-free paper.

Library of Congress Cataloging in Publication Data

Language and Theme.

Obiechina, Emmanuel N., 1933–
    Language and theme : essays on African literature / Emmanuel N. Obiechina.
        p. cm.
    Includes bibliographical references.
    ISBN 0-88258-045-0 : $26.95.—ISBN 0-88258-064-7 (pbk.) : $14.95
    1. African literature (English)—History and criticism.   2. Oral tradition—Africa.   I. Title.
    PR9340.O25 1990
    820.9'896—dc20   90-34189
                                                                                CIP

CONTENTS

PREFACE

THESE ESSAYS have appeared at various times during the past sixteen years. Taken together, however, they constitute a view of African literature unified by certain central concerns of the works studied and the impulses that gave rise to them. The African writers' fidelity to experience, history, and culture has itself provided a unifying principle from which critics could, and do, distill the themes, ideas, and preoccupations of the works.

The texts used in these essays were themselves published in the last thirty years. I have tried to extract from them those insights which I consider central to African literature, insights that include the efforts by Africans to come to terms with the physical, emotional and psychic problems of their environment. The social, cultural, and historical background of the works is constantly emphasized because the authors' themes and their reflected attitudes are centered on them. The coexistence of oral and literary traditions as a conditioning factor of life and experience is also stressed in the essays; in fact, it is so important that it is given thematic status in a number of essays.

Interest in themes inevitably draws attention to the language in which those themes are expressed. *Language* is used generically here to encompass those technical and stylistic devices adopted by the authors to further their creative purposes. It should be remarked, however, that no detailed literary criticism of the works has been intended or undertaken. Nevertheless, enough incidental criticism is included to sustain a balance between the discussion of the themes and the modes of exploring them.

One problem remains. It is the problem that every critic of African literature has to face: the number of texts in African literature is continually growing. Its preoccupations are also growing to match the pressures of a rapidly changing world. Every critic in the field of this literature has, of necessity, to make certain choices and to attain his critical objectives within the limitations of those choices. My own approach here has been to select my texts from the area of African writing best known to me. I have not attempted to include all the works that treat any of the themes discussed. However, it would be right to say that, within the limits of this choice, the texts selected adequately reveal some of the main themes that hold a fascination for and are of value to readers of African writing.

E. N. O.

vii

ACKNOWLEDGMENTS

Grateful acknowledgments are made to the following:

Présence Africaine for permission to reprint "The Growth of Written Literature in English-Speaking West Africa," first published in *Présence Africaine* (Paris) 66 (2d Quarterly 1968); and "Amos Tutuola and the Oral Tradition" from *Présence Africaine* 65 (1st Quarterly 1968).

The Conch for permission to reprint "The Problem of Language in African Writing: An Example of the Novel" from *The Conch* (Spring 1974).

Ufahamu for permission to reprint "Perceptions of Colonialism in West African Writing" from *Ufahamu* 1 (Spring 1974).

C. O. D. Ekwensi, ed., for permission to reprint parts of "Politics in Select African Novels" from the *Festac Anthology of Nigeria: New Writing* (Lagos, 1977).

Institut Für Ethnologie Und Afrika-Studien, Universität Mainz, for permission to reprint "Post-Independence Disillusionment in Three African Novels," from *Neo-African Literature and Culture: Essays in Memory of Janheinz Jahn* (Mainz, West Germany, 1976).

Okike for permission to reprint from "The Theme of Victimization in Select African Plays and Novels," *Okike: An African Journal of New Writing* 3 (September 1972); and "Art and Artifice in Okara's *The Voice*" from *Okike: An African Journal of New Writing* 1, 3 (1973).

Nsukka Environment for permission to reprint "Literature—Traditional and Modern—in the Nsukka Environment" from *Nsukka Environment* (1978).

Fourth Dimension Publishing Co. Ltd. for permission to reprint "Christopher Okigbo: Poet of Destiny" from *Christopher Okigbo: Poet of Destiny* (Enugu: 1980).

Cambridge University Press for permission to reprint pages 108–109 and 171–74 from *Culture, Tradition and Society in the West African Novel* (Cambridge, 1975).

CHAPTER 1

The Growth of Written Literature in English-Speaking West Africa

THE GROWTH of written literature in West Africa is a process that is, often erroneously, associated solely with the introduction of Western-oriented literacy into West Africa. The truth is that the Arabic script had already been in existence several centuries before the arrival of the Roman script in West Africa. Furthermore, there were, in parts of West Africa, certain "embryonic" scripts, one of which, the Nsibidi, is reputed to be one of the very few original world scripts.[1] However, the introduction of the Western script, with its more democratic application and greater facility for diffusion into West Africa, made the spread of popular literacy and the consequent growth of written literature possible. The other forms of writing were either too restrictive or too underdeveloped to have the same kind of literary impact.

Nevertheless, no discussion on the growth of written literature in West Africa can be regarded as full if we completely ignore the place of Arabic in the evolution of the literary tradition in West Africa, or the place of the "embryonic" scripts in the history of writing in this region. I shall start with the underdeveloped and the Arabic scripts before proceeding to the main subject, which is the growth of written literature in West Africa as a result of the introduction of Western-oriented literacy.

The tendency for groups of human beings to evolve forms of graphic communication that would eliminate verbal exchange must be as old as the human desire to share secret thoughts and intelligences among distinct groups by converting them into esoteric symbols and secret signs. This tendency gave rise in West Africa to numerous local "scripts" that amounted to local devices by groups of people, sometimes cult groups, through which those who shared their secret symbols communicated among themselves on certain issues about which they wished to keep the generality of the people ignorant. This phenomenon was quite widespread in West Africa.

David Diringer devotes a whole section of his book, *The Alphabet*, to these "scripts" embodying secret codes and symbols among restricted groups of West Africans.[2] They are called "ideographic" scripts because their symbols do not represent sounds or letters, as with the alphabetic scripts, but ideas. Mention should also be made, in passing, of the "Aroko" or the symbolic epistles of the Yorubas that show how, by tying together different numbers of cowrie shells in different well-established ways, the users of the "Aroko" system could convey different messages to one another. The same passing mention will be made of the ideographs of the Ewe people that were used by those initiated into the system to represent "symbolic" proverbs. These examples are taken at random, but there is no doubt whatever that the tendency by small sections of society to evolve secret means of communication must have been widespread in West Africa, especially nearer the coast, where for a long time there was no widely diffused writing. Those whose childhood was spent in rural Igbo areas will attest to there being some kind of meaning in the chalk marks drawn by elders on the floor when they visit one another in the mornings. Another elder coming into a place later in the day can always say, looking at these markings, that so-and-so has been there.

These "scripts" remained at best esoteric and strictly limited in application and were often shrouded in mystery. Of course, this in itself is not surprising. Early efforts at writing anywhere in antiquity had often been associated with secret cults and mysterious (including religious) activities. "Among the Sumerians and Akkadians" according to Goody and Watt, "writing was the pursuit of scribes and preserved as a mystery, a secret treasure."[3] The Anglo-Saxon writing, Runes, receives its name from *rūna*, a Gothic word for mystery, secret.[4]

It is not possible, of course, to particularize the comparison of the Aroko or the Ewe scripts with the Runes or the ancient Near Eastern scripts (because they represented varied stages of development), but we can at least draw attention to the quality of mysteriousness and secrecy that surrounded them. The West African "scripts" have not reached the stage in which they could be regarded as anything more than mere pictorial representations of ideas.

The Nsibidi is the only truly ideographic script in West Africa: that is, the only system of conventionalized signs used to represent definite ideas. Some of its ideas could be generally interpreted while most of the others are only known to the members of the Nsibidi secret society into which men were and still are being initiated after a period of preparation.[5] It is a largely amatory writing but it is also used to give public notices or private warnings. The messages are cut or painted on split palm stems: David Diringer has an extract of the Nsibidi writing as well as its corresponding translation in *The Alphabet*.[6] Elphinstone Dayrell has also recorded some Nsibidi writing in an article entitled "Further Notes on Nsibidi Signs, from the Ikem District, Southern Nigeria."[7]

The origin of Nsibidi is uncertain, but it is considered by Talbot, a knowledgeable administrator, anthropologist, and author of *The Peoples of Southern Nigeria*, to be "of considerable antiquity." Its existence was discovered independently by two District Commissioners in Calabar—T. D. Maxwell in 1904 and J. K. Macgregor in 1905—and was thought to have been invented by the Uguakima people, an Igbo group in the Cross River area of Nigeria. The Ekoi of the Cross River also claim the credit for having invented it. The precise truth will be hard to establish because of the mixed nature of the Cross River area. Jones and Forde have clearly shown in their ethnographic study, *The Ibo and Ibibio-Speaking Peoples of South-Eastern Nigeria,* that this region is inhabited by mixed peoples, among whom are Igbo, Ekoi, and Efik-Ibibio groups.

The importance of Nsibidi, as Moorhouse has rightly commented, is that it reached a stage of development from which other "primitive" scripts matured into full-fledged writing systems. Who knows whether its further development, had it not been inhibited by the introduction of Western writing, would not, in the fullness of time, have become a widely diffused system of writing?

There are other West African scripts, the invention of which has been stimulated by the introduction of the Western or Arabic script, or both. Here, what is often copied is not the particular system of writing but the idea of writing. This is a phenomenon that sociologists call *idea-diffusion* or *stimulus diffusion*. This is said by Diringer to have given rise to the Celtic picture writing known as Oghams, and by G. P. Murdock as accounting for the script invented by the Cherokee Indian chief, Sequoyah, for the use of his subjects.[8]

The best example of the idea-diffusion script in West Africa is the Bamum script that was invented by a Cameroonian chieftain, Njoya. It is conjectured that the idea of inventing a system of writing occurred to him after he had considered the numerous public and private uses to which such invention could be put. He could, for example, use it to communicate with his subordinate chiefs while evading the colonial government's censorship. An additional incentive must have been a desire to extend his people's cultural repertoire by adding a system of writing to it. Both motives must obviously have been greatly reinforced and sustained by a third: personal ambition to become an inventor. Whatever his real motive may have been is not very important. What is important is that Chief Njoya, borrowing the idea of writing from users of both the Western and the Arabic scripts within the former German Cameroons, developed his own artificial and original script.

Njoya's script began as a combination of pictographic and ideographic writing with one thousand symbols, but was periodically reformed and simplified until it was reduced to only seventy signs in 1918 and became almost phonetic. The script was taught in the local schools and employed by the Bamums as the official script of their state. When Njoya died in 1932, his invention survived him; but since then has been dying out and is being replaced by the Western script.

The other idea-diffusion scripts in West Africa are the Vai script, invented by a chief of the Vai in Liberia,[9] and the Oberi Okaime script, which was invented in Ikpa, near Kyere, in the Itu Division of Calabar Province. The latter is closely modeled on the Western script even though the experts have not been able to establish direct identifications. The view was formerly held that it was just mirror writing, but this has been convincingly refuted by R. F. G. Adams in "Oberi Okaime: A New African Language and Script."[10]

All these scripts—the Nsibidi, the Bamum, the Vai, and the Oberi Okaime—could be regarded as protoliterate systems, in the sense in which Kramer uses the term to describe the Sumerian phase of writing in Lower Mesopotamia when writing was first invented, rather than the sense in which Goody and Watt use it when referring to the fully developed Sumerian, Egyptian, or Chinese systems, which, though restricted to a relatively small proportion of the total population, of an elite literati, were already being utilized for religious, administrative, and technological purposes.[11] The Bamum, Nsibidi, and Vai scripts obviously showed considerable promise of further development, but their rather local and limited application meant that they were doomed in the face of the advancing cosmopolitan Western and Arabic scripts. They could be compared to the Germanic Runes and the Celtic Oghams, which were also restricted scripts, the former used mainly in Scandinavia, Germany, and Britain and the latter in the Celtic areas of Britain, and which disappeared with the introduction and diffusion of the Roman script in the areas in which both scripts had previously been in use.[12]

Neither the West African nor the European scripts are known to have been used extensively in communication, nor were they used to create written literature. Their comparison cannot, of course, be sustained all the way. Both the Runes and the Oghams are alphabetic scripts, while the local West African scripts are, with the exception of Oberi Okaime, either pictographic or ideographic and obviously much more local and restricted. Even if the local West African scripts had been more widely diffused than they actually were, their being pictographic or ideographic places them at a distinct disadvantage vis-à-vis the fully-developed Western and Arabic scripts since, as Goody and Watt have rightly pointed out, the alphabet with its system of single signs for individual sounds, has always proved more economic and convenient than any other system of writing.[13]

The "embryonic" scripts place this region right in the mainstream of a universally observed phenomenon. When it is misguidedly argued by a certain school of European thought that any people who have not, among other things, invented writing, must be regarded as primitive, it is not always apparent to them that Africans have not been behind the rest of the world in experimenting with some systems of symbolic representation of objects or ideas for communication, record, or ritual purposes. If the opinion of experts is to be believed, then West Africa ought to be proud of having one of the five original scripts of the world, a distinction to which Europe, in spite of its great civilization, cannot lay claim. We can only speculate on what could have become of the Nsibidi if its development had not been arrested by the introduction of the Western alphabet. Any such speculation would of course be irrelevant since no one who has turned his mind to the question could seriously regret the replacement of such an underdeveloped script by the more efficient alphabetic system. At a time when even China is seriously considering replacing its centuries-old ideographic writing with the alphabetic script, it would be altogether unrealistic for any West African to lament the passing away of the embryonic scripts. No one regrets their being superseded any more than any Englishman or Irishman or Welshman regrets the super-session of the Runic and Oghams by the Roman. The local scripts have become casualties of the ever-widening sweep of a world civilization trans-mitted through cosmopolitan scripts and the agency of cosmopolitan and proselytizing religions.

At any rate, what has happened in West Africa is largely what Chadwick has established as being a near-universal phenomenon.[14] In Europe, as else-where, the early phase of writing consisted of crude scribblings on objects of wood, bone, metal, and stone in "native" scripts, to denote ownership, memorial notices, magical formulae, and so on. There was no attempt to use writing for extensive communication or literary expression. The second phase sees the introduction of a cosmopolitan script that is used for communication, record-keeping on a massive scale, and creation of written literatures. The Nsibidi script and its use fall within the first stage, the stage of the Anglo-Saxon Runes and the Celtic Oghams. The second stage, that of the intro-duction of the Roman script, West Africa shares with Anglo-Saxon Britain and with every other place where the Roman script has been introduced.

The introduction of the Arabic script into West Africa has this in common with the introduction of the Roman script: it had a very close association with a cosmopolitan and proselytizing religion, and its dissemination was also fostered by the dissemination of this religion. Moreover, both the Roman script and the Arabic script are ancestrally related, both being derived from the Egyptian syllabary. Out of the Egyptian syllabary grew the Semitic al-phabet, one of whose scions is the Arabic script. The Greeks borrowed the Phoenician branch of the Semitic alphabet, a wholly consonantal system, and converted some of its consonants not needed by them to the vowels which they did need. From the Greeks, the alphabet passed on to the Etruscans, and from the Etruscans to the Romans. After some further modifications, the Romans and (with the fall of the Roman Empire) the Christian Church, spread it throughout Europe, whence it was later introduced into the other parts of the world. Thus, even though we may not be immediately aware of the fact, the Arabic and the Western scripts, the two dominant writing systems of West Africa, are related. It is obvious, therefore, that both the West Africans, who use the Western or the Arabic script, and Europeans and Arabs, who introduced these scripts into West Africa, owe their possession of al-phabetic writing ultimately to the ancient Egyptians.

As a result of the introduction of Islam, Arabic scholarship, based on the use of the Arabic script, and drawing sustenance from the scholastic tradition of the Maghreb, Egypt, and the Middle East, flourished in the Western Sudan long before the introduction of Western learning to West Africa. The tre-mendous importance of this scholarship is only just being fully realized, as the manuscripts embodying the writings of learned marabouts and other

Arabic scholars are increasingly unearthed by different researchers and assembled in the departments of Arabic studies in West African universities and elsewhere.

The vintage period of Arabic scholarship in West Africa is, however, associated with the Fulani jihad in Northern Nigeria in the nineteenth century. Hodgkin has rightly designated this as a period of Islamic literary renaissance in West Africa because the literature produced during that period covered the entire range of traditional Islamic sciences, including theology, exegetics, law, literature, grammar and mysticism. This renaissance is essentially a product of the Shehu, Uthman dan Fodio, the leader of the jihad, and his sons, Sultan Bello and Abdullah, all of whom were accomplished Islamic scholars. The most outstanding literature of this period is Sultan Bello's *Infaq al-Maysur*, which is written in the tradition of the Arabic tracts of the times. Apart from histories, chronicles, and jihad tracts, there are also large collections of letters, some of which were recovered from some native officials by British administrators during the pacification of the North. The most famous of the letters are those composed by Muhammed Bello during his delightful polemics with the Sultan of Bornu. The letters are easily the most interesting of the body of West African Arabic literature. They reveal an elaborate ceremonial mode of address that is typically Eastern, as well as a ruthless logicality of thought, keenness of wit, and an astounding mastery of figurative language. They contain great masses of oily rhetoric, within which is craftily embedded much barbed vituperation. In addition, there are also praise-poems, such as those addressed to particular dignitaries. Hodgkin regards these praise-poems as examples of a form of literature common throughout the Western Sudan.[15]

Evidence points unmistakably to the numerous influences of the Arabic-Islamic culture on the Moslem areas of West Africa, influences that were made possible by a fully developed alphabetic script that the introduced culture brought with it. Proficiency in the use of Arabic writing has remained at all times the prerogative of a small section of the population, the scribes and the learned men; it was never diffused among the entire population. The production of literature in the Arabic script, as well as its use for communication purposes, has remained largely the preserve of a tiny intelligentsia of religious and administrative dignitaries.

We may see in the restricted diffusion of Arabic writing a reflection of the feudal nature of the societies in which it is employed in West Africa,[16] societies in which acquisition of literacy and literary education is regarded as the privilege of the ruling classes.

There is, however, another reason why the diffusion of the Arabic writing system has been very slow in West Africa, why, in spite of its arrival several centuries before the Western script, the latter has mainly superseded it and taken its place for record-keeping and communication except in Islamic religious matters. The acquisition of proficiency in it is a long and tedious process because it is a purely consonantal system and therefore requires longer time and great effort to master. One is reminded, in this respect, of the anecdote often told by Moslem scholars. When Mohammed, according to them, was asked to say how long he thought an individual would take to master Arabic writing thoroughly, he was reported to have answered that it would take two hundred years. Only a few people can hope ever to attain anything approaching mastery over the system. These few are made much of in Islamic societies because the rest of the population has to depend on them and their labors for intellectual, religious, and administrative leadership.

This also explains why much of the literature of the Arabic tradition has to be put into verse and made as easy to commit to rote as possible—there is in this tradition a blending of the literary and the oral impulses. We notice, for instance, the passage in Abdullah dan Fodio's autobiography, *Id al-nusukh man 'akhadhtu' anhu min al-shuukh*, in which, after enumerating the large number of sheikhs "from whom I have acquired knowledge," he proceeds to turn his composition to verse[17] in order to make the memorizing of it easy for his great-niece.

Goody and Watt tend to corroborate the two reasons stated here why the Arabic script has not been more widely diffused: "As regards the Semitic system—the evidence suggests that—in part, perhaps because of the intrinsic difficulties of the system, but mainly because of the established cultural features of the societies which adopted them—the social diffusion of writing was slow. There was, for one thing, a strong tendency for writing to be used as a help to memory rather than as an autonomous and independent mode of communication. . . ."[18]

Arabic laudatory poetry, chronicles, philosophical tracts, and, in fact, every other literary genre, are couched in the form of language that is easily accessible to memory. Hence, what has clearly distinguished Arabic literary output in West Africa has been its highly formalized cadence and poetic, rather than prosaic, linguistic structure.

Despite the fact that the Arabic script has been in use in West Africa for the past seven centuries, it has continued to be a minority script and has become increasingly so since the introduction of the Western script. This is so despite the past, and continuing presence of numerous Koranic schools in the Islamized parts of West Africa. As Sir Alan Burns informs us, in Islamic schools the pupils learn the Koran by heart, and are instructed in their religion, but there is little or no education in the Western sense.[19] With the introduction of Western-type schools, Moslems have also begun to acquire Western-type education to furnish themselves with the knowledge and skills necessary to make a living and to satisfy their ambitions in a modern technological society. The citadels of Islamic feudalism will collapse one by one before the advance of Western-type literacy, with its democratic appeal and infinitely greater ease of articulation, not only for record-keeping and communication, but also for the production of all types of creative literature, including the most complex of them all, the novel.

The introduction of the Western script into West Africa was consequent upon the introduction of Western-type education. The use of the Arabic script to produce a written literature and for communication purposes is, as we have noted, very much limited to a privileged minority of religious and administrative personages. The few pictographic and ideographic "native" scripts, we have also seen, were too rudimentary, underdeveloped, and restricted to be of any use for the production of literature or for communication. The introduction of the Western script with its wider appeal, however, ushered West Africa into the mainstream of the literary tradition by making available the most efficient medium for the production of literature and a most highly developed means of communication among the largest possible number of people. The process of literary development, which began with the spread of the Roman script by Christian monks and teachers all over Europe during the Dark Ages and after and gave rise to the profound transformation of the oral cultures of Europe, had at last begun in West Africa, with the spread of Western-oriented literacy and the initiation of literary activities from the late eighteenth century onward. In West Africa, as in Europe, the Christian Church has been the chief agent in the spread of literacy and the introduction of literary activities.

It is, however, not altogether true, as is often assumed, that modern education was first introduced into West Africa by the Christian missionaries. Captain John Adams, a British merchant and adventurer who made ten voyages to the west coast between 1786 and 1800, describes the educational situation in Calabar at the end of the eighteenth century. He notes that the presence of European traders along the coast had stimulated a desire for literacy among the native inhabitants, who therefore devoted considerable efforts to acquiring it, long before the missionaries began to arrive.[20] This is how Captain Adams saw the situation:

> Many of the natives write English; an art first acquired by some of the traders'
> sons who had visited England, and which they have had the sagacity to retain
> up to the present period. They have established schools and schoolmasters
> for the purpose of instructing in this art the youths belonging to families of
> consequence.[21]

From existing records, it is also obvious that some of the coastal West African traders were already able to read and write a form of pidgin English referred to by Daryll Forde as "trade language," a type of hybrid language with a largely English vocabulary and Ibibio syntax, which had developed within the Oil Rivers. One of these traders, Antera Duke, a leading Calabar trader, kept a diary written entirely in "trade language" about his trading and social activities toward the end of the eighteenth century. In spite of the efforts by coastal individuals to establish schools and teach literacy, formally organized and systematic education was first introduced by the missionaries, and rather than being exclusively restricted to families of consequence, was open to all who desired it. In fact, it would appear that at the beginning, especially in Igboland, modern literary education appealed mainly to the outcasts of traditional societies. The well-born and socially integrated were too secure in their traditional way of life to face the uncertainties of the new ways introduced by modern education. The Christian missions played a most crucial role in the development of a modern Western-oriented education that contributed more than any other factor in changing the face of West African society and introducing West Africa into the mainstream of a world literary tradition.

The need for Christian missions to spread Christianity as well as a civilization was of immense significance for the growth of written literature in West Africa. Of the two objectives, the generality of the missionaries would obviously place great emphasis on the conversion of the people. To facilitate their evangelical aspiration, the early missionaries had of necessity to learn the West African vernaculars and to reduce them to writing; they translated the Bible, hymn books, and other religious works into these vernaculars and taught West Africans to read and write so that they could avail themselves of the Christian message embodied in the translated texts.

Each aspect of these contributions is vital to the development of written literature in West Africa. The missionaries, by adapting the West African vernaculars to the Western script and using diacritics to mark tonal inflections, made a permanent contribution of the greatest importance to the study of African linguistics. In fact, it is obvious that the tools of linguistic research set up by them have not been superseded by modern linguistic research. In addition to translating the Bible and religious books into the vernaculars, the Christian missions participated actively in the compilation of dictionaries and grammar books on the vernacular languages.[22] The missionaries also encouraged the collection of African oral traditions: folktales, fables, myths, proverbs, riddles, songs, and historical fragments and their permanent recording in writing. Their interest in these things also stimulated others, such as colonial administrators and European travellers, to similar activities. We may even go so far as to suggest that the establishment of departments for the study of African languages in European universities and the tremendous interest in the anthropological study of the oral societies of Africa, which began in the late nineteenth century and gathered strength in the twentieth, owe much of their inspiration to the interest of the early missionaries in the languages and cultures of the African peoples they went out to convert.

Apart from the positive contributions of European missionaries to the growth of vernacular literature, the growth of written literature in English has also been largely stimulated by them. Of particular significance is the fact that, by teaching reading and writing to West Africans, they equipped them with the necessary tools for creating written literature. Many West Africans trained in mission schools have written grammar books, dictionaries, school readers, plays, short stories, poetry, biographies, and extended prose works, both in the vernaculars and in the English language.

Most of the early written works in West Africa were, in fact, by West Africans engaged in the Christian ministry. We have already seen that the Reverend Crowther, a Yoruba ex-slave who became the first Anglican bishop of Onitsha, produced dictionaries, a grammar, and school textbooks in both the Yoruba and Igbo languages. In fact, so expert is his tonal description of Yoruba in his *Yoruba Dictionary* that it is still regarded by present-day students of Yoruba as an authoritative work. It is also of particular interest that the two earliest history books written in West Africa should have been by native Christian clergymen. The Reverend C. C. Reindoorf, a Ghanaian minister of the Basel Mission, wrote the first systematic history of Ghana (then Gold Coast) entitled *History of the Gold Coast and Ashanti* (1895), while the Reverend Samuel Johnson, a Yoruba, wrote *The History of the Yorubas* in 1897. The latter book was posthumously published by the Reverend Johnson's brother, Dr. O. Johnson, in 1921. In all these works, the writers draw heavily from the oral tradition that compounds much of what could be called pure historical information with legend and myth. Therefore, one of the most enduring contributions the missionaries have made to the growth of written literature in West Africa has been to stimulate interest in their local cultural traditions in native West Africans, and the desire to record these in history books, school textbooks and, later, to assimilate them into creative literature.

There was, of course, a certain ambivalence in the attitude of missionaries to the traditional African culture. There was much in it they rejected outright with a singlemindedness that came to influence in a profound way the attitude of many of their converts to this culture. This negative aspect of the missionary attitude to African culture has often engendered much deserved censure of the missionaries by many West Africans. We have, however, in our eagerness to assign blame, forgotten the positive contributions made by the Christian missionaries to the spread of modern learning and the restoration of our local oral cultures to a position of dignity by their incorporation into our written literatures and records, for our own edification and for posterity.

There are striking analogies between the introduction of literacy and the growth of written literature in West Africa and in pre-medieval peasant societies elsewhere. We have already seen how the spread of literacy and the development of written literature in Europe were carried out by the Christian missionaries after hordes of marauding Northern Europeans had overrun the old Roman Empire. These Teutonic invaders were illiterate and possessed an oral rather than a literary tradition. When they settled within the former Roman Empire, which already possessed a well-developed literary tradition, there were Latin or Greek clerks ready to write letters for their chieftains, or to record their laws, histories, and oral traditions—not in their own languages, be it said, but in Latin. Their native prose was choked by Latin competition, as R. W. Chambers has observed, before it could spring up.[23] Elsewhere, as in Britain, Ireland, and Scandinavia, which were partially or not colonized at all by the Romans, and where literacy and the literary tradition were introduced de novo by the Christian missionaries fleeing from the disintegrating Roman Empire, both Latin and the native languages were established as literary languages. The native laws, local history, chronicles, and oral traditions were written down.

In Britain, for example, Latin remained the language of high scholarship as well as the language of the church, and was to maintain this position until the Reformation when English officially dethroned Latin as the language of the state, the church, and literature. During this period, the English language was gaining in importance. Even though the literary tradition developed in Greece and transmitted through Rome to the rest of Europe was actively cultivated in British grammar schools, largely through the medium of Latin, an English prose and poetic tradition was also being nurtured by its side. The development of prose is traced by literary historians to King Alfred's *Anglo-Saxon Chronicles* and was continued for centuries by subsequent contributors to the *Chronicles* until the eleventh century when, as a result of the Norman conquest of Britain, English was submerged by French for official and literary purposes. Even during this period of near eclipse of English, the English literary tradition continued to flourish in the people's common speech while the pulpit (because preachers had to translate their sermons into English to get them across to their non-French-speaking audiences) continued to promote the English tradition from where the chronicle writers had left off. A few centuries after the conquest, the effect of French began to wane and English began to reassert itself as a literary language, especially in the mass of homiletic and edificatory literature written by pious churchmen. By the fifteenth and early sixteenth centuries, the English literary tradition had recovered its vigor and presence in the writings of Englishmen. With the Reformation and the breakup of the monasteries, English became the main national, administrative, and literary language, while Latin receded further into the realm of classical and antiquarian scholarship. The outburst of literary activity that marked the Renaissance found expression in Britain in the English tongue. The Norman influence, which earlier on had emasculated the creative impulse in medieval Britain, at last wore off, allowing currents of fresh literary influence to flow in from Italy, France, and Spain, and to be assimilated into the English native tradition based on the English language.

Thus, we can see that the introduction of the Roman script and the development of written literature in Britain went through three stages: the first in which Latin only was the literary language; the second, in which the native language (as well as Latin—we may here ignore the brief interlude of the Norman period whose influence was on law and politics mainly) was used for writing religious, historical, and literary works derived from Roman sources or based on Roman models (witness the large numbers of chronicles, histories, biographies, poems, etc., which belong to this stage) and the third, in which purely native works were written.

All this has considerable interest for any one interested in the introduction of alphabetic writing and the development of written literature in West Africa. The analogies between the growth of written literature in premedieval Europe and the growth of written literature in nineteenth-century West Africa are clearly marked. In both cases Christian missionaries were largely instrumental in the introduction of an alphabetic script. In both cases, also, they brought with them a cosmopolitan language and a literary tradition in a developed state from their original base—Saint Augustine and his missionaries took Latin and Greco-Roman literary models to late-sixth-century Britain while the British missionaries brought the English language, together with European written literature, into West Africa in the nineteenth century.

In this respect, we may rightly say that there is some kind of continuity in the literary tradition, from the time the Greeks borrowed the Semitic alphabet and transformed it into an adequate instrument for communication and production of written literature, to the introduction of the Western script and European literary models by the Christian missionaries into West Africa.

We can see the whole thing as a continuous process of adjustments and incorporation of fresh elements from one stage to another in historical evolution, with different peoples joining the mainstream of the literary tradition whenever they were, by accident or by design, brought into contact with it. Britain and much of Europe entered this stream after the breakup of the Roman Empire. Africa entered it in the nineteenth century; but, in either case, Christian missionaries had been the main agents. Having entered the literary tradition at a much later stage than Europe, West Africa is a happy beneficiary of the contributions Europe had made to this tradition. In spite of the fact that Europe, an earlier arrival to this tradition, helped considerably in its development, both Europe and modern Africa share a common belonging to it; the main difference between their individual positions and their contributions to this literary tradition lies in the historical facts of Europe's early arrival and the circumstances under which West Africa was brought into it.

The early stage of the development of written literature in West Africa roughly coincides with the same stage in Europe. There was a mass of grammar books and dictionaries written by both European missionaries and the first educated West Africans. The main West African languages were written down and the Bible, religious books, and songs were translated into them. There is this difference, however: the greater secularization of education, which followed the breakup of medieval Christendom in Europe, has had the effect in West Africa of transferring much of the emphasis from religious to secular subjects. The result is that, along with the teaching of the scriptures and the catechism, the missionaries had also to teach grammar and composition, history and geography, mathematics, science, English, and classical literature. They set up schools patterned on European models and with a content based largely on that of the English schools.

There was from the beginning some argument as to the suitability of the content of Western-oriented education to West Africa. This argument centered on the question of how much each of local and foreign elements should be incorporated into the school syllabuses to ensure a balanced development of students and prevent their wholesale alienation from the indigenous culture.[24] The debate in this argument does not matter too much here. What is of interest is to note that West Africans were brought into contact with the various written forms already established in Europe through Western-type schools, and that when they came to produce written literature, they readily used these forms as their models in the same way that the British had adopted the Greco-Roman models after the introduction of the Roman script.

The first West Africans to produce written literature were actually expatriates who found themselves, as a result of the slave trade, in Europe long before the missionaries came to West Africa in large numbers. The most widely known of them was Gustavus Vassa whose real name was Olaudah Equiano. He was kidnapped at eleven along with his sister by slave hunters and sold into slavery in the United States. Bought by a British sea captain, he was taken to England. Later he bought his freedom and became a Christian and a respected gentleman. In 1789 he published his autobiography, *The Interesting Narrative of the Life of Olaudah Equiano or Gustavus Vassa, the African*,[25] a fascinating account of his life and what he remembered of his childhood and life in his village. Toward the end of the book he makes a strong plea against the slave trade. His book was made much of by those English people engaged in the antislavery movement. The style of the narrative with its dignified prose is typically eighteenth century. The eighteenth-century English convention also shows in the foreword in which he offered his book to the Lords Spiritual and Temporal, and the Commons of the Parliament of Great Britain, writing: "Permit me, with the greatest deference, to lay at your feet the following genuine narrative, the chief design of which is to excite in your august assemblies a sense of compassion. . . . I am sensible I ought to entreat your pardon for addressing to you a work so wholly devoid of literary merit as the production of an unlettered African. . . ."[26] The undoubted importance of Equiano's narrative from the literary, historical, and social-anthropological angles has been acknowledged by the prominence accorded it in nearly all the anthologies of African literature that have appeared up to the present time.

The other West African expatriates are much less known in West African literary circles than Equiano. One of them, however, Ignatius Sancho, a Ghanaian who was born on a slave ship as his pregnant mother was being taken into slavery, was brought to England and, at the age of two, handed over to a household containing three sisters. It must have been the sisters who nicknamed him Sancho in remembrance of Don Quixote's charming squire. He entered the service of the duke and duchess of Montague as butler, educated himself, and later had his letters against the African slave trade published. Other West African expatriates include the Ghanaian Anton Amo, who became a great scholar and philosopher, and published, among his works, *De Jure Maurarum in Europa*, a thesis vindicating the humanity and intellectual integrity of the African. Like Equiano's and Sancho's works, *De Jure Maurarum* was directed against the African slave trade. These writers were greatly influenced by the European intellectual tradition although, unlike the first two writers who knew only English, Amo's knowledge of Hebrew, Greek, Latin, and French, in addition to Dutch and German, must have made him an intellectual of international repute.[27]

In West Africa for a long time, apart from the spate of grammar books, dictionaries and translated religious texts, there was little or no creative writing. One of the situations, however, in which literacy was put to practical use from its early inception was in letter writing. We have since grown accustomed to the public letter-writer as a ridiculous figure of fun in West African prose fiction, which has the effect of diminishing our appreciation of his importance at the earliest period of the introduction of literacy. His efforts, crude and often deficient in many ways, sustained some kind of communication between those at home and their kinsmen, who were venturing out of their rural isolation into the new urban settlements springing up everywhere under Western stimulus. His scribblings helped to ease the pain arising from the tremendous disjunction of the old stable community that followed the movement of peoples from country to town.

In a way, these early letter-writers could be regarded as the forerunners of later creative writers. They were the most creative early professional group that emerged after the introduction of Western education. They had to grapple with the problems of transmitting the oral style of communication into writing for the benefit of a third party. It required imaginative exertion to render vernacular expression into a foreign language, and to capture, through the proper kind of phrasing, the mood, tone, and gestures of their clients. The essential difference between scribes and modern creative writers proper is that the latter have absolute choice of their subjects and a greater freedom to order them. The letter-writers had had their material provided for them to order and their success at communicating depended on their sense of the dramatic, their grasp of human situation, and their skillful use of language to recapture the mood and the emotional nuances of their clients.

Not everyone, however, felt very kindly toward the professional letter-writers and their trade. Governor Clifford of Nigeria, for instance, roundly vilified them in his address to the Nigerian Council in 1920. After attacking "the mushroom growth of 'hedge' schools in Southern Nigeria," he goes on to comment on the products of these schools: ". . . too many of them, no matter how imperfectly educated they may be, thereafter regard themselves as superior to agricultural pursuits and prefer to pick up a precarious and demoralizing living by writing more or less unintelligible letters for persons whose ignorance is even deeper than their own."[28] It is difficult to imagine what the governor found so disreputable about the profession of letterwriting. If anything, these letter-writers, as we have seen, were performing an essential social function at a time when extensive physical mobility unprecedented in the life of the small-scale, self-contained traditional communities was in progress, and there was a very real need for members of the community to keep in touch with their absent relations (and vice versa) by letter.

One of the phenomena associated with the spread of literacy and the growth of written literature in West Africa was the tremendous interest in African culture they gave rise to, as reflected in the number of history books by Africans appearing between the late nineteenth and early twentieth centuries. The Reverend Reindoorf's *History of the Gold Coast and Ashanti* and the Reverend Johnson's *The History of the Yorubas* incorporated what could be regarded as history proper with myths and legends. There were other educated West Africans who were beginning to be interested in the local history and social anthropology of their areas and who wrote about these in the cultural magazines established by the British administration in the various British West African territories. Some published essays dealing with such subjects in the local newspapers, while others produced theirs in pamphlets issued by local printing presses or as books published in the United Kingdom.[29]

This interest in local history and cultural institutions gathered strength in the first decade of the twentieth century and has continued to the present day. The mass of historical and social-anthropological writing, not surprisingly, appeared first among such West African peoples as the Yoruba, the Fanti, and the Sierra Leoneans, who received Western education earlier than the other West Africans. Modern West African historians such as K. O. Dike and J. F. A. Ajayi of Nigeria and Arthur Porter of Sierra Leone, sociologists such as Kofi Busia of Ghana and the late Nathaniel Fadipe of Nigeria, legal scholars such as T. O. Elias of Nigeria, and theological scholars such as Drs. Lucas and Idowu of Nigeria who have emerged since the 1930s, and whose scholarship has a distinctly West African bias, are therefore continuing and sublimating a process begun in an earlier period. To the coastal intellectuals of the later nineteenth-century West Africa, like Africanus Horton and Edward Blyden, African culture was a kind of abstraction they championed because they felt it belonged to them even though, in fact, they did not belong to it. After them, however, and as education spread farther inland, there followed a generation of fairly educated Africans with a background in this culture, people who had lived part or all of their lives within a purely African environment, and felt the urge to describe this traditional way of life, not only in order to reassure themselves but also in order to record it before the oncoming cosmopolitan modern culture obliterated it.

Apart from historical and cultural interests, the writing of biographies was beginning to excite the imaginations of members of the literate class. We have already seen that in the late eighteenth century Olaudah Equiano wrote his autobiography—for English readers—and that Antera Duke of old Calabar also wrote his fascinating but brief account of his trading life about the same period; but nothing in the nature of a true biography seems to have appeared after these until Adeoye Deniga's *West African Biographies* in 1914.[30]

Deniga was an Ondo man living in Lagos. In 1914, he began a series of lectures spaced over a period of years on African leaders in West Africa. Each lecture, dealing with the lives of eight or more prominent people, was published as a pamphlet, and later a number of these pamphlets were formed into a book. In 1934, Deniga published another volume containing about double the number of biographies in the earlier book. Deniga wrote about his characters with great enthusiasm and undoubted sympathy. He tried to be as factually accurate as possible by interviewing known descendants of those he wrote about and asked for the most relevant information about them.

Another publication of African biographies was *The Red Book of West Africa*, which appeared in 1920 but ceased publication after a few years. No general biographical sketches of this nature appeared again until the publication of the modern *Who's Who: A Biographical Dictionary* (Lagos, 1956), and more sustained biographies. Since Mbonu Ojike's autobiography, *My Africa* (1946), the genre has become so popular that it is the ambition of every prominent West African politician to cap his political triumphs with an autobiography or inspired biography.[31]

The first creative work of any significance produced by an English-speaking West African appeared in 1939. This was D. O. Fagunwa's *Ogboju-ode ninu igbo Irunmale* (The skilled hunter in the forest of the spirits), which is a long prose narrative in the tradition of Yoruba folklore.[32] From the beginning, it was very popular among Yoruba readers, but those who could not read Yoruba only came to know of its existence when extracts from it in English began to appear in recent times in African anthologies. It is a work of imaginative vigor and narrative excellence that will no doubt reinforce the existing body of African literature in English, especially since Wole Soyinka translated it into English under the title *The Forest of a Thousand Daemons: A Hunter's Saga*.[33]

Thirteen years after Fagunwa's first book was published, Amos Tutuola's first work, *The Palm-Wine Drinkard*,[34] was issued. It became an instant success in Europe but was to cause more argument and greater diversity of views among West African readers than any other book by an English-speaking West African. Tutuola writes in the same tradition as Fagunwa and may, in fact, have been influenced by Fagunwa, but he is more widely known because he writes in English, whereas Fagunwa is only now being "discovered" by the non-Yoruba reader through translation.

In the late 1940s a spate of creative pamphleteering began that was to dominate the realm of popular literature in the fifties and sixties. This mass of popular pamphlet literature took root in Nigeria. Its development was a postwar phenomenon that coincided with the tremendous spurt in the growth of literacy in the southern part of Nigeria and the rapid growth in urban population, the spread of locally-owned and operated printing presses, and the diversion of much of the energy and money previously devoted to the war effort into commercial, industrial, and technological development. All these factors were evident in Onitsha, the seat of this pamphleteering writing.

Cyprian Ekwensi, the versatile Nigerian novelist, pioneered this species of writing. In 1947, while still a practicing pharmacist, his two booklets, *When Love Whispers*, a love story, and *Ikolo the Wrestler and Other Igbo Tales*, a collection of Igbo folktales, were published by Tabansi Bookshop in Onitsha. Soon after followed Chike Okonyia's *Tragic Niger Tales*, two sharp attacks on marriage by proxy. The output of the pamphlets continued to grow and by the mid-sixties anyone could buy a couple of hundred different titles from the Onitsha market and the large towns of Nigeria.[35]

In 1954, two years after Tutuola's *The Palm-Wine Drinkard* appeared, Cyprian Ekwensi's *People of the City*, the first true novel in English by a Nigerian, was released. Since then, more and more novels, plays, books of poetry, anthologies, and other literary works have been published by West Africans.

It is obvious, therefore, that the growth of written literature in West Africa has followed the same pattern that it had in medieval (or earlier) Europe. In either case, we notice the introduction of an alphabetic script by Christian missionaries through a formal, literary education, followed by the writing down of the vernaculars and their being used (side by side with the cosmopolitan languages) to produce written literature. There is this difference, however: whereas the European vernaculars like English, Russian, or Swedish came with time to replace Latin, in West Africa, English and French have persisted as literary languages and have tended to drive the West African vernaculars into the corner. This is so because English and French have become "link" languages among the heterolingual peoples of West Africa.

Finally, we see that the development of written literature has followed models existing in the original base from which the writing system, cosmopolitan language, and system of education have been transplanted to the new place. In Europe, Christian monks brought the various literary genres that had existed in the old Greco-Roman classical period—chronicles, histories, biographies, grammars, poems, as well as religious and legal works. In West Africa, European missionaries inculcated the various forms of written literature developed in Europe.

In addition to the forms borrowed from ancient Greece and Rome by the rest of Europe that crystallized into the European literary tradition, West Africa has also inherited other literary forms that were to develop later within the Western literary tradition. Thus, West African writers have not only cultivated such literary forms as history, biography, grammar, poetry, as well as composing religious, legal, and philosophical works, they have also inherited and are imitating the novel, a post-Renaissance European contribution to the literary tradition.

West Africa has, on the whole, gained from the technical improvements in the production of literature (such as the development and spread of the printing press) achieved in Europe, and this, in turn, has hastened the growth of literacy and the pace at which West Africans have begun to create written literature and to pass from a purely oral to a largely literary tradition. This is amply proved by the fact that it took much longer for the novel to emerge in Europe after the introduction of alphabetic writing than it did in West Africa. Between the arrival of Augustine and his missionaries in Britain and the emergence of the novel, there passed no less than eleven centuries, whereas between the arrival of European missionaries and their establishment of Western-oriented schools in the mid-nineteenth century in West Africa and the appearance of Ekwensi's *People of the City* in 1954, there passed only a hundred years.

NOTES

1. See A. C. Moorhouse, *The Triumph of the Alphabet: A History of Writing* (New York, 1953), 47.

2. Ibid., 148 ff.

3. Goody and Watt, *Consequences of Literacy*, 314.

4. David Diringer, *The Alphabet* (London, 1947), 143; Moorhouse, *Triumph of the Alphabet*, 78.

5. Ibid.

6. Diringer, *Alphabet*, 148–53.

7. See: *Journal of the Royal Anthropological Institute* (1911).

8. See Diringer, *Alphabet*, 527; Murdock, "How Culture Changes," in *Man, Culture, and Society*, ed. H. L. Shapiro (New York, 1971), 256–57.

9. See A. Klingenbehen, "The Vai Script," *Sierra Leone Studies* 14 (1933).

10. *Africa* 17 (January 1947).

11. Goody and Watt, *Consequences of Literacy*, 313.

12. For a discussion of the origin and uses of the Runic Script and Oghams, see H. M. and N. K. Chadwick, *Growth of Written Literature*, vol. 1, 476; Diringer *The Alphabet*, 516; and Moorhouse, *Triumph of the Alphabet*, 145.

13. Goody and Watt, *Consequences of Literacy*, 313–16.

14. Chadwick, *Growth of Literature*, 476ff.

15. See Thomas Hodgkin, *Nigerian Perspectives: An Historical Anthology*, 2d ed. (London, 1975), 191–205.

16. M. G. Smith, *Government in Zazzau* (Oxford, 1960) and S. F. Nadel, *A Black Byzantium: the Kingdom of the Nupe of Nigeria* (London, 1942) present a clear picture of post-jihad Northern Nigeria. Their works provide a background to the literature produced in this part of West Africa and explain how the most literate class emerged. In the Nupe Emirate, described by Nadel, the *imams*, or religious leaders, and the *alkalis*, or judges, form the core of the scholarly class.

17. See M. Hisket, "Material Relating to the State of Learning Among the Fulani Before the Jihad," *Bulletin of the School of Oriental and African Studies* 19 (1957): 550–78.

18. Ibid.

19. Alan Burns, *History of Nigeria* (London, 1965), 225.

20. In the fifteenth and sixteenth centuries, Roman Catholic missions were established at many points on the West Coast by the Portuguese, but they disappeared before the modern period. See L. D. Turner, "The Impact of Western Education on the African Way of Life" in *Africa Today*, ed. C. Groves Haines (Baltimore, 1955), 100.

21. Captain John Adams, "Remarks on the Country Extending from Cape Palmas to the River Congo," in *Efik Traders of Old Calabar*, ed. Daryll Forde (London, 1956), 8.

22. The language of the Akan people of Ghana has been written down for the past hundred years. By the end of the nineteenth century, the major West African languages had been committed to writing. In 1848, parts of the Bible were translated into Yoruba—a complete Yoruba Bible followed in 1854, an Efik Bible in 1858 and 1868, and an Igbo Bible in 1860 and 1906. The Rev. J. G. Christaller of Basel Mission, after reducing Twi (1859) and Ga (1863) to writing, compiled his first Twi dictionary in 1874. Notable among the early grammars and dictionaries were Bishop Ajayi Crowther's *Yoruba Dictionary* (1843), *Grammar and Vocabulary of the Yoruba Language* (1852), *Vocabulary of the Igbo Language* (1882); J. F. Schon's *Oku-Igbo*, (1861); Hugh Goldie's *Principles of Efik Grammar* (1868).

23. R. W. Chambers, "The Continuity of English Prose from Alfred to Moore and his School" in Harpsfield's *Life of Moore*, ed. Elsie Vaughan Hitchcock, vii–ix.

24. See J. F. A. Ajayi, *Christian Missions in Nigeria, 1841–1891: The Making of a New Elite* (London, 1965).

25. *The Narrative* went through sixteen editions before the twentieth century and was favorably reviewed by the leading journals of the day. See Wilfred D. Samuels's introduction to the bicentennial edition, vol. 1 of Equiano's *Narrative* (Coral Gables, Florida, 1989), xviii. See also Paul Edward's introduction to *The Life of Olaudah Equiano* (Essex, 1988), xiii.

26. Equiano, *Life*, iii–iv.

27. See W. E. Abraham, *The Mind of Africa* (London, 1962), 126–27 and Abbe Henri Gregoire, *An Enquiry Concerning the Intellectual and Moral Faculties, and Literatures of Negroes, Followed with an Account of the Life and Works of Fifteen Negroes and Mulatoes, Distinguished in Science, Literature and the Arts* (New York, 1810).

28. Sir Hugh Clifford's attack on "hedge" schools and letter-writers is to be found in his address to the Nigerian Council in 1920.

29. A few examples of this kind of writing in West Africa are NIGERIA: Adesola's "Burial Customs in the Yoruba Country," *Nigerian Chronicle* (1908–10); Ajisafe's *Laws and Customs of the Yoruba* (Lagos, 1924); O. Keribo's *History of the Yoruba People* (Abeokuta, 1906); M. I. Ogumefun's *Yoruba Legends* (London, 1929); Ojo Coles's *The Wisdom of My Fathers: Yoruba Folk-Wisdom, Conception of Manhood* (London, 1929); A. Azikiwe's "Nigerian Political Institutions," *Journal of Negro History* 14 (1929), and "Fragments of Onitsha History," *Journal of Negro History* 15 (1930); E. Erokwu's "The Musical Instruments of My District," *Nigeria Field* 5 (1932); P. Anekwe's "Une Fable des Igbos de la Nigeria," *Anthropos* 31 (1936). GHANA: A. B. Papafio's "Native Tribunals of the Akras of the Gold Coast: Law of Succession Among the Akras or the Ga Tribes Proper of the Gold Coast"; "Use of Names Among the Gas or Accra People of the Gold Coast," *Journal of African Society* (1910, 1911, and 1913); J. B. Danqua's *Akan Law and Customs* (London, 1928); SIERRA LEONE: Esu Biyi's "The Temne People and How They Make Their Kings," *Journal of African Society* (1913); B. Juga's "Ceremonies on the Death and Crowning of a Paramount Chief in Temne Country," *Sierra Leone Studies* 11 (1919).

30. Adeoye Deniga, *West African Biographies* (Lagos, 1934) and S. R. B. Attoh Ahuma, *Memoirs of West African Celebrities* (Liverpool, 1905) were meant to answer racist assertions of black intellectual and moral inferiority.

31. Among the outstanding examples of works in this genre are Nnamdi Azikiwe, *Zik: Selections from the Speeches of Nnamdi Azikiwe, Governor-General of the Federation of Nigeria* (Cambridge, 1961) and *My Odyssey* (London, 1970); Obafemi Awolowo, *Awo: The Autobiography of Chief Obafemi Awolowo* (Ibadan, 1960); Adegoke Adelabu, *Africa in Ebullition* (Ibadan, n.d.). There are scores of biographies, popular and intellectual, of politicians and public figures in West Africa. At least twenty of them are about Dr. Nnamdi Azikwe, an African nationalist and the first president of Nigeria.

32. D. O. Fagunwa, missionary educated schoolmaster, wrote four fictional works in Yoruba in addition to *Ogboju-Ode ninu Igbo Irummale* (Lagos, 1938; Edinburgh and London, 1950). These are *Igbo Olodumare* (Edinburgh and London, 1946, 1949, 1961), *Adiitu Olodumare* (Edinburgh, 1961), *Ireke onibudo* (Edinburgh, 1949), *Irinkerindo Ninu Igbo Elegebeje: Apaketa* (Edinburgh, 1954, 1961)

33. Wole Soyinka translated *Ogboju-Ode ninu Igbo irunmale* from Yoruba into English as *The Forest of a Thousand Daemons: A Hunter's Saga* (London, 1968). He supplies an introduction and a glossary for the benefit of non-Yoruba readers.

34. It was published by Faber and Faber of London in 1952.

35. For extended studies of the popular pamphlet phenomenon, see E. N. Obiechina, ed., *Onitsha Market Literature* (London, 1972) and Emmanuel Obiechina, *An African Popular Literature: A Study of Onitsha Market Pamphlets* (Cambridge, 1973).

CHAPTER 2

Amos Tutuola and the Oral Tradition

AMOS TUTUOLA is the first West African writer of fiction to attain international recognition. When his first book, *The Palm-Wine Drinkard*, appeared in 1952, it was received with enthusiasm in Europe and America. The book has now been published in French, Italian, and German. Since *The Palm-Wine Drinkard*, Tutuola has written five more books: *My Life in the Bush of Ghosts, Simbi and the Satyr of the Dark Jungle, The Brave African Huntress, Feather Woman of the Jungle*, and *The Wild Hunter in the Bush of Ghosts*.

It seems quite ironical but it is true that the more popular Tutuola's books became abroad, the more unpopular they became (at least until recently) at home. There are many reasons for this, but the main one seems to be that he deals with a world that European writers, especially "the crocodile writers," had exploited in the past from a motive of sensationalism at a time when little that was authentic was known about African cultural life. That world was one of witches and wizards, of magic and magicians, of jungle life, ritual murder, and mumbo-jumbo.

Tutuola, however, is no lineal descendant of creative European writers on West Africa. It is obvious that a hiatus exists between European and indigenous writers on West Africa, the first group writing essentially for a European audience and about situations which they only saw from the outside, and the second group writing for a West African and non-West African audience about situations seen largely from the inside. Anybody familiar with West African writing will readily agree that Tutuola's work has a greater affinity with the writing of the latter group than with that of the former because it is based largely upon the oral tradition of West Africa represented in the works of indigenous West African writers but hardly in those of non-West African writers.

The more open objection to Tutuola by some Nigerian critics[1] is that he has merely collected and rehashed folktales known to everyone and put them into semiliterate English. In this sense, he is, in their opinion, no more original than a stamp collector. His work, they say, has the fascination of novelty for Europeans that it could not possibly have for indigenous Nigerians. By this kind of criticism they try to deny him any creative merit or originality. The ensuing discussion will prove this criticism to be both misguided and misleading. The concept of originality within the oral tradition is not the same

21

as it is within the literary tradition, and I conceive of Tutuola's writing in the context of a transition between the oral and the literary tradition.

ORAL TRADITION

Cultural continuity within the nonliterate traditional societies of West Africa (and still to a very large extent after the introduction of literacy) is carried on largely by oral transmission. Goody and Watt emphasize this statement in respect of all nonliterate societies when they write, ". . . all beliefs and all values, all forms of knowledge, are communicated between individuals in face-to-face contact; and as distinct from the material context of the cultural tradition, whether it is cave-painting or hand-axe, they are stored only in human memory."[2] Storytelling is one of the ways in which this oral transmission of culture is carried on. In traditional African communities storytelling provides entertainment, moral instruction, and an opportunity to express collective solidarity. It is one of the methods of educating young people by introducing them to the material culture, customs and usages, beliefs and philosophies of their people. Traditional African narrative can therefore be said to embody more than the art for art's sake philosophy.

Storytelling is part of the seasonal rhythm of life in Africa and is closely related to the ecology of any particular area.[3] Among all agricultural village-dwellers in Africa, the ideal storytelling period is after the harvest when people are free at night to assemble round a fire or in an open courtyard when there is moonlight. Sometimes children gather together while adults sit apart, conversing and smoking pipes or taking snuff; sometimes adults join children. Sometimes the group is composed of the members of the same compound— the father, his wives, their children, the father's and often the mother's relatives living within the compound. Very often the gathering is a larger one and includes people from other compounds and adjoining villages.

There is a definite solidarity by way of shared response and stimulus between the narrator and his audience. The story itself is often well known to everyone present and has been told often. The audience therefore anticipates every move of the narrator in the singing of the ditties where these form a part of the story. People are not bored because they already know the story. Apart from feeling the pleasure of recognizing the details of the story, they can be thrilled by the competent narrator, who enhances the effect of his story by his manner of narration, his gestures, verbal command, and voice modulation.

There are different types of traditional stories, with varying contents, patterns of narration, and significance. There are also what, for lack of a better nomenclature, are called "verbal arts." Verbal arts are not stories but are an essential part of traditional lore. They depend on verbal command, association of ideas, and the ability to establish naturalistic links among objects. They include proverbs and riddles.

Proverbs are the kernels that contain the wisdom of a people. They are usually philosophical or moral expositions reduced to a few words, and form a mnemonic device in societies in which everything worth knowing and relevant to the day-to-day life of the people has to be committed to memory. The speeches of old men are usually spiced with them and it is certainly considered an index of traditional wisdom to apply them appropriately in one's speech. The pronouncements of divination are often couched in proverbs since they confirm that the diviner is both an intellectual and a philosopher in the traditional African society. In contemporary West African novels the proverb features prominently as one of the ways West African authors recapture traditional speech atmosphere and wisdom.

Riddles are briefly stated questions, the answers to which are to be guessed by the listener. They are essentially intellectual exercises that provide an outlet for training the powers of observation and imagination. They are very popular with young people and provide a welcome diversion when storytelling becomes monotonous. They are usually telegraphic, that is, they are formed with a minimum expenditure of words, with conjunctions and prepositions almost always left out.[4] They are in the form of statements even though they require answers, for example: "Elephant dies, Jamu-Jamu eats him; cow dies, Jamu-Jamu eats him; Jamu-Jamu dies, there is no one who eats him." Most of the riddles are enigmas or paradoxes presented by balanced statements that appear mutually contradictory, incongruous, or impossible, as, for example, "A black ram goes to the river; it turns white." Riddles, apart from affording training in observation and sharpening the imagination, introduce young people to the material culture of their society. They are also an essential element in cultural orientation and moral training. A Yoruba riddle, such as "Who is it that goes down the street without greeting the king?" makes children aware that when they walk by the king's palace they must go in and greet him. Proverbs and riddles are not stories, properly speaking, but they are so vital a part of the oral tradition that they cannot be left out of even the most cursory discussion of that tradition.

Linguistic development within the literary culture of Europe seems to lean toward discouraging the use of fossilized expressions such as proverbs, saws, apothegms, and even epigrams. They are either regarded as clichés and therefore vulgar or as signs of affectation and pedantry. At the core of this attitude is the modern concept that originality and individuality are expected to be reflected in individual speech and writing style. In traditional nonliterate societies, however, the appropriate application of these set expressions is regarded as a mark of rhetorical virtuosity and traditional wisdom. Riddles do not seem to have had a very important place within the English literary tradition except in balladry, which, in any case, belongs essentially to the oral tradition. Shakespeare's use of the casket riddle in *The Merchant of Venice* obviously indicates the close touch his age still had with oral traditional lore. The verbal arts are an essential feature of nonliterate societies. They are very highly developed in traditional West African societies.

Traditional stories can be differentiated into folktales, legends and pseudo-history, and myths.[5] These are distinctive in their content, narrative form, and significance. They are easily confused one with another, and much misunderstanding of Tutuola's writing, as will appear later in this discussion, arises from the failure to realize the underlying differences among these narrative types and the content within which Tutuola was writing.

Legends and pseudo-history are usually stories about tribal heroes and the significant events and places with which they are associated. These stories deal with, among other things, military exploits, magical prowess, singular economic fortunes, feats of strength, skill, and wit.

In traditional African societies, legends embody the main historic records of the people's past and are passed down from generation to generation by oral transmission. Old men are often the renowned chroniclers of the community and are highly revered as a result of their being the repositories of traditional historical records. Legends form an essential part of communal religious celebrations, not in the sense of being an integral part of the ritual activity, but in the sense of fulfilling the same role during communal eating and drinking that background music and conversation would at a modern European dinner party. The respected elder (sometimes one who stands to gain in reputation from the story being told, either because he took part in the incident being described or because he is lineally descended from the hero) refurbishes the imagination of the young people with these legendary tales. These he delivers as a series of reminiscences or reported accounts of what he learned from his father or another respected elder when he was young. While he narrates his story, a few words are thrown in occasionally by some of the adult males to jog his memory, or a few friendly noises are made to indicate that the people are still "with him." Sometimes arguments develop on a point of detail but these are rarely pressed hard enough to spoil the conviviality of the occasion. In these gatherings traditional African diplomacy, sense of decorum, and good breeding permeate everything that is said or done. Women and children sit still and say nothing. Traditional African society has this in common with Victorian English life––women and children should be seen but not heard on such important occasions.

Legends and pseudo-history perform a dual function for the community that possesses them. First, they give the members of the community a collective solidarity by linking their present with their past, by enabling the living members of the community to identify themselves and their aspirations with those of the dead members. This is so because most traditional societies are small-scale societies within which oral dissemination of information presents no difficulty. Second, legends and pseudo-history provide the legalistic basis for settling the problems or rights and obligations within the social system; for, the doings of traditional heroes become precedents and norms by which present action can be judged.

In terms of creativity, the freedom of the traditional chronicler is restricted by the material he is using. He must be loyal to the fact as he saw it or as it was handed down to him by his father or another reliable elder. In spite of that, the manner of his narration will reflect his capability as a competent narrator. His use of words, which are likely to evoke distinctive emotional responses in his listeners, his gestures, bodily movements, the expression of face, and even his judicious pauses and inflections cannot but add to the effects that his narratives produce. In some traditional African societies, especially those with greater specialization and division of labor, the chronicler becomes a professional court poet and historian. His method is often declamatory and his language highly formalized and rhetorical. His material, however, remains of communal interest and derives from the legends and pseudo-history of the community. He cannot alter the facts, though he can use his imagination to enrich and vivify their color. These professional chroniclers have been variously designated as griots, orators, linguists, or remembrancers. The most famous of them is the Asantehene's linguist.

Myths are stories of a sacred nature that treat of the ultimate mysteries like death, the afterlife, creation, and the gods. They are not only regarded as true but have a pseudo-religious significance. They are not just important for their story content but much of their value derives from their giving purpose to the mysteries of existence—they give meaning, as the anthropologist Malinowski has observed, to the cosmic order. Without them, traditional society would lose the rationale and the confidence that hold it together. Let us take belief in God as an example. Nietzsche's gloomy prophecy that there will be universal madness on the day the world wakes to discover that there is no God may appear to be a cynical hypothetical speculation, but it cannot be doubted that belief in God is one of the great influences in the lives of individuals. The power of this belief is reflected in the horror with which believers regard confessed atheists. It is as if in his unbelief the atheist is threatening the very foundation and security of the believer's world. There is no doubt whatever that myths provide security to the people in traditional societies. They are not just symbolic expressions of some detached realities, they *are* the realities and the charters for their own existence. They permeate the lives, beliefs, attitudes, and values of the people who profess them. They live in their mores and rituals, control their conduct, and govern their faith.[6]

It must be said, of course, that the preponderance of myths in traditional African societies can be explained by the relative absence of skepticism among their peoples. Modern skepticism is an essential aspect of the modern scientific outlook that has been most developed within a literate tradition. But that is not to say that there is absolute conformity to and acceptance of the generally defined beliefs in traditional societies. Within them there are bound to be those whose minds are disturbed by little ripples of doubt. The fact that some of the sanctions against nonconformity and disbelief appear too severe by modern standards goes a long way to indicate that the traditional African societies have their heretics and free-thinkers against whom priests and kings have evolved inquisitorial machines and repressive laws. An encounter with some of the priests and diviners often reveals cleverly concealed skepticism that sometimes makes them too vociferous in the assertion of beliefs they inwardly disavow. In spite of the growth of modern skepticism, however, myths continue to express, enhance, and modify belief, safeguard and enforce morality, vouch for the efficacy of ritual, contain practical rules for guiding behavior, and impart a general direction to the ideologies that seem to dominate the modern age.

Myths, by their very nature and collective significance, are always the product and property of the whole community, or a self-identified section of the community. They cannot belong to individuals in the sense of being formulated by them out of their own personal needs; for myths very often refer to things that are supposed to have happened in the past, and therefore provide a precedent or warrant for present actions and usages. They have a dynamic quality only insofar as fresh and decisive events in the present lead to a gradual reinterpretation or reformulation of an old myth to reflect the new situation. For instance, where an autochthonous people have been conquered and effectively subjugated by an invading group, old myths are reinterpreted to embody the new situation. Even in this circumstance the myth-makers or interpreters are not doing anything original or individual but are merely giving expression to the collective experience. The social function of myths is too closely tied up with the collective experience to be within the ken of individual creativity.

Folktales are distinctive imaginative stories told for amusement, entertainment, and education. They may deal with the experiences of individual human beings or of animals. They often contain some moral or clinching exemplum—even though they are told essentially to provide entertainment, a strong didactic purpose is implicit in them. They form the largest group of traditional narratives and have well-known and recurrent motifs and stereotyped characters.

The stock-characters include the trickster who is often something of a rogue. He manages to extricate himself from intriguing and sometimes dangerous situations by a display of mental agility. He is often associated with the forces of disorder within society—he breaks laws, tramples on customary usages, and subverts established social conventions, relying on the nimbleness of his wits to get him out of difficulties. Sometimes, he falls victim to his own cleverness, for in his attempt to trick others he very often gets tricked himself.[7] Among many West African tribes the trickster is often an animal. The Igbo have the tortoise, the Yoruba, the rat, and the Ashanti, Anansi the spider. Anansi stories are also popular in the Caribbean (notably in British Guiana and Jamaica) and among black Americans of the South. There are also human tricksters and trickster gods. The Dahomean Yo is among the outstanding divine tricksters in West Africa. Other folktale heroes have a varying degree of cleverness and stupidity according to circumstance and the

exigencies of plot development, but the trickster alone evokes definite anticipation of a tale of villainy, daring, cunning, and intellectual gymnastics. One
could observe in passing that the trickster type of folktale hero has a universal
distribution. Within the European folktale tradition, Reynard the Fox and
Brer Rabbit are among the celebrated rogue heroes.

Another popular folktale character in West Africa is the quest hero. He
goes in quest of something or some ideal and usually undergoes harrowing
ordeals before attaining his objective, then emerges full of confidence and
triumph. He owes his escape from disaster and defeat to personal courage,
chance, divine intervention, or magic. The dark horse is also a common
folktale hero. Often a victim of persecution at the hands of an unkind uncle,
a wicked aunt, a scheming stepmother (or, if a girl, an invidious and jealous
elder sister), the hero manages to steal the show in spite of his obvious
handicaps, much to the discomfiture of his hostile relatives. The Cinderella
heroine of the European folktale is the nearest equivalent to the dark horse.
The villain or persecutor is a very common character. He is usually an an-
tihero. He is ruthless, cunning, and physically menacing and constitutes one
of the task-masters of the quest hero.

West African folktales also have stereotyped motifs. The same motifs occur
in different parts of West Africa and, in fact, in different parts of Africa, as
has been shown by comparative folklorists who have made a study of folktales
in different parts of Africa.[8] Some of the common folktale motifs are the
stubborn child motif, the crime-does-not-pay motif, the unfaithful friend
motif, the fairy godmother motif, the good-versus-evil motif, and the pride
goeth-before-a-fall motif. These motifs derive essentially from traditional cultural values, the norms of behavior, and the strains and stresses that originate
from day-to-day individual relationships. In traditional West African societies,
with their sedentary agricultural occupation, there exists a widespread so-
cialization of beliefs, moral values, and modes of behaviour, and consequently
an acceptance of a common standard of what comprises an ethically justifiable
action or its travesty. This social homogeneity seems to explain the wide
distribution of identical folktale motifs among the agricultural cultures of
Africa.

The world of the traditional West African folktale is an undifferentiated
world, within which the dichotomy between the natural and the supernatural,
the abstract and the concrete, the physical and the metaphysical, does not
exist. Here, animals, plants, objects, natural forces, and abstract entities like
song, laughter, and dance are humanized. All creation is spectacularly imbued
with vital force, and this force is constantly strengthened by magic. This
world has much in common with that of the European ballad. "The ballad,"
writes M. J. C. Hodgart, "is peopled with animals and birds that speak, with
fairies and witches, and with ghosts who return from the grave. There is no
clear line of demarcation between such creatures and ordinary mortals. The
supernatural is treated in a matter-of-fact and unsensational way, and to the

ballad singer there seems to be no question of a suspension of disbelief."9 For the traditionalist and his audience, too, there is no question of suspending disbelief. In spite of the assumption that many people make (no doubt because of ignorance of the folktale tradition), this world is not irrational, illogical, or prelogical. On the contrary, it is a world within which the laws of cause and effect operate scrupulously. Given certain basic postulates as, for instance, the logicality of magical belief, it will be seen that the world of the traditional storyteller is a more ruthlessly logical one than the world of the modern realistic novel. One of the essential requirements of traditional storytelling is that the competent narrator must make a series of etiological explanations as he unfolds the plot of his story. Plausibility is not only implicit in the plot, as in the case of the realistic novel, it is explicit in folktale narrative. Because the traditional storyteller has a greater freedom in his use of words for elaboration and explanation, and because he uses tonal inflections, gestures, facial expressions, and even brief rhythmic movements of the body to convey some dramatic elements in his story, he is in a far better position to tell a more convincing story than his counterpart who is using writing.

MAGIC AND FOLK IMAGINATION

The logicality of magic is central to any discussion of the world of the traditional folktale and, in fact, of the traditional world itself, because the rejection of this world by modern scientific realism sometimes seems to embody a fundamental assumption not only that it does not stand the test of true scientific and empirical verification but also that it lacks an intrinsically logical application worthy of a rational human system. In this discussion, the meaning that is assigned to *logic* seems most pertinent and forms the focal point around which much else revolves. Should we regard *logic* here as that "branch of philosophy that treats of the forms of thinking in general, and especially of inference and scientific method," or as "the science or art of reasoning as applied to a department of knowledge" or should one apply *logic* in an attributive and descriptive sense to include any kind of systematic and comprehensive development of action and thought? It is obvious from several discussions which have taken place on the subject that different people have had one or the other of these definitions uppermost in mind while discussing the subject of traditional magic. Frazer and Tylor, who pioneered the study of magic especially within pre-technological, nonliterate societies, had the scientific basis of *logic* in mind in their discussions.10 On the implicit assumption that these societies evolved their magical practices after a process of rational consideration and scientific observation, they imposed an intellectual construction on magic by a severe application of the scientific methods of induction and deduction. In their opinion, even though the pre-technological and nonliterate man has an essentially functional and utilitarian interest in magic, his magical beliefs and practices are capable of analysis based on the abstract principle of scientific and empirical investigation. Tylor and Frazer postulated the view that the nonliterate mind draws from two fundamental laws of association of ideas in its conceptualization of magic—the law of contiguity and the law of similarity. From these two laws they derived two principles of thought on which magic is based—first, like produces like, or an effect resembles its cause, and second, things that have once been in contact with each other continue to act on each other at a distance after the physical contact has been severed. To differentiate one mode of magical operation from the other, Frazer invented the terms *homeopathic* and *contagious* as applied to Frazer and Tylor's magic.

Imposition of a purely scientific construction on magic was bound to lead to unsatisfactory results because the analogies between science and magic are bound to break down. Even though both the magician and the scientist appear to make certain fundamental assumptions based on end-means formulations, the scientist attains his end through a process of experimentation and verification, whereas the magician, believing in the unfailing efficacy of his magical formulae, has no means whatsoever of verifying and modifying them because magic is supposed to operate with the aid of a mystical agent. In his frustration, Frazer dubbed magic "bastard science" and the magician a counterfeit scientist because he attempts to reach empirical ends through irrational means.

Later investigators of traditional magical practice departed from the intellectual approach of Tylor and Frazer and concentrated on the study of magic as a social phenomenon that can only make sense when seen in the context of the society within which it obtains. As Gluckman says, it is absurd to compare the modes of nonliterate, preindustrial thought with the modes of modern scientific and philosophical thought.[11] Discarding the idea of traditional magic as a science or even a pseudo-science, modern investigators make on-the-spot studies of its application by treating it as essentially a part of the cultural content of pre-industrial societies, a part of what Levy-Bruhl calls the "représentations collectives"[12] of those who practice it. Using the Azande society as a test case, Evans-Pritchard shows that magic, witchcraft, and oracle form a trichotomic structure upon which a considerable part of social behavior depends.[13] The principle of magical causality, he finds, does not invalidate a purely rational explanation but often tends to extend it. For instance, the farmer who, after consulting an oracle, employs magical preparations to ensure a good harvest does not so much assume that the preparations will stimulate plant growth as that they will counteract the pernicious influence of any enemy's witchcraft that is capable of destroying the crops; for, it is reasonably argued, the crops are going to do well anyway unless witchcraft interferes with them. The logic immanent in this case is the consistent belief in a notion of causality embodying the idea of mystically directed action. This notion of causality does not preclude an empirical explanation. Again, if a granary under which a man is resting falls down and kills him, no one doubts that he has been killed by the falling granary. The question goes beyond that. Why should this particular granary have fallen when this particular man was sitting under it and not before or after? This is a question that a scientifically-oriented mind would shrug off. The Azande would take the matter to an oracle who would probably find the answer in the malevolent intervention of an evilly disposed neighbor exercising a psychically malevolent influence on the victim. Therefore, to defend himself from such an influence, the individual arms himself with protective magic. In nonliterate, preindustrial societies of Africa, magical belief provides the means of reconciling man to the unfortunate events that overtake him and a ready-to-hand method for reacting to those events. It also affords him the necessary confidence for meeting the exigencies of nature by making available to him mystical power he can invoke in a particular circumstance by performing the proper rites and using the appropriate spells.

A more fruitful discussion of traditional magic should pay attention to the intent rather than the content of magic. Magic has a utilitarian purpose in traditional societies within which organized, efficient police service or proper techniques of crime detection do not exist. Magic, by coordinating beliefs and regulating personal relationships, helps to prevent the disintegration and collapse of these societies. By providing the pre-technological man with some semblance of power, magic rescues him from the final despair that comes from powerlessness. A nonliterate society, not being self-analytical and handicapped by a lack of written records, cannot anatomize its institutions in terms of the logical and the nonlogical, the empirical and the ritual, or the scientific and the mystical. These are distinctions made by the outside observer, who is very often steeped in modern scientific thought and notions. Nonliterates actualize rather than intellectualize their beliefs.

In viewing the "magical" world of the traditional folktale, it should be borne in mind that it is altogether futile and unrealistic to employ the standard of modern scientific realism, which is a by-product of technological development and literacy. Traditional magic should be regarded as a mode of social behavior in a different kind of society from the modern technological society and not as an intellectual curiosity, which is what it becomes when viewed through the "représentations collectives" of the modern industrial culture. Its pertinacity in nontechnological societies must be taken for granted much in the same way as the pertinacity of science is in modern industrial societies. It should be conceded that a thing may be logical without necessarily being scientific, that is, without being amenable to easy analysis by the scientific processes of deduction and induction. It may even fail the test of elementary empiricism; that is to say, it may appear irrational, judged from a conventional scientific point of view, or nonrational, where it defies such a judgment. Nevertheless, it can still be said to be logical if it has an internal unity, consistency, and a structural coherence of its own. The logicality of the "magical" world of the traditional societies and their representative literatures depend upon these qualities of internal unity, consistency, and structural coherence. The traditional folktale world implicitly assumes the logicality and efficacy of magic, hence a large proportion of action within it is magically determined.

The world of traditional storytelling is not supposed to be a contemporary world. Even though the story has contemporary material and allusions, the narrator makes it clear from the beginning that his story relates to an age in the remote past when man and the rest of the universe could intercommunicate verbally and experience a more direct intimate relationship, a time when animals lived and talked like human beings. The shattering of this folktale world, which must have been as extensive as the confusion of tongues in Babel, is often a narrative theme.

It must be obvious from the folktales themselves that the traditional attitude to that "golden age" has nothing of the Rousseauist sentimentalism about it. That a greater intimacy is purported to have existed among all its various components does not mean that there was also a greater harmony. It was a world within which the everlasting conflicts between good and evil raged with as much intensity as they do today.

This is, of course, as it ought to be because the distancing of the action is actually an aesthetic device that gives the narrator an absolute freedom to incorporate material that may appear incredible to the audience. Since contemporary allusions are often incorporated into the stories, the aesthetic remove of the time-setting of a story makes it difficult for the narrator to be accused of slander even when the audience recognizes a contemporary allusion made at someone's expense.

The distancing device and the consequent humanization of all the elements of nature imbue the folktale world with immense vitality and excitement, beside which the modern "scientific" world must appear tame and anemic, because within the modern "scientific" world the trees are rooted helplessly to the ground, the stones are dead, and the animals are banished permanently to the jungles and only a few docile ones are allowed by sufferance to approach human (and therefore refined) society. The dead are securely imprisoned in their tombs, and spirits communicate only with an eccentric few, and then in secret cells and darkened hideouts.

Folk-beliefs as reflected in traditional folktales and ballads have tended to disappear from the European written tradition as a result of the growth of a modern intellectual outlook, which dichotomizes experiences on the basis of the physical and the spiritual, the natural and the supernatural, treating them as polarities rather than as a continuum as they have been regarded in folk societies. A cursory investigation of English literature up to and including the Renaissance will show a blending of literary impulse and folk belief during that period. In much Elizabethan writing, for instance, the natural and the supernatural, the human and the spiritual, are often found woven into a fabric of great literature. The world of witches and wizards, of fairies and magicians, was a very real one to the Elizabethans, and some Elizabethan works were greatly reinforced by the injection of folk belief and practice. Puck in *A Midsummer Night's Dream*, the ghost in *Hamlet*, *Macbeth*'s witches, all these readily come to mind as examples of Shakespeare's effective use of folk material in literature, and Prospero is certainly one of the most fascinating studies in the exercise of mystical power in English literature. Spenser's *The Fairie Queene* is a great repository of Elizabethan demonology and nymphology.

More recently still, folk material still survives in a residual form in European and American literature.[14] It usually manifests itself as folk motifs that are merely used for the purpose of exploring contemporary reality, as in T. S. Eliot's use of the Garden-of-Eden motif in *The Waste Land* and Herman Melville's employment of the quest motif in *Moby Dick*. William Butler Yeats, especially the early Yeats of the "The Celtic Twilight," could say of the impact of folklore on his poetry: "All my art's theories depend upon just this—rooting of mythology in the earth." [15]

By and large, however, the modern European intellectual outlook, stimulated by the industrial revolution, has encouraged the growth of rationalism and the rejection of folk beliefs that cannot be empirically verified. Because many African societies are relatively insulated from urbanization, industrialism, and mass communication media, they still enjoy a considerable measure of stability, leisure, and traditional communalistic life, and folktales still remain an essential part of the social life of the people. The expressions "relatively insulated" and "considerable stability" are used advisedly, because no part of Africa, not even the remote rural areas, has altogether escaped the effects of the superimposition of the modern technological culture on the traditional agrarian cultures of Africa.

About three-quarters of contemporary Africa is still rural and agricultural. Within it, folktales still remain an essential element in the recreational and educational life of the people. Most people in the traditional part of Africa have at some time or other taken part in storytelling sessions. They have listened to these stories as part of an active and responsive audience and have more likely than not taken their turn as narrators. Amos Tutuola, whose books will be discussed herein, confessed to the Reverend Parrinder, one of the first Europeans to draw attention to the unique imaginative merits of his writing, that as a child he had been an active participant in storytelling sessions in his village.

AMOS TUTUOLA AND THE ORAL TRADITION

A fairly detailed discussion of the distinction among folktales, legends, and myths is necessary for a proper appraisal of Tutuola's works. Many of his critics have taken it for granted that he is a purveyor of myths.[16] This opinion could not possibly be correct. Myths are a collective possession of the people, and no single individual can lay claim to having invented them. If the West African reader of Tutuola rejects his claim to originality on the mistaken assumption that he has merely rehashed existing mythology, then Tutuola has the ignorance of his admirers to thank for it. His stories fall into the category of folktales. Myths are to a great extent sacred tales; Tutuola's writing belongs to profane storytelling. As a result of their pseudo-religious significance, myths are rigid in form and content and so do not yield much to individual creativity, whereas legends are only slightly less rigid, since the need to stick to the facts embodied in them has a limiting effect on the creative freedom of the narrator. Individual artistic creativity finds the greatest outlet in folktales, because they have neither a ritual significance, like myths, nor a factual necessity, like legends.[17] As a result, folktales not only form the largest group of traditional narratives but they also have the greatest popular appeal.

Within the scope of the folktale there is plenty of room for the exercise of individual imagination and originality. Only the outline of a story needs to be known. The narrator takes this outline and is completely free to embellish it with as much invention as he can muster, and, in fact, much value is attached to his resourcefulness in improvising new and interesting variations. His mode of delivery, dramatic gestures, and verbal dexterity are the essential qualities that mark him out as a good storyteller. In view of this, it is difficult to see why anyone should refuse to acknowledge Tutuola's right to originality and inventiveness. The conventional procedure at storytelling gatherings is something like this (and every West African who has lived in a village will agree): the person whose turn it is to tell his story announces to the audience that he has a story to tell. The audience asks him to tell it. He then proceeds to do so.

The text of any story is public property until the individual whose turn it is to tell a story picks it up. Then it becomes his story. It can be suspected that the reverse process probably applied in balladry and epic narrative. These, requiring a more rigid formalistic structure than the folktale, probably depended on an original transmuting genius who, even though drawing heavily upon the cultural repertoire of the community, had to give formalistic shape to the material before it was ready for absorption into folk literature. An epic narrative must therefore be the product of an original bard, and a ballad, that of an original ballad-maker.[18] The folktale, on the other hand, belongs in its bare outline to the community until the individual picks it up and, during his process of narration, makes it his own. There is therefore no single authentic text. The skeletal text, which embodies the well-known motif, is there, and sometimes, the underlying exemplum. The individual narrator, using the former, builds it up by the use of his own methods. There could therefore be as many texts of one story as there are narrators, some of them very good, some indifferent, and others downright poor, depending on the competence or lack of it of the individual.

In written tradition, with its fixed texts, it is possible to determine the indebtedness of one text to another. It is, for instance, easy to see to what extent La Fontaine's *Fables* incorporate details from Aesop's *Fables* by comparing the two. In the oral tradition, within which the quality of a story depends not only on verbal manipulation but also on dramatic devices such as gestures, facial expressions, and voice modulation, textual comparison is not only unprofitable but impossible. Each text can be regarded as original because it bears a distinctive stylistic stamp. What Tutuola has done in his writing is to refurbish old tales by employing well-known motifs and narrative techniques. He is doing in writing what is perfectly justified in oral tradition—embellishing texts from his replete imagination. These tales have become his own, even though he has had to write them down. This process is similar to "borrowing" and adaptation in Elizabethan literature. Some of the best work produced in this period was by those who "borrowed" their themes from well-known classical and folk texts, or even from the work of living authors, and imaginatively transformed them. Shakespeare made use of existing texts, and in spite of Robert Greene's catty denunciation of "the upstart crow" who decked himself in others' feathers, the world is certainly much the richer for having Shakespeare.

The Palm-Wine Drinkard and *Simbi and the Satyr of the Dark Jungle*, which most people regard as Tutuola's best books, will be discussed here in order to show how much his writing owes to oral tradition. For the purpose of brevity, the titles are abridged to *The Drinkard* and *Simbi*.

◆

The Drinkard deals with the search by the hero for his dead palm-wine tapster. After a series of harrowing adventures, he succeeds in tracing him to Deads' Town. He does not bring him back, however, but instead receives a gift of a magic egg, with which he is enabled to produce anything he wants by merely requesting it from the egg. After further adventures, the Drinkard returns home and settles a dispute between the Sky God and the Earth Goddess, thereby putting an end to the drought that the Sky God caused to spite the earth. *Simbi* is the story of a pretty peasant girl and the daughter of a well-to-do mother who becomes dissatisfied with a life of slothful ease and decides, contrary to her mother's advice, to explore the real meaning of poverty and punishment. After stormy adventures, during which she experiences a great deal of both poverty and punishment, especially at the hands of the noxious Satyr of the Dark Jungle, she returns home a sadder and wiser woman.

The world of these stories is the undifferentiated universe of the traditional folktale, within which intercourse between the living and the dead is possible. In this universe, all nature is humanized. Tutuola recaptures the atmosphere of the immense intimacy between the different elements in nature in his description of the great carnival celebrating the resettling of the Red-people in a new town:

> When the day that they appointed for this special occasion was reached, these fellows (Drum, Song and Dance) came and when 'Drum' started to beat himself, all the people who had been dead for hundreds of years rose up and came to witness 'Drum' when beating; and when 'Song' began to sing, all domestic animals of that new town, bush animals with snakes, etc. came out to see 'Song' personally, but when 'Dance' started to dance, the whole bush creatures, spirits, mountain creatures and also all the river creatures, came to the town to see who was dancing. When these three fellows started at the same time, the whole people of the new town, the whole people that rose up from the grave, animals, snakes, spirits and other nameless creatures, were dancing together with these three fellows.[19]

Such outbursts of vitality recur throughout Tutuola's stories. Man has to struggle hard to ensure a place in the universe. He must compete with the rest of animated nature. He is no absolute monarch exerting untrammeled authority over the rest of the universe. Fortunately, he is able to reinforce his vital force with magical power. He is able, by magic, to change himself into something else when hard-pressed by his adversaries. Metamorphosis offers him both a means of protection and a facility to display his magical power. Tutuola employs the technique of metamorphosis extensively in both *The Drinkard* and *Simbi*.

As a result of this, some enthusiastic critics have referred to his writing as Kafkesque. Kafka also uses the technique of metamorphosis in some of his short stories. The comparison between Tutuola and Kafka, even in respect to their use of metamorphosis, appears tenuous if not altogether misleading. In Kafka's stories, metamorphosis is a process of deenergization, a process demonstrating the deflated state of man when confronted with inexplicable and portentous forces. Tutuola's tales reveal man as possessing the power and the ability to face up to or circumvent the menaces of those inimical forces. Man is not just a helpless and self-pitying cockroach, utterly isolated and rendered incommunicado with his kind; he is not a wretched lamb who is "left in the lurch," or the lost soul hovering perpetually and hopelessly between heaven and earth. In Tutuola, man becomes the consummate strategist who can turn himself into a bird, a lizard, or a self-propelled pebble, with the purpose of getting the better of his adversaries. In Kafka, man is the impotent victim of inexorable fate; in Tutuola, he is the proud possessor of great magical powers with which he defies even fate itself. Kafka's metamorphosed men foreshadow the millions of helpless people in Europe who were to be trodden under the heels of the most ruthless dictatorships. Tutuola's metamorphosed heroes and heroines show them struggling against the fearful and formidable forces of wild nature and the supernatural but who, though often wounded and bruised in the struggle, nevertheless emerge victorious. Whereas metamorphosis in Tutuola emphasizes the dignity and vital energy of humankind, in Kafka it stresses human futility and despair. Finally, Kafka uses metamorphosis parabolically for the purpose of giving a peculiar insight into the predicament of doomed man; Tutuola uses it literally to demonstrate man's hope for survival even in the teeth of the hostile forces that surround him.

An aspect of the world of Tutuola's books is the complete blending of fantasy with conventional realism, a quality that is also very characteristic of the traditional folktale. This aspect is clearly brought out in situations within which the principles of economic rationalization are seen to operate within magical contexts. For instance, when pressed for hard cash, the Drinkard uses his inherited magical powers to turn himself into a canoe, which his wife uses to ferry people across a stream at the rate of 3*d* per adult and 1½*d* per child. Making an average daily turnover of £7.5*s*.3*d*, the Drinkard and his wife are able to amass a handsome sum of £56.11*s*.9*d* at the end of one month. Again, just before the Drinkard and his wife enter the home of the Faithful Mother in the White Tree, they carry out a brisk business transaction with "somebody at the door," selling their death to him for £70.18*s*.6*d*. and lending him their fear on the interest of £3.10*s*.0*d*. When they finally leave the White Tree, they collect their capital (fear) and interest from the said "somebody at the door." They, having sold their death, cannot from now onward be afraid of dying though they still possess the quality of fear, not having sold their fear at the time they sold their death. Within the arcadian Wraith-Island, and again in the new town of the Red-people, the Drinkard becomes an agricultural landlord making use of the mysterious little creature, the Invisible Pawn, to cultivate his extensive farm. Death is shown in *The Drinkard* as leading a sedentary and retired life on his farm, and when the Drinkard visits him, he is busy tending his yam crops. Being Death, of course he is living alone and is both his own master and laborer. In *Simbi*, the heroine pawns her services to the decrepit iconophile in return for shelter, food, and clothing at a time when she is almost completely indigent in the Dark Jungle. She has to work very hard and devotedly to satisfy even her most elementary needs.

This essential economic rationalization, which operates on the formula that material needs must be paid for either in cash or in kind, exists side by side with a magical determinism that appears entirely antithetical to it. By possession of the appropriate magical object (such as the egg which the Tapster gives to the Drinkard) and application of the proper spells, a man is able to procure his needs without physical labor or money payment. Very often, however, it turns out that fantasy merely subserves the interest of realism, and magical determinism in economic affairs only goes to strengthen the realistic principles of the *homo economicus*. To take the example of the magical egg again, after the parasitic neighbors of the Drinkard have been fed for some time through the agency of the magic egg, an accident occurs and the egg breaks. The Drinkard patches it up but when it is commanded to produce food and drink, it produces whips that lash the idle parasites back to their homes. In the final analysis, this episode seems to suggest that there is really nothing like honest labor for honest returns. The predominance of economic rationalization—whether by way of employment of labor, money lending, or commercialism—over magical determinism in economic matters is an essential aspect of the blending of fantasy and realism within the folktale tradition.

Another aspect of this blending is shown by the fact that, within the seemingly amorphous structure of Tutuola's universe, there are clearly defined boundaries as fully demarcated as modern national boundaries—and a good deal more rigid since the folktale world, having no provision for the visaed traveler, has no means of admitting him from the outside except on hostile terms. Within the Tutuolan jungle, therefore, the inhabitants, whether they are human trees, human animals, or even spirit beings, know the extent of their own territory and do not violate the territorial integrity of their neighbors. Both the Drinkard and Simbi owe much of their suffering to their not respecting these "national" boundaries. But it is also an essential attribute of the protagonist that he cannot respect these boundaries because, if he does, the scope of his action would be unnecessarily narrowed. In fact, the action could not even be expected to begin at all because the protagonist cannot leave his own territory if he is afraid of violating the integrity of other people's territory. The effect of a great immensity and variety of color, character, and idiosyncracy derives essentially from this geographical differentiation. Even though the unaccustomed eye of the hero cannot immediately recognize them within the dream like half-light of the Tutuolan jungle, the inhabitants are acutely aware of them. Thus, the Faithful Mother stops short of the stream that separates her domain from the next territory when she sees off the Drinkard and his wife. When the Drinkard and his wife are attacked by the army of horrible children along Deads' Road, they escape into the forest, which turns out to be the territory of the wicked giant, who catches them in his net and makes them his slaves. Again, when the Drinkard and his wife change into a pebble and propel themselves across the stream, they automatically put themselves beyond the reach of the angry mountain creatures hot in their pursuit because, by conventional usage, the latter cannot cross the stream that forms the boundary between their territory and another.

There are distinctive physical and idiosyncratic differences between the inhabitants of the different parts of this world, and Tutuola gives the reader a quick insight into these differences by the use of remarkably cryptic descriptive terms such as the Sinners' Town, the Path of Death, the Town of the Multi-Coloured People, the Town where Nobody Sings, the Satyr of the Dark Jungle, the Red-People of the Red-Town, Deads' Town, and so on. Differences in behavior exist between different groups, as shown in the absurd ways of the people of the Unreturnable Heaven's Town, who would climb the ladder first before leaning it against the tree. Differential behavior also exists between the living and the dead, as the Drinkard learns to his cost in Deads' Town. Differences in physical appearance sometimes form the basis for discrimination against the foreigner as shown by the racist king of the Multi-Coloured People telling Simbi and her fellow refugees: "We don't hate yourselves but your mono-colour." The Tutuolan world is therefore an un-differentiated universe only in the sense that within it all nature is humanized. In other respects, it shows clearly defined geographical and national bound-aries and racial differences. It is a part of the hero's prerogative that his activities carry him across these various barriers. His cosmopolitanism and absolute freedom from physical constraint enable him to move freely through the rigidly partitioned world of the traditional folktale.

The hero, however, is no brazen anarchistic revolutionary, contemptuous of customary usages and impatient of established procedures. He violates the territorial rights of others because he is impelled by the circumstances of his single-minded pursuit to do so. He recognizes himself as an outsider in the new communities where his adventures take him. He is suspected and feared because, as a stranger, he is reputed to have a malignant and potentially dangerous influence over the well-being of the indigenous community. Not being a revolutionary, the hero does not set out to subvert the strange com-munity, but the hostility of the natives puts him on the defensive and, in his effort to defend himself, he soon brings calamity upon them. The community is never quite the same again after the hero has made his way into it. The fate of the Red-People seems to justify the apprehension with which for-eigners are regarded, for the Drinkard turns out to be the instrument of their destruction after he has settled in their midst in the new town, and Simbi's arrival in the Dark Jungle robs it of its colorful proprietor, the Satyr.

Hostility to the stranger is not just a case of morbid irrational xenophobia. The stranger is supposed to possess the evil eye, which makes him a source of great danger to the community, and the earliest opportunity is taken to get rid of him either by expulsion or by some more wicked means. Here, as in most other cases, cruelty stems from fear and apprehension. In a significant way, however, the attitude to strangers in folktales differs from the attitude to strangers in traditional society. Whereas in the former the stranger is an outsider and remains an outsider even after he has settled down, in the latter he could be, and often is, ritually incorporated into the community and ceases to be regarded as an outsider, in much the same way as an alien who has been granted a country's citizenship ceases to be regarded as such. By the rites of incorporation, the erstwhile outsider now shares the common mystical bonds that bind the community. In folktales, he remains outside these mystic bonds and therefore has a destiny that is different from, and often in conflict with, the destiny of the community. This lack of a common destiny is the root cause of the inevitable disaster the folktale hero brings to the community in which he finds himself.

This distinction between attitude to strangers in folktales and in traditional African societies is of some importance in view of the opinion sometimes expressed, especially by Western observers, that the tribe in traditional Africa is a closed association that recognizes only itself and its own interests and maintains purely negative and hostile relations with outside associations and persons. The concept of "them" and "us" is certainly strong in these societies (as in all others because it is by having identified common interests of its own that a society regards itself as an entity in contradistinction from others of the same kind), and communities are aware of themselves by means of the common bonds of custom, beliefs, political identity, and ritual obligations that unite their people in the same way that the possession of a national flag and anthem, common allegiance to a political authority and, to some extent, the existence of a national ethos, marks out and defines the existence of a modern nation-state. But a traditional society is not quite as closed as it is made out to be; neither is it necessarily in a perpetual state of hostility toward outsiders. Apart from the possibility of ritual incorporation of strangers, a traditional community has economic and sometimes ritual ties with neighboring communities, and this makes it imperative that friendly relations exist between collaborating groups. The practice of exogamy further increases the need for peaceful and friendly relationships and leads to the lessening of conflicts between different communities and peoples.

The "foreign wife" motif in folktales hardly applies in traditional society. According to this, the foreign wife is marked out for discriminatory treatment, and her children are victims of the injustice to which those of indigenous mothers are not subjected. In *Simbi*, for instance, we are told that the heroine has to leave her woodcutter husband because the townspeople have sacrificed her two sons to their gods because she is not "a native." Such wicked injustice is hardly possible in a traditional society, and least of all in the Yoruba society to which Tutuola belongs. The Yoruba have a patrilineal system and marriage among them is patrilocal. The children of a marriage belong to the father's lineage group, and there is no question whatever of their being regarded as strangers within their father's community.

The folktale world is therefore not a verisimilitude of the actual traditional world in every detail. What happens is that the potential tensions and stresses in traditional society, which are taken care of by cleverly patterned social behavior, are sometimes played up in folktales with the purpose of heightening the emotional effect of the narrative. From this point of view, exaggeration and sensationalism are the keynotes. Petty jealousies between siblings, co-wives, and parents and children are constructed into elaborate machinations often ending in murder, and fear and suspicion of strangers lead inevitably to a monstrous sadism such as Simbi experiences as the woodcutter's wife. This sensationalism elicits feelings of horror, wonderment, and fascination from the audience. Tutuola's genius as a storyteller manifests itself in his easy grasp of this aspect of storytelling.

His stories recapture the essential humanism of the world of the folktale. Within it, all nature is not only imbued with vital force and is humanized, but Homo sapiens is the pivot round which the drama revolves. He, in all his goodness and nastiness, is the real center of the Tutuolan world. Even where an animal is the hero of a story, it is invested with human qualities. As Léopold Senghor writes: "In the fable, the animal is seldom a totem; it is this or that one whom everyone in the village knows well: the stupid or the tyrannical or wise and good chief, the young man who makes reparation for injustices . . ."[20] In Tutuola, we see man at grips with hostile elements, the jungle, vicious monsters, and supernatural beings, struggling often to save himself by the skin of his teeth from the evils that surround him. Unlike the ballad, whose preoccupation is with the thing done or the event that happened, Tutuola's story is important in reference to the personality of the protagonist.

This should be emphasized because the popular image of the traditional African as the helpless victim of his hostile environment is contrary to that held by the African of himself as reflected in traditional folktales. The African is aware of the problems, physical and otherwise, which surround him and threaten his survival, but he is immensely confident in his ability to face up to these problems with courage and mental resourcefulness. This basic confidence is dramatized in many folktales, where the triumph of the hero over hostile forces represents the triumph of mankind. The triumphant hero sees himself as a member of a community whose well-being and survival are also his own. Even though he recognizes himself as an individual with an individual destiny, he is also aware that he cannot work out that destiny outside the framework of his community. The concern of the community becomes his concern and his egocentricity is strongly tempered with altruism. The traditional African draws strength from his group and then helps to sustain the group by his individual contribution. Both Simbi and the Drinkard are essentially individualists working out their personal salvation with courage and resourcefulness, but they also realize that personal achievements, to be worthwhile, must be linked to the overall well-being of the community. Both therefore clinch their adventures by performing some service of immense social advantage: Simbi, by saving her town from the ravages of Dogo, the notorious slave-raider, and the Drinkard by settling the quarrel between the Sky God and the Earth Goddess and thereby putting an end to the famine that torments his town.

Judging from the folktale world, the individual's awareness of his membership in, and responsibility to, his society does not automatically make him a slave to its institutions. The individual is not a mere pawn within a rigid and ruthlessly authoritarian society, a blind, unquestioning slave to his tribal institutions, with neither individual will nor freedom of action and personal responsibility. Obviously, the traditional society provides ethical and social guidance to its members through its mores, prohibitions, and sanctions; but the individual has freedom of action and does exercise full responsibility for this. Both Simbi and the Drinkard's wife follow their own paths in spite of parental advice, and they fully shoulder their responsibility. Of necessity, the hold the community has over the individual cannot be so constrictive that the expression of individuality is completely frustrated; conversely the individual cannot be so individualistic that he regards his interests as entirely independent of those of the community within which he lives. Either case would inevitably lead to the complete impoverishment of both. In traditional society, a happy mean exists that imparts strength and unity. Its essential humanism, as exemplified in folktale narratives, arises from the awareness of an individual destiny within a larger, more inclusive communal destiny. The exploits of the folktale hero are expected to inspire the audience with courage, daring, and mental alertness—qualities that are possible only within the context of a society that recognizes the existence of individual will and freedom of action. Without this important element, traditional societies would have perished from a lack of stimulus and inspiration to overcome the hostile forces that surround them.

Tutuola makes use of the stereotyped characters found in the folktale. Both Simbi and the Drinkard are quest protagonists, and the quest-type character is one of the best known in West Africa. The pattern is very clear: first, there is the hero, then the well-defined objective of the quest, and, finally, the taskmasters who are consciously or unconsciously operating to hinder the hero from attaining his objective. Among the most striking episodes of the two books are the rescue of the old man's daughter from the home of the skulls by the Drinkard, the trapping of Death, the birth of the Terrible Infant from the left thumb of the Drinkard's wife, the meeting with the Faithful Mother in the White Tree (all in *The Drinkard*), and Simbi's protracted and epic battle with the Satyr of the Dark Jungle (*Simbi*). The essence of the quest tale is that everything is built on a heroic scale. The tasks imposed on the hero are formidable and dangerous, and he succeeds in performing them by a characteristic combination of personal power (physical and magical), intelligence, and bluff. Thus, in his mission to capture Death (a task imposed on the Drinkard by an old man in return for having shown him the way to his dead Tapster), the Drinkard displays these qualities. On his way to Death's house, he reaches a crossroad. To find out which way to follow, he lies down in the middle of the road with his head, legs, and hands pointing in different directions. When, soon afterward, some market-women arrive, their comments (as one may expect) solve the hero's dilemma.

"Who was the mother of this fine boy, he slept on the roads and put his head towards Death's road," they shouted. That is all the hero wants to know—his head is pointing "towards Death's road." In Death's house, his struggle with Death is not only a matter of displaying physical or magical power, it is also a battle of wits, and the Drinkard triumphs because he proves to be more nimble-witted and resourceful. In her struggle with the formidable

Satyr of the Dark Jungle, Simbi displays great agility and astuteness. For instance, she confuses the Satyr by saying she would metamorphose into Iro instead of Iromi. The Satyr knows that Iromi means a waterfly but he has never heard of Iro (which at all events does not exist). When Simbi changes into a waterfly, the Satyr is at his wit's end.

In this display of intellectual dexterity, the quest-hero shows an aspect of another kind of folktale hero—the trickster (or Picaro). The essential difference between the two is that the latter is something of a rogue; the former is not. Both move from one adventure to another (hence the term "picaresque" to denote the exploits of a traveling rogue-hero), but, whereas the trickster's adventures are directed towards the aggrandizement of deep-seated perversities, the quest-hero is single-mindedly bent upon achieving a worthy objective. He is courageous, bold, resourceful, intelligent, and pleasant, whereas the trickster is clever, sly, intemperate, and given to phallic obsessions.

Tutuola's *Simbi* and *The Drinkard* have a picaresque quality without the rogue element. This is the sense in which the term was applied in the eighteenth century, especially to the prose epics of Fielding. Evidence of the picaresque nature of Tutuola's plot is that, while structurally having a beginning, a middle, and an end, it does not conform to the Aristotelian criterion of the well-constructed plot—that is, it does not represent a unity so closely knit that the transposal or withdrawal of any of the incidents would disjoint or dislocate the whole. It derives its unity essentially from the protagonist, whose participation in the incidents holds the plot loosely together. In this respect, the quest-tale plot is more structurally akin to the Spanish picaresque than to the eighteenth-century English imitations, with their more coordinated plots. In *Tom Jones*, for instance, the characters converge in London by a series of coincidences leading to the denouement. Transposition of incidents (especially the middle ones) in Tutuola would not be of great structural consequence.

Tutuola makes use of the quest-type folktale because, depending as it does on the marvelous and the sensational, and having a great deal of room for episodic development, it allows his creative imagination the fullest play. One of the ways he exploits its possibilities is by building not only his protagonists but also his antagonists on a gigantic scale and imbuing them with immense supernatural powers (much in the same way that Milton builds up his Satan in *Paradise Lost*) to give a heroic quality to the ensuing struggle. Here, for example, is the description of the totemic Red Fish to whom the Drinkard is about to be sacrificed, and whom he ultimately kills:

> . . . its head was just like a tortoise's head, but it was as big as an elephant's
> head and it had over thirty horns and large eyes which surrounded the head.
> All these horns were spread out as an umbrella. It could not walk but was only
> gliding on the ground like a snake and its body was just like a bat's body and
> covered with long red hair like strings. It could only fly to a short distance,
> and if it shouted, a person who was four miles away would hear. All the eyes

which surrounded its head were closing and opening at the same time as if a man was pressing a switch on and off.[21]

We see the hero faced with a being physically gigantic and appalling, endowed with an immense, undefined power. Its grotesque shape, combined with its gliding-flying propensities, its electric-torch eyes, and its loud voice reinforce the atmosphere of terror. This use of the grotesque and larger-than-life aspect is a universal characteristic of the epic narrative. The Red Fish reminds one of Bunyan's Appolyion, the hideous giant with scales like a fish, wings like a dragon, and a mouth like a lion, out of which he belched fire and smoke. The loudness of its voice can be likened to that of Stentor which, as Homer says, could drown the waves.

The heroic stature of Tutuola's protagonists and, to some extent, the adventures in which they are involved, have sometimes led to his being compared with Dante and Bunyan. One can, in fact, see some resemblances to these authors, though one has to keep the comparison within reasonable limits without attempting to make normative judgments and realize that his writing belongs to a different tradition. His heroes and the heroes of the representative works of Dante and Bunyan are involved in some kind of peregrination: the Drinkard goes from the world of the living to Deads' Town in search of his dead Tapster; Christian goes to the Celestial City in search of salvation; Dante makes an imaginary journey that takes him to Hell, Purgatory, and Heaven in search of spiritual experience. These journeys span the natural and the supernatural worlds. Dante's poem and Bunyan's prose fiction derive their motifs and inspiration from a Christian world view and are clearly eschatological whereas Tutuola's writing derives them from the traditional African weltanschauung. The Christian works are allegorical, whereas Tutuola's is immersed in the cultural consciousness of traditional Africa as embodied in cosmology, moral values, and attitudes. Finally, all three writers, within their different cultural milieux, have successfully applied their creative imagination, to producing works of outstanding vigor, vividness, and beauty.

Apart from stock characters, Tutuola also uses well-known motifs and themes that are derived from traditional values, ideas of morality, and norms of personal relationship. The motifs include that of the enfant terrible, derived from a belief that the abnormal child has a peculiar relationship with some supernatural agencies as a result of the circumstances surrounding his birth. The enfant terrible is often a source of affliction to his parents in particular and the community in general. Within this category fall twins, revenants, and abnormally born children. The Drinkard's son, born from his wife's left thumb, and Bako (the Siamese twin in *Simbi*) belong here. The first is as much a source of torment and affliction to his parents as is Bako to Simbi and the other "refugees." Tutuola also makes use of the "popular godmother." This motif deals with the character of those benign old people who help the young and needy with material sustenance. In folktales, they are often kindly, elderly women who emerge as if from nowhere to render succor to the hard-pressed hero. In *The Drinkard* the hero and his wife are much relieved by the Faithful Mother in the White Tree, and Simbi is saved from starving to death by the decrepit iconophile.

Tutuola ingeniously employs the quarrel between the Sky God and the Earth Goddess to tie up the plot of *The Drinkard*. The myth of the Sky God, the *Deus otiosus*, is widely held in West Africa.[22] He is supposed to be the Creator of the Universe but has detached himself from this universe because man has polluted it with his sins. As a result of his distance from the world, he does not permeate the people's religious consciousness to the same degree as the ancestral spirits and minor gods. As a result, the Sky God has no shrines, no priests, and hardly features at all in religious worship. People appeal to him only as a last resort when human justice has been denied to them and the other gods have turned their backs on them. To invoke the Sky God is, in reality, a final gesture of despair and disillusionment. The explanation is that, by banishing himself to the sky, the Sky God puts himself beyond the immediate sphere of activities in purely agricultural communities where the Earth Goddess and the gods that control rain, fertility, diseases, and so on, are of more immediate significance. Christian missionaries, such as the Reverend John Taylor, who guardedly admires the "this-worldliness" of traditional African religion,[23] are intrigued by its materialistic orientation, essentially because the Sky God, who is held to be at the head of the Pantheon, is hardly made much of while the inferior gods and the ancestral spirits are much revered because they are directly involved in the people's struggles for material well-being.

Tutuola employs this belief to resolve the plot of his book. The Earth Goddess and the Sky God, once friends, are now involved in a quarrel over primacy, and the latter has withdrawn rain from the earth to demonstrate his superior power.[24] As a result, the earth is afflicted with drought and there is a famine. The Drinkard returns from his quest to find his country in a hopeless and piteous condition. Full of self-confidence built up during his quest, he arbitrates the quarrel by sending a tribute from earth to the sky, thereby establishing the primacy of the sky over the earth and ending the famine.

It is typical of Tutuola's close adherence to traditional belief that the carrying of the mediation sacrifice to the Sky God is assigned to a slave, because direct confrontation with the divine is held to be highly dangerous. Everyone refuses to carry the sacrifice except the slave, who has no free choice. The accomplishment of the mission excludes him from any further communion with other people: he has dealt directly with the divine and his person has, as a result, become sacred and dangerous to the security of ordinary folk.

This view applied to the Osu, a slave caste in Igboland which, in the remote past, formed a high priesthood that performed mediational rites to the gods. As a result, their persons were regarded as sacred, and it was forbidden to shed their blood, shave their heads, or have any sort of physical or social contact with them. The sacred nature of their functions, which was transferred to their bodies, made them social outcasts. Until quite recently, the predicament of their descendants was one of the most painful social problems facing the Eastern Nigeria government, and legislation had to be passed forbidding discrimination against them.

In both *Simbi* and *The Drinkard* we are made aware of a society in which sacrifice is an important aspect of religion, not just as a means of currying favor with the gods but as an essential part of the pattern of life. Divination plays an active part in the unraveling of the unknown. The Drinkard's wife, who fulfills the dual function of philosophical companion and prophet, expresses herself in gnomic pronouncements typical of professional diviners. Simbi consults a diviner to know what the future has in store for her. Kings play an important social role as the benign protectors and counselors of their people: they are not bloodthirsty, arbitrary tyrants, and when they have to offer human sacrifice, they have often opted for foreigners who do not partake of the mystic bond that unites the indigenous people. Human relations count for a great deal in traditional African societies and folktales emphasize their importance in sharply-pointed morals. Ingratitude, regarded by Dante as one of the most reprehensible sins, is severely punished. The whole population of Red Town in *The Drinkard*, and the ungrateful hunter in *Simbi*, pay for this sin with their lives, while the ungrateful parasites of the Drinkard's town undergo severe flagellation. Obedience to parents and elders by children is a cardinal virtue; disobedience is often visited by punishment and remorse. The whole story of *Simbi* is an extended moral treatise on the theme of parental obedience. The woman who later becomes the Drinkard's wife has to go through the horror of marrying a mere skull posing as a complete man after borrowing human parts from several clients. This combination of didacticism and entertainment satisfies one of the canons of traditional literary expectations: namely, that good literature should instruct as well as please.

A consideration of the didactic aspect leads to the moral dilemmas that are sometimes posed. Tutuola presents two of these at the end of *The Drinkard*. The first, dealing with a professional debtor and a professional debt-collector, is not, in my opinion, nearly as good as the second—the love-trial. According to the latter, three women and their husband are going on a journey when the husband suddenly stumbles and dies. The first wife instantly dies in order to keep him company in the other world; the second sets off to discover a wizard who can revive the dead; while the third stays by the bodies to keep away wild beasts that would otherwise maul them. Later, the second wife brings back a wizard who revives the bodies. Asked what the fee for his labor is, he demands to be given one of the wives. None agrees to be given away and the dilemma, therefore, is which one should be given to him? Here, the audience recognizes, or is expected to recognize, that the three wives have, each in her own way, demonstrated their affection for their husband, one by dying with him, another by bringing his reviver, and the third by protecting his body from harm. They have shown that they love him in life and in death and are prepared to make any sacrifice to be with him. He alone gives meaning to their sacrifice. To go with the wizard would mean being cut off physically and spiritually. Such a sacrifice would no longer have any meaning: it is as if Christ had allowed himself to be crucified only so man could be claimed by the devil—a case of stupid self-immolation and a repudiation of reason. The audience is made both judge and jury in the case, but everyone knows that there cannot be a just and equitable decision.

It may be asked why "dilemma stories" form a considerable part of the African folktale corpus. Alta Jablow's view that dilemmas abound in West African narrative because West Africans are interested in legal problems[25] can be quickly dismissed, because the image of the African as the incorrigible litigant who spends most of his time talking "palavers" is one of those clichés that have no basis in fact. It is naive to imagine that indigenous African societies, not having had the literate facilities for drawing up deeds and agreements, must have been in a chronic state of disorder. Every society evolves ways and means of reducing potential conflicts among its members, and in ours there are well-established sanctions, apart from the purely legalistic ones, for preventing anti-social tendencies and the possibility of people having their rights trampled underfoot. At all events, the idea of the dilemma being used to inculcate legal expertise is unfounded. The problems are very often not legalistic in nature but are always part of human life. People are constantly faced with choices, the making of which may not only be difficult but often tragic. The Kantian differentiation between the absolute and the categorical imperatives as the basis of the tragic dilemma no doubt has a universal application, but many dilemmas of the African folktale have no immediate divine or ethical basis that could help to arbitrate in making a choice or at least point a way to a final resolution. They are not always as clear-cut as, for example, Antigone's choice between a religious duty to a dead brother and her duty to the state. Tutuola asks which of these wives, whose loyalty and affection to their husband have been proved, ought to be sacrificed to the wizard?

Dilemmas of this nature are posed here to remind the audience that life contains many moral imponderables that cannot be resolved by making a facile or an apparently clever judgment. The question transcends mere intellectual juggling: it touches the very depths of our emotional being. In short, many of these dilemmas cannot be resolved and are not meant to be. Whereas the literary artist attempts to explore the complicated implications of a particular moral dilemma for the purpose of revealing his own individual insight, the duty of the traditional storyteller is to enunciate it in the clearest way possible and to leave each individual to reach his own solution, if he can. This is exactly what Tutuola has done.

◆

The folktale as a well-developed narrative can be examined not only on the basis of its structure and content, but also on the basis of style. Its stylistic quality derives essentially from its spoken rather than its written form and is therefore more akin to drama. The competent raconteur uses the possibilities offered by the oral nature of his narrative to immense advantage. By the modulation of his voice, facial expressions, and gestures, he can express varied emotional nuances that are difficult to recapture in written form. The use of songs and ditties not only heightens and vivifies the narrative, it establishes a rapport between the storyteller and his audience. It is expected that the loss of these dramatic devices and songs, as a result of committing what is essentially an oral form to writing, will weaken Tutuola's stories. Anyone who is brought up within the oral tradition cannot fail to notice some gaps in the plot of a written version. In *Simbi*, for instance, the absence of song is often felt because Tutuola tells us from the beginning that Simbi is an expert singer who has delighted the people of her village. However, he goes some way toward capturing the effect of song by the simple colloquial rhythm of the speeches. This effect comes out in the scene when Simbi narrowly escapes being sacrificed to the wicked gods of the people of Sinners' Town. Several of Simbi's companions have already been sacrificed, and now that it is her turn, she bursts into a long sorrowful song, part of which is an appeal to the people to save her life and the lives of her surviving colleagues. She sings and the king responds in song also:

> "Please the King, set the rest of us free."
> "Ha!-a!-a! don't you know you have become the slave of these gods this midnight . . . ?"
> "Please, the chiefs deliver us from these gods!"
> "Ha!-a!-a! you chiefs, don't you hear her plead now . . . ?"[26]

Then the king, the chiefs, the prominent, and all the common people who were outside the shrine replied to Simbi's request by singing loudly: "Don't you hear, she asks the chiefs to deliver her. But she is not aware that she has become the slave of the gods this midnight, gods who are going to drink her [Simbi's] blood in just one or two minutes' time."

"Having heard like that . . . she changed that song to a kind of melodious song."

She soon has the whole congregation swaying and dancing. One may say that the reporting of the singing here, like the reporting of an action in the theater, is no adequate substitute for the real thing, and that in a storytelling session the alternate singing by the victim and the congregation would have produced an operatic effect that cannot be adequately recaptured in writing. Nevertheless, the colloquial rhythm of the speeches, especially the interjected remarks and repetitions, does give the *feel* not so much of traditional folktale singing, which can be extremely lively, but of the kind of irregular incantatory singing that one sometimes hears at a place of ritual sacrifice, a general stirring within the taut, sacrificial atmosphere like the rustling of dry leaves under a dark, overcast sky.

Tutuola achieves his best storytelling effects by a simple, direct, and almost bald narrative method. He goes straight to the story without any preambles or circumlocutions. In four brief opening paragraphs, he sets the stage for the long adventure in *The Drinkard*:

> "I was a palm-wine drinkard since I was a boy of ten years of age. I had no other work than to drink palm-wine in my life. In those days we did not know other money, except COWRIES, so that everything was very cheap, and my father was the richest man in our town.
>
> "My father got eight children and I was the eldest among them, all of the rest were hard-workers, but myself was an expert palm-wine drinkard. I was drinking palm-wine from morning till night and from night till morning. By that time I could not drink ordinary water at all except palm-wine.
>
> "But when my father noticed that I could not do any work more than to drink, he engaged an expert-palm wine tapster for me: he had no other work than to tap palm-wine every day.
>
> "So my father gave me a palm-tree farm which was nine miles square and it contained 560,000 palm-trees, and this palm-wine tapster was tapping one hundred and fifty kegs of palm-wine every morning, but before 2 o'clock P.M., I would have drunk all of it; after that he would go and tap another 75 kegs in the evening which I would drink till morning. So my friends were uncountable by that time and they were drinking palm-wine with me from morning till a late hour in the night. But when my palm-wine tapster completed the period of 15 years that he was tapping the palm-wine for me, then my father died suddenly, and when it was the 6th month after my father had died, the tapster went to the palm-tree farm on a Sunday evening to tap palm-wine for me. When he reached the farm, he climbed one of the tallest palm-trees in the farm to tap palm-wine but as he was tapping one he fell down unexpectedly and died at the foot of the palm-tree as a result of injuries."[27]

In these few paragraphs we are given, in a graphic way, the time-setting of the story. This, as has been stated earlier, is one of the few stylistic requirements of folktale narrative, the temporal remove that helps to give plausibility to incidents that would otherwise seem incredible in a contemporary setting. Then we are given a brief insight into the character of the Drinkard. He is obviously utterly spoiled by his father. We are shown by facts and figures his obsessive addiction to palm-wine and then, of course, we are told of the death of the Tapster, which necessitates the quest.

◆

Tutuola's humor and sensitive nose for the kind of detail that gives beauty, power, and immediacy to writing are illustrated in almost every page of his books. Simbi's conversation with Dogo the slave-raider along the Path of Death and with the Satyr of the Dark Jungle at the first encounter are handled with delicate humor that is greatly reinforced by the deadly menace lurking behind the apparent innocuousness of the situations. Tutuola's imaginative inventiveness is at its best in the description of the masque cunningly staged by the Satyr of the Dark Jungle as a trap for capturing Simbi. The magic hall within which the masque is staged, the phantom orchestra, and the ultra-beautiful ladies are all described with engaging ease and ample imaginative detail. The last arrivals at this colorful pageant are the six fearful ostriches who wear white shoes on their hooves and cover their faces with masks. The image conjured up by the entire masque is one of a great variety of color and ornament and a sort of fairy-tale ballet whose effect is increased by the knowledge that hidden in an obscure corner, ready to pounce at any moment and dissolve the whole scene, is the implacable Satyr. The ability to produce a fascinated response behind which there is a background of dread and horror is one of the most outstanding qualities of Tutuola's genius as a storyteller.

Finally, an aspect of his writing that has intrigued many readers is the incorporation of several elements from modern culture. In the dark jungle, time is measured in hours and minutes, as though the protagonists are carrying their pocket watches, distance is gauged in miles, and business is conducted in pounds, shillings, and pence. The skulls chasing after the Drinkard are likened to a thousand petrol-drums pushing themselves along a hard road. Bombers, buoys, technicolor, telephones, electric switches, and the other paraphernalia of modern civilization, all find their way into these stories. A bewildered German reader asked me why this is so and even compared Tutuola's stories with those of the Brothers Grimm to show that "pure" examples cannot incorporate "foreign" cultural elements.

An explanation for this phenomenon must be sought in the nature of the traditional African folktale. It is a very free narrative form and the narrator has ample scope to incorporate whatever elements within the experience of the community he thinks will make his story effective, especially since these elements do not alter plot, setting, or moral purpose. Even though Tutuola's stories (like all traditional folktales) refer to a remote age, the fact that he was writing in the second half of the twentieth century meant that he would have to incorporate some modern elements that have become part of the everyday reality of Nigerian life. Even an illiterate person in the streets of Lagos has seen a clock, a petrol-drum, and a torch, and may have heard of bombers, telephones, and technicolor. Tutuola's life in the capital must have made him aware of the buoys in the harbor, and his Christian education must have familiarized him with angels, and so on.

These things cannot correctly be regarded as "foreign" and are as much part of the composite culture of modern Africa as are the purely traditional elements. In the words of Kofi Busia: "Survivals of extremely old cultures can be found alongside recently borrowed inventions and ideas. The old and the new are both a part of Africa as it is today. The talking drum belongs as much to contemporary African cultures as does the telegraph or the jazz band; the baby at its mother's back as much as the baby in the pram; the lineage or clan as much as the trade union or the political party; the chief as much as the president. All have been accepted and incorporated into the ever-changing and growing cultures that constitute Africa's way of life."[28]

Because the folktale narrator builds his story essentially from contemporary material even while asserting that his story refers to a remote past, it must be conceded that Tutuola is perfectly justified in incorporating such elements of modern industrial civilization as have become part of neo-African culture. The analogy with the stories of the Brothers Grimm does not therefore apply. In that Tutuola's education has not gone beyond the elementary school, it is something of an advantage, because he is much nearer to traditional society than if he were better educated; cultural contact operates mostly through education, and the more highly educated are likely to be the more acculturated.

Reading Tutuola's stories, anyone who has grown up within the oral tradition cannot but be impressed by his effort to capture the real folktale effect. One can almost hear the speaking voice and discern the emotional nuances as one is carried along from one adventure to another. He thinks his stories in the vernacular and writes them in English much as he would have told them in the vernacular to a group of listeners. We can appreciate them if we see them within this context. But this is not all. Although he has drawn his material largely from oral tradition, he has also succeeded in using the immense possibilities offered by writing to build his stories on a scale that would have been impossible for an illiterate narrator to do.

Non-West African readers who do not understand the chief influences in Tutuola's writing tend to invest him with qualities of excellence he has largely obtained from the living tradition of village storytelling. His West African readers, on the other hand, recognizing his close identification with this tradition, have all too frequently refused to acknowledge his real imaginative merits (by utilizing the facilities offered by the alphabetic script) in producing works whose scope, beauty, and variety would have been impossible within the narrow, formal potentiality of the former.

The typical traditional narrative form is built around a single theme and is self-sufficient in all its relevant details of structure, style, and didactic purpose. For instance, the theme of the obdurate daughter who marries a demon-lover is by itself enough to make a full story. The story of Ogilisi Akwalaka in C. O. D. Ekwensi's *Ikolo the Wrestler and Other Ibo Tales*,[29] which is a true folktale form, and the story of the girl who marries a skull in *The Drinkard*, which is just an episode in a long chain of adventures, simply illustrate this. Whereas Ekwensi's story is sufficient unto itself, Tutuola's is just an episode that is strung on to many others to make a bigger, more complex story.

The uniqueness of Tutuola's work rests on his ability to assimilate elements peculiar to the oral tradition with elements peculiar to the literary tradition: in other words, to impose a literary organization upon essentially oral narrative material. He thus represents an example of a transitional stage in the formal artistic evolution from a purely oral narrative tradition to a purely literary narrative one.

NOTES

1. Wale Olumide, "Amos Tutuola's Reviewers and the Educated Africans," *New Nigerian Forum* (New York, 1960), 5–7.

2. Jack R. Goody and Ian Watt, "The Consequences of Literacy," *Comparative Studies in Society and History* 5 (April 1963): 306.

3. Obviously oral storytelling is an essential aspect of life in agricultural and rural communities. In *Gods, Demons and Others* (New York, 1948), 1–10, R. K. Narayan has given an important insight into the storytelling tradition of rural India. The world of his stories is strikingly similar to the African world in its storytelling tradition. Although his stories are based on manuscript texts, the mode of their delivery is essentially oral. H. M. and N. K. Chadwick have elaborately documented the oral traditions of various peoples of the world that have been written down after the introduction of literacy. See their great work, *The Growth of Literature*, 3 vols. (Cambridge 1932–40).

4. For a study of style in West African riddles, see William Bascom, "Literary Style in Yoruba Riddles," *Journal of American Folklore* 62 (Jan.–March 1949).

5. Jan Vansina has a more elaborate typological identification of African oral tradition in his *Oral Tradition* (London, 1965). The three categories above are adequate for our purpose.

6. F. Boas has rightly asserted that the mythology (and tales) of a people constitute "the autobiography of the tribe," 31st Annual Report, *Bureau of American Ethnology* (1909–10):27–37.

7. For the qualities of the trickster character, see Paul Radin, *The Trickster, A Study in American Indian Mythology* (London, 1955).

8. Paul Radin, ed., *African Folk-tales and Sculpture* (New York, 1952). Also, for world distribution of folk motifs, see Stith Thompson, *Motif-Index of Folk Literature* (Bloomington, Indiana, 1955–58).

9. M. J. C. Hodgart, *The Ballad* (London, 1950), 116.

10. James G. Frazer, "The Magic Art," *The Golden Bough* (London, 1922), 52–214. See also Edward B. Tylor, *Primitive Culture: Researches into the Development of Mythology, Philosophy, Religion, Art, and Custom*, vol. 1 (London, 1871), 115–21.

11. Max Gluckman's inaugural address as professor of social anthropology in Manchester University.

12. Lucien Lévy-Bruhl, *The Soul of the Primitive* (New York, 1966).

13. E. E. Evans-Pritchard, *Witchcraft, Oracle, and Magic Among the Azande* (Oxford, 1937). See also Max Gluckman, *Custom and Conflict in Africa* (Oxford, 1963), especially the section titled "The Logic in Witchcraft," 81–108.

14. See "Folklore in Literature—A Symposium," *Journal of American Folklore* 70 (1957).

15. Richard Ellman, *Yeats: The Man and the Masks* (London, 1961), 267.

16. Gerald Moore's *Seven African Writers* (London, 1962); K. E. Senanu in *The Commonwealth Pen*, ed. A. L. McLeod (Ithaca, New York, 1961); Dr. Geoffrey Parrinder's foreword to the Faber and Faber edition of *My Life in the Bush of Ghosts* (London, 1954); and Janheinz Jahn, *Muntu* (London, 1961).

17. This distinction was pointed out to the Herskovits by a narrator during their

research into Dahomean oral literature. See Melville J. and Frances S. Herskovits, *Dahomean Narrative: A Cross-Cultural Analysis* (Evanston, Ill., 1967), 16.

18. For a discussion of the problem of epic-making, the so-called Homeric Problem, see Albert B. Lord, *The Singer of Tales* (London, 1960), 124. Also, Senghor's preface to Birago Diop's *Les Nouveaux Contes d'Amadou Koumba* (Paris, 1958) and *The Making of Homeric Verse*, ed. A. Parry (Oxford, 1971).

19. Amos Tutuola, *The Palm-Wine Drinkard and His Dead Palm-Wine Tapster in the Deads' Town* (London, 1952), 84. The title is always shortened for convenience to *The Palm-Wine Drinkard*.

20. Quoted by Janheinz Jahn in *Muntu*, 221.

21. Tutuola, *The Drinkard*, 79–80.

22. See James O'Connell, "The Withdrawal of the High God in West African Religion: An Essay in *Interpretation*," *Man* 1 (May 1962): 67–69.

23. John Taylor, *The Primal Vision* (London, 1963), 90.

24. In the Philippines, India and the Malay Peninsula, the quarrel is not between the sky and the earth but between the sun and the moon. See *Folklore Studies* 12–14 (1953–55).

25. *Anthology of West African Folklore* (London, 1962), 35.

26. Amos Tutuola, *Simbi and the Satyr of the Dark Jungle* (London, 1955).

27. Tutuola, *The Drinkard*, 7–8.

28. K. A. Busia, *The Challenge of Africa* (New York, 1962), 39.

29. See Cyprian Ekwensi, *Ikolo the Wrestler* (Onitsha, 1947), 65–68.

CHAPTER 3

Language and the African Novel

WRITING IN ENGLISH presents the West African writer with a problem the English writer does not have. Stated simply, it is how to express the African experience in a language that was originally evolved to embody a different kind of experience and to convey a different kind of sensibility? How can the novelist render his characters' words, feelings, and attitudes in English and still retain their idiomatic quality and authenticity?

This, in a way, is the problem of all translations; but, for the West African writer, the problem is more immediate and acute than in ordinary cases of translation. To the West African living in one of the ex-British colonies, English is the national, administrative, legal, and (along with the vernaculars), literary language. The writer using the English language is therefore bilingual and expected to be "at home" both in English and in his own language.

Whereas the literary reputation of European novelists translated into English has been made in the language in which they originally wrote, West African novelists, by an ironic twist of history, have to make their literary reputation in a language that traces its development as a literary language to King Alfred and his Anglo-Saxons in the sixth century A.D. In other words, if an English translation of *Crime and Punishment*, or *Mastro-don Gesualdo* fails to convey the idiom of the Russian or Italian original, or the setting, experience, and inner atmosphere and vision the writer intended to convey, there is some consolation that the original is still there, to be translated at any future time by someone more competent. With West Africans writing in English, the process of translation is part and parcel of the process of creation and determines summarily whether the completed book is a success or a failure.

The problem for the West African writer is that bilingualism in Africa, that is, the situation in which people speak one of the European "colonial" languages with as much ease and fluency as they speak their native tongues, is a phenomenon associated with a small (if continually growing) minority. In spite of the strides made in education since the early fifties, less than one-quarter of the population of any of the West African countries in the sixties and perhaps the seventies, is truly bilingual in English and the vernaculars. This means that a large section of the West African population still thinks, feels, and reacts in the vernaculars and is more deeply affected by the oral tradition than by the introduced literary tradition. The writers, because of their peculiar privilege of belonging to "both worlds," are in a position to use their literary gifts and to exploit the advantages of their bilingual knowledge to make available to the world at large the culture, traditions, and heritage of their people. Their knowledge of a "world" language, coupled with their background of African life, qualifies them to interpret this life through fiction. It is a fact that West African writers using the English language are conveying the West African experience that has distinguished West African literature from English literature proper.

There is common ground in the writings of West Africans and their English counterparts in the same genre, since West African writers base their writing on Western models; but there are also significant differences that derive from differences in culture, experience, language, outlook, and so on. Thus, because the social and cultural background of the West African novel and the major impulses that bring it about differ from those of the English novel, we notice obvious differences between them.

English writers convey their English experience in a language that has evolved specifically to bear the full weight of this experience. Their stylistic efforts do not demand fundamental changes in the pattern of their language to fit it into a new structure of thought, feeling, and expression. The West African writer has to recast his material in a fundamental way if his West African experience is to remain West African, while at the same time making sure that the English in which it is expressed remains intelligible to users of the English language all over the world. This problem has been identified by Ngugi wa Thiong'o in respect of all African writers using English. Contrasting their position with that of native English writers and even West Indian writers in English, he observes:

> The African writer in fact, has got his added problem . . . [that] . . . whereas people like George Lamming or an English writer can get narrative value from 'slang' from twisting of language from his community, we have got to get the slang and the twists of language in a different language and then try to put that into English. . . . Not many Africans speak English . . . and even those who speak don't use it as their normal language. It is not what they use every day, at breakfast, lunch, when they make jokes and so you're getting nourishment, linguistic nourishment in a different medium and then trying to use the English medium to create.[1]

Indeed, the comparison between West African writers in English, and American and West Indian writers is quite instructive. People have often, erroneously it would appear, compared West African writing in English or French with American, Caribbean, and Latin American writing; for, in each of these cases, the writers are using the language of a former colonial master for literary purposes. Leaving aside the Indians in the Americas and the Caribbean Islands and the West Indies, neither the American nor the Latin American writer, nor even the West Indian is bilingual or multilingual. The

American has his American English, the Brazilian has Portuguese, the Chilean or Cuban has Spanish, and the Jamaican or Martiniquan has his own local variations of English or French. In West Africa, we have vernaculars spoken by large sections of the populations of individual nation-states. In Nigeria alone, six major language groups—Hausa, Yoruba, Igbo, Kanuri, Fulani, and Efik-Ibibio—account for 85 percent of the population, but more than fifty other language groups account for the remaining 15 percent. Of the whole Nigerian population of around one hundred million people, not more than 25 percent speak English at all. To the preponderant majority of West Africans, the vernaculars are the first language and English (French, Portuguese, and other metropolitan languages) a mere second. West Africa is in the same position, as far as language is concerned, as India, Pakistan, Ceylon, and Burma, which are multilingual, combining a number of vernaculars with one or more metropolitan European languages that function as "link" languages.

For the West African writer, the problem of translation from the vernacular into English is a crucial matter. In an article, "Problems of Linguistic Inequivalence in Communication," L. F. Brosnahan throws light on some of the main differences between English and West African languages, like Yoruba and Bini, and emphasizes the kinds of problems involved in translation from the vernaculars into English.[2] For the professional translator, these problems probably have more obvious as well as specialized answers worked out for them. For example, Malinowski, speaking from the point of view of a trained ethnographer, puts forward this broad blueprint for translators:

> The object of a scientific translation of a word is not to give its rough equivalent, sufficient for practical purposes, but to state exactly whether a native word corresponds to an idea at least partially existing for English speakers, or whether it covers an entirely foreign conception. That such foreign conceptions do exist for native languages and in a great number, is clear. All words which describe the native social order, all expressions referring to native beliefs, to specific customs, ceremonies, magic rites—all such words are obviously absent from English as from any European language. Such words can only be translated into English, not by giving their imaginary equivalent—a real one obviously cannot be found—but by explaining the meaning of each of them through an exact ethnographic account of the sociology, culture and tradition of that native community.[3]

Such a blueprint is of little practical use to the creative writer, even if it may prove valuable to the ethnographer or professional translator. The creative writer's medium requires a greater subtlety of procedure than that suggested here. Indeed, experience has shown that where the writer has adopted the ethnographic approach suggested by Malinowski, as Nzekwu has done in his novels, the result has proved less than happy. The social scientist's interest in surface factuality could easily become a crippling weakness in the creative writer who, in addition to being expected to be faithful to surface truths about society and people, is also under the pressures of art and form. These demands on the creative writer's loyalties ought not to clash, but sometimes they do, as in this matter of fidelity to sociological fact and the exigencies of art. The similar conflict confronting the Marxist writer, between the maintaining of the Marxist ideological line and artistic integrity, has been defined by Mao Tse-tung in his famous "Talks at the Yenan Forum on Art and Literature":

> What we demand is unity of politics and art, of content and form, and of the revolutionary political content and the highest possible degree of perfection in artistic form. Works of art, however politically progressive, are powerless if they lack artistic quality. Therefore we are equally opposed to works with wrong political approaches and to the tendency towards so-called "poster and slogan style" which is correct only in political approach but lacks artistic power.[4]

The advice is pertinent to the West African writer in his need to render cultural effects, ideas, thoughts, feelings, and sensibilities from the vernacular culture into English, but the other oversimplified suggestion that the artist maintain his artistic integrity at the expense of social realism has also to be rejected because the African writer's artistic purpose in this context includes the ability to transfer sets of realities from the vernacular into the operative linguistic medium, which in this case is English.

Translation itself is an art. We talk of the art of translation, which determines the ends as well as the means for reaching them. Certain clearly discernible techniques dictated by an intuitive, and imaginative grouping are adopted in translation in order to attain ends that include transference of "meaning" from one autonomous language to another. What confers the quality of art on the operation is not the ordinary mechanical aspect of the activity but the bringing to bear on it of the powers of the imagination. Calling the imagination into play is necessary because the definition of "meaning" in translation transcends the direct, symbol-referent structure and includes structures of feeling and association. The good translator not only achieves literal transference of meaning, but evokes equivalent feelings and associations. There is another reason why the matter of fidelity to social and cultural fact in transferring meaning from the vernacular into English is critical for the African writer. One of the major impulses in African writing is the desire to portray African life and experience realistically in order to refute formally the centuries of slander and misrepresentation by European and American commentators. Writers are directly or indirectly influenced by this consideration when they represent African traditional life in literature. Therefore, the least that will be expected of them by their African audience is truth to cultural life. Earlier, when many of them wrote with a largely European and foreign audience in mind, the need to justify the African way of life was a strong pressure for a projection of traditional realities, but even now that a home audience has come more and more to be assumed, the need to represent faithfully realities of which vast numbers of people have intimate knowledge remains very strong, to obviate a writer's being accused of misrepresenting these realities. This is not just a hypothetical fear: books can be given a hostile reception by readers and reviewers, as was Aluko's *One Man One Wife*, which was condemned for distorting traditional life.

In the final analysis, however, the main problem remains a linguistic one, that is, how a writer can render vernacular experiences into English and still retain a valid and convincing degree of vernacular authenticity. It is futile to pretend that this problem does not exist for West African writers or to give the impression that it disappears once the West African writer has mastered English. If, as philologists and anthropologists tell us, a language is the medium by which the culture and collective experience of a people are transmitted from generation to generation and also a means whereby the people organize and pattern their thought-processes, concepts, and categories, then the West African writer who is attempting to translate the West African experience into English needs to be thoroughly "at home" in both languages to bring off the difficult exercise.

Most West African writers recognize this problem of linguistic transference and attempt to meet it in their different ways, depending on their general grasp of the idiom, rhythm, and structure of the English and vernacular languages, and on how intimately they have perceived their West African subjects.

Achebe is most successful in expressing his African experience in English and still preserving its African authenticity. Here is a passage from *Arrow of God* in which the chief priest is telling his son why he is sending him to join the Christian church, contrary to what might have been expected of him as the custodian of the traditional religion:

> "I want one of my sons to join these people and be my eyes there. If there is nothing in it you will come back. But if there is something there you will bring home my share. The world is like a Mask, dancing. If you want to see it well you do not stand in one place. My spirit tells me that those who do not befriend the white man today will be saying had we known tomorrow."[5]

The language here is English, but the rhythm of its prose and the structure of feeling behind it are West African; both reflect the oral tradition of West Africa. To illustrate how Achebe has managed to preserve the Africanness of what he is saying in English that is clear, lively, and intelligible, here is the passage translated back into Igbo. This will give us an idea of what transformations are thought necessary by Achebe and how he accomplishes them while remaining close to the original experience in language and in feeling.

Here is the Igbo translation:

"A Cholu m ka ofu n'ime umu m sonyelu ndi-a ka o bulu an"a m n'ebeafu.
Obulu na o nwero ife di n'time ya, I putabakwa. Ma obulu na o nwelu ife di
n'ebeafu, I wenatalu m nke m. Uwa di ka nmo egwu. Onye cholu ifu ya ofuma
a d'akwu n'ofu ebe. Nmo m gwalu m na ndi obuna n'aburo oyi ndi
ocha tata ga nasi echi, n'obuluzidi na fa ma."

Translated literally into English, this would read:

"I want me that one inside children my join people these that he becomes eyes
my inside place—that. If that it has not something be in the inside it, you
come out again. But if it be that it has something be inside place—that, you
bring back me own my. The world is like spirit [masquerade], dancing. Person
wants to see it/him well he not stands in one place. Spirit my tells me that
persons any that not become friend persons white today will be saying tomorrow that if it had been that they know."

If we compare how the passage would have read if Achebe had translated
it literally into English with how he has sensibly rendered it, we see that he
has made obvious concessions to the syntax of the standard English. For
instance, where the syntactical sequence in Igbo would be noun plus adjective
as in *anya m* "eyes my," Achebe respects the English syntax by the sequence
reversing to "my eyes."

Apart from the minor changes in the order of words, it is clear that the
language of Achebe's novel translates very easily back into the vernacular
and, in fact, preserves the speech of the vernacular. When the chief priest
says that he would send one of his sons to become "his eyes" within the
Christian camp, he is using a figure of speech every Igbo speaker will recognize. Again, when he clinches his intention by backing it up with a well-
known and appropriate proverb, he is doing something that is integral to
the oral tradition of West Africa in the context of which we must see the
passage. He interferes minimally with the actual words of his characters, and
when he does, it is merely to put them in the normal standard English word-
order to produce intelligible English. He could, for example, have para-
phrased the proverb in this passage, but instead he transfers it into English,
exactly as an ordinary nonliterate Igbo would say it. To take another example,
Achebe makes Ezeulu say, "My spirit tells me . . ." (*Nmo m gwalu m*), which
is how an Igbo man would say it, and not "I have a feeling that . . ." which
is a more likely English paraphrase. Achebe's close adherence to the actual
speech of his characters gives an oral quality to his narrative and establishes
its African consciousness.

Most writers attempt the same thing in their writings, with varying degrees of success. For example, Gabriel Okara, in *The Voice*, goes a stage further
than Achebe in trying to transfer some of the syntactical features of the Ijo

language into English. Here is a passage in which the hero's dying father gives him a few parting words of advice:

> "Let the words I am going to speak remain in your inside. I wanted you to know book because of the changing world. But whiteman's book is not everything. Now listen, son, believe in what you believe. Argue with no one about whiteman's god and Woyengi, our goddess. What your inside tells you to believe, you believe and, always the straight thing do and the straight thing talk and your spoken word will have power and you will live in this world even when you are dead. So do not anything fear if it is the straight thing you are doing or talking."[6]

Even though this is written in English, the content of the passage is less "English" than the passage from *Arrow of God*. It is not just that there are expressions like "your inside," "to know book," "whiteman's book," which are direct translations from Ijo, but the word order of "always the straight thing do and the straight thing talk" seems more Hebraic than English, though it is actually an Ijo word order. As an exercise, the present writer translated the passage into Igbo (which belongs to the Kwa group of West African languages to which Ijo also belongs) and found that Okara not only translates directly from the vernacular into English, but adheres more to the vernacular word order than does Achebe in any of his narratives. Obviously Okara has to have most of the English word order to make his writing intelligible at all in English. How far he is prepared to go in introducing the vernacular word order can be seen in a sentence like "He is a madman be . . . ," which occurs a few lines after the passage quoted above.

Many commentators on the language of *The Voice* have found it hard to accept. The same kind of dry, unimaginative, grammatical purism that attempted to deny Tutuola's language any redemptive virtue could be seen at work again. One academic literary critic at least, Geoffrey Walton of Ahmadu Bello University, has already written off Okara's language in *The Voice* as "no language at all."[7] In reality, however, Okara's language is a deliberate medium for conveying the kind of experience embodied in his novel. That such a strategy of language is essential for an African writer using a cosmopolitan language is clear to him, as his article in *Transition*, "African Speech . . . English Words," clearly shows.[8] What matters finally is whether the strategy serves the author's interest well. The effect of Okara's effort to translate both the lexical and syntactical forms from Ijo into English is to give his prose a heavy, solemn cadence, which seems to fit the serious moral tone and the mood of pessimism that pervade his novel.

Elechi Amadi's *The Concubine* owes much of its success to the author's skill in transferring the speech peculiarities of its vernacular characters into English. Its simple, unassuming style and rhythm of colloquial conversation do more to give peasant immediacy to the action of the novel. There is no mistaking the traditional nature of the society in the close bonds of linguistic relationship. People are addressed by their names, which are often accompanied by some kinship term that indicate their status, age, and degree of kinship relationship. For example, in the opening passage of chapter eleven of *The Concubine*,[9] Wigwe exclaims when he sees Nnenda, a neighbor's wife, "Nnenda, my daughter, I have not seen you for some time," while Wigwe's wife greets her with, "I see your eyes at last, Nnenda, my daughter." The use of the term "daughter" here is generalized. Nnenda is indeed not a daughter to the Wigwes in the strict, narrow kinship sense, but from the generalized point of view in which the village becomes one vast family of interrelated people with interlocking, interrelated interests, the term is appropriate in its extended meaning. Everyone assumes a certain degree of responsibility for everyone else—the elderly members assuming a generalized parental responsibility toward the younger ones. Nnenda reciprocates by referring to Wigwe as "Dede," or "father." Again, the oral nature of the narrative, and the fact that those involved in the conversation are vernacular characters and not educated in English, is quite clear from the sentence, "I see your eyes at last, Nnenda, my daughter." A speaker educated in English idiomatic usage would not say it like that; he would probably say, "Nnenda, my dear, I haven't seen you for ages" or "I'm awfully glad to see you again." Less English still is the expression, "On the evening of the brother of tomorrow," which is the answer given by Nnenda when Ekwueme asks her the question: "When will you bring me word again?" "On the evening of the brother of tomorrow" is a direct translation from Igbo of *"n'ime ugbede anyasi nwanne echi."*

Amos Tutuola is the example par excellence of a West African writer whose writing is closest to the oral tradition because his sparse formal education has denied him the degree of familiarity with the English language enjoyed by other West African authors. Whenever he is translating his story from the Yoruba language into English, his effort is often very conspicuous. When he describes the feet of the terrible animal in the Wraith-Island in *The Palm-Wine Drinkard* in this way: "His four feet were as big as a log of wood,"[10] it is quite clear that he is making his comparison in Yoruba and then translating it into English. What he is emphasizing about the feet is their quality of bigness, hence the "log of wood" could be used to indicate this quality whether of the feet individually or collectively. English, with its "scientific" outlook, would not be content to stress the quality of bigness, it would also indicate the number involved. Thus, a proper English equivalent would be: "Each of his four feet was as big as a plank" or "His four feet were as big as planks." West African languages, to use Dr. Johnson's famous image, merely remark "general properties and large appearances" while the European languages "number the streaks of the tulip." The distinction is basic to oral languages (such as the vernaculars in West Africa) and "literary" languages such as the European, which have been employed for hundreds of years to transmit a literary tradition and a technological culture.

Occasionally, Tutuola creates his "own" vocabulary which, though not strictly "English," is quite adequate for his narrative purpose. He talks, for instance, of "alives," and "deads," and of "Deads' Town," all of which seem to fit into the context of the semifantasy world of his tale. Tutuola is using the expressions in a context in which they do not exist in English. The term "deads" expresses the concept of dead people as active individuals who inhabit a place known as Deads' Town and who go about their business in the world of *The Palm-Wine Drinkard* like ordinary people except that, unlike living people, they walk backward instead of forward. The English concept of dead people is of a sort of lifeless collectivity labeled "the dead." For Tutuola, as well as the ancestor-worshipping West Africans, there is nothing like the English concept of "the dead"; dead people, in their view of the world, are immensely alive in "the other world," in what Tutuola calls "Deads' Town."

For Tutuola, the invention of the right word to convey his concept of dead people in their special country does not present any difficulty. The common English usage of forming plurals is to add *s* or *es* to the singular form. Thus, if he chooses to call a dead person "dead," then more than one dead person logically becomes "deads." As for "alives," it is clear that language and its rules have a way of breaking down just when they are most expected to be consistent.

Tutuola's language is highly idiosyncratic, for, apart from his obvious effort to fit his narrative into a language, the technique of which he has not fully mastered, and his success in creating a style that is very close to the oral narrative style, he is also capable, as with the example of "deads" and "alives" of striking out on his own and producing something original, graphic, and quaint, which charms his foreign readers but displeases the more snobbish of his West African readers. His publishers, of course, ought to have corrected the more glaring of his grammatical and spelling mistakes, as they did the nineteenth-century English "peasant" poet, John Clare, who had his spelling and punctuation made "genteel."[11] The use of words like "deads" and "alives," which contribute to a fuller realization of his world and art, ought to be left alone in spite of their seeming quaintness. Obviously, fastidious grammarians would not agree with this view, but it should at least be recognized that Tutuola is essentially a storyteller, not a grammarian.

Achebe, Okara, Amadi, and Tutuola have been selected here for discussion because they represent a fair cross-section of the variety of ways in which West African prose writers are dealing, with considerable success, with problems of writing in a second language. There are, of course, occasions when the problem is really quite serious, such as when a word with built-in conceptual meaning in the vernacular with no equivalent in English has to be translated into English. Such, for instance, is the problem the word *chi* presents to the West African writer.

No single English word can adequately translate this word that is built into the very center of the African's concept of individual identity, destiny, and the place he occupies in the general ordering of the universe. It is often as elusive as the Western concept of the individual "soul." A vague and generalized description of *chi* as "destiny" or "fate" is totally inadequate to convey the fullest meaning of the word. And yet this word is a key to understanding the African mind and its reactions to reality. The exploration or appraisal of a character's state of mind, his motives and aspirations, his fears and frustrations, may, in the long run, hinge on an understanding of this three-letter word. It is, perhaps, as relevant to understanding the African character as the two words *arête* and *hubris* are to understanding the classical Greek one.

How do West African writers solve the problem of conveying, in a fairly concrete and full term, the meaning and significance of the concept of *chi* in the development of character and moral outlook? In the first place, they tend to leave it as *chi* and follow it with brief explanatory parenthetic remarks or let the meaning reveal itself in the context. When unaccompanied by any explanation whatever, the word will probably not carry the significance it is expected to carry in a story. What, for example, would a non-West African reader make of this dialogue in Nkem Nwankwo's *Danda*? The hero, Danda, has just fallen afoul of the community and become a source of anxiety to his father. His father, Araba, ruminates over this and blames his son's social failure on his (Araba's) *chi*, with which his companion completely agrees. Araba: "It is my misfortune, I have a weak Ikenga. . . ." The Okelekwu: "One's *chi* brings one so many troubles. . . ." The non-native reader may rightly feel cheated of the meaning of this exchange.

Achebe, on the other hand, provides adequate guidelines to the reader. Here are two passages that deal with the hero and his father, two very different types of characters with two opposite kinds of temperament:

> (a) Unoka was an ill-fated man. He had a bad *chi* or personal god, and evil
> fortune followed him to the grave, or to his death, for he had no grave. He
> died of the swelling which was an abomination of earth goddess. When a man
> was afflicted with swelling in the stomach and the limbs he was not allowed to
> die in the house. He was carried to the Evil Forest and left there to die.[12]

> (b) If ever a man deserved his success, that man was Okonkwo. At an early
> age he had achieved fame as the greatest wrestler in all the land. That was not
> luck. At the most one could say that his *chi* or personal god was good. But the
> Igbo people have a proverb that when a man says yes his *chi* says yes also.
> Okonkwo said yes very strongly; so his *chi* agreed. And not only his *chi* but
> also his clan too, because it judged a man by the work of his hand. (*TFA*, 13)

Achebe goes to great lengths to introduce this idea concept to the reader because it is one of the few highly complex religious and psychological concepts that must be assumed by any one who wishes to understand traditionally oriented African characters. The main concepts of *chi* are present here—the fatal aspect, the "luck" aspect, and the anti-destiny aspect.[13] This third aspect is stressed by Achebe in respect to Okonkwo's life because it is central to the understanding of the character and his temperament. Most non-West African commentators on the concept of *chi* tend to emphasize the first two aspects of it to the exclusion of the third. This implies that in spite of the obvious intervention of blind anonymous forces in the lives of individuals, a man still can and does have a large measure of responsibility for what he does and for the results of his actions; things do not only happen to him, he also makes things happen.

Achebe has rightly devoted considerable space and effect to expounding the concept of *chi*, as is clearly shown in the above passages, because it is an important theme in *Things Fall Apart*. The fact that he has had to do so in a fairly conscious manner is a necessity imposed on him because he is writing in a language in which the concept of *chi* cannot be assumed but must be explained to be perceived. This is so because the West African writer in English is addressing a nonlocal as well as a local audience. The nonlocal audience would, of course, include all those West Africans who share the concept of *chi* with the Igbo but who refer to it in different words according to their different languages. Thus, to all intents and purposes, it has become a cardinal necessity that the West African writer in English transmit his West African experience, not only through action, but occasionally by consciously interpolating information that is vital to the foreign reader's appraisal of this experience.

This necessity creates undoubted dangers and pitfalls for the writer. The greatest danger is that the story's interest may be sacrificed to the exigency of supplying factual information. After all, a novel or any other kind of prose narrative is a story first and foremost, not an anthropological analysis.

The writers have, in a great majority of cases, managed to strike a balance between their narrative interest and the necessity to put the non-native reader into the picture of locally tinged experiences, ideas, or concepts. In a few cases, the effort has not been altogether happy. Some of the writers, in their anxiety to "inform" the reader as well as tell him a story, have included too many burdensome factual explanations, which do not greatly improve the reader's perception and unnecessarily retard the progress of the narrative. When the explanation is brief and unobtrusive, the writer can carry it off without irritating the reader. Achebe does a lot of explaining in this unobtrusive manner in the first two or three chapters of his *Things Fall Apart*. Such sentences as, "The elders, or *ndichie*, met to hear a report of Okonkwo's mission," and "His own hut, or *obi*, stood immediately behind the only gate in the red walls," contain brief explanations that help the non-native reader without retarding the progress of the narrative. When the device is not skilfully used, it tends to ruin the narrative quality of a novel.

This passage from Nzekwu's *Blade Among the Boys* illustrates the kind of situation in which the eagerness to explain things to the reader slows down the pace of the narrative, while failing to advance the reader's perception to any appreciable degree. Here a group of young boys, of whom the hero is one, is attracted to a spot where a man, surrounded by a small gathering of people, is digging a hole in the ground. The hero, who is not yet fully familiar with some of the local customs and beliefs, has to have things explained to him:

> He learnt from his companions that the man digging the hole was a herbalist. He was digging out a sick girl's *iyi-uwa*, objects with which the sick girl sealed her promises to a club of gambolling souls to which she belonged. Unless the objects were dug out and hidden from her she would sicken and die. No herbalist, doctor or sacrifice was good enough to save her if the object were not dug out.[14]

This description of *iyi-uwa* is certainly interesting information, especially for the non-Igbo reader, but the question that immediately suggests itself is, does this explanation advance the narrative? Does it improve the reader's perception of the characters and situations in the story, apart from telling him that the people of Ado (among whom the story is set) believe in *iyi-uwa*? This is the kind of knowledge that could be gleaned from Margaret Green's *Ibo Village Affairs* or C. K. Meek's *Law and Authority in a Nigerian Tribe* or any other competently written anthropological study of the Igbo people and their culture. At any rate, the explanation could be included in a glossary at the end of the novel, or as a footnote. (This has indeed been done to an immense advantage by Soyinka in *The Interpreters*.) It is a serious technical flaw that such pieces of factual information should be allowed to protrude from the main flow of narrative. We notice, of course, that Achebe also has an explanation of *ogbanje* (which is the name of one of the "gambolling souls") in *Things Fall Apart*, but his explanation is integral to the story and actually adds something to the elucidation of personal relations in the novel. Okonkwo and his wife, Ekwefi, have had to exorcise the scourge of "one of those wicked children who, when they died, entered their mothers' wombs to be born again," before Ezinma was born and could survive. The story shows the circumstances under which Ezinma was born, the underlying reason for the current of sympathy and affection uniting father, mother, and an only daughter, and, to a large extent, the shaping of the domestic background of *Things Fall Apart*. All this is directly relevant to the story in *Things Fall Apart* in a way Nzekwu's description of the *iyi-uwa* incident is not in *Blade Among the Boys*. The impression that emerges is that Nzekwu uses Patrick's ignorance of the traditional beliefs as a pretext for lecturing the reader on these beliefs.

The problem of language in the West African prose narrative is also obvious in the writers' efforts to translate into English the concept of the African extended family, which is very different from the nuclear European family system of today. To express this idea in English, Achebe and Nzekwu have gone to anthropology for precise, though specialized, terms. Achebe talks, in *Things Fall Apart*, of "the clan," and Nzekwu of "the patrilineal lineage," in *Blade Among the Boys*. Both of these terms are far removed from ordinary everyday speech, and their highly specialized connotations tend to disqualify them as language of creative literature, though it is quite obvious that "the clan" is much less objectionable than "the patrilineal lineage."

Nkem Nwankwo made a more suitable translation of the African family idea in *Danda*. His characters refer to the members of their extended families as "sons of our fathers," or "children of our fathers." These expressions immediately tell the reader that he is among a people for whom the family is much larger than the father-plus-mother-plus-children. And, more important still, "children of our fathers" (*umunna-ayi*) is an exact word-for-word translation from Igbo for the members of one's family on the father's side, just as "children of our mothers" (*umunne-ayi*) applies to one's relations on the mother's side.

Sometimes, the desire to communicate absolutely the precise meaning of a local word to nonlocal readers may lead the writer into absurd expedients. Even a writer as competent as Elechi Amadi does now and again get caught in this clumsy posture. Here, for example, is a typical illustration: "'Ihuoma, are your yams dry enough to be tied into ekwes?' (An ekwe is a vertical column with yams dexterously tied along it.)"[15] The sentence and its explanation represent a dual disaster from the point of view of what one may regard as a reasonable approach to a real problem. The only suitable place for such an explanatory sentence is in the glossary. But looking at it where it stands, the one word that gives it away altogether is "dexterously." It is not really an explaining word but one that indicates fascination on the part of the author. The author is not only trying to convey practical knowledge but is also attempting to infect the audience with his interested response. And here it must be said that the writer is going beyond reasonable bounds. It is not for him to suggest a response to readers, especially where he has not done a scrap of work to justify such a response. Superfluous as the information is, one might still have permitted it on the vague assumption that the readers of *The Concubine* might be somewhat better equipped to understand its world by knowing that yams are tied in columns on sticks. But this tolerance cannot be extended to the author when he implies that all tying up of yams is "dexterously" done, or that all tied-up yams look artistically satisfactory. As for the word "ekwes" in the main sentence, it just does not exist. "Ekwe" is both a singular and a plural form of Igbo. At least this form ought to be adhered to, even when the word is carried over into English. Otherwise we shall be back to a Tutuolan expedient totally at odds with the linguistic mode of *The Concubine*.

These observations on the use of language in West African prose narratives are made in good faith, not out of a complacent pedantry or censoriousness. The problems the writers face are formidable indeed. It is an amazing achievement that they have succeeded so well in conveying in English African experiences that lie outside the English cultural environment.

In view of the pragmatically successful way the writers have gone about using the English language to express their African subjects, it is somewhat surprising that Obiajunwa Wali, a former university lecturer in Nigeria, should seriously question the wisdom of using English for creative purposes in Africa. In a highly controversial article in *Transition*, "The Dead End of African Literature," he argues that African writing, if it is to have any future, must be carried on in the African languages. This started a series of lively exchanges among African writers and critics of African literature, which goes to show that Wali touched upon a subject that is of considerable interest to all those involved in the literary life of contemporary Africa.[16]

The debate need not be gone into here. The question seems highly irrelevant since English is the national language of Nigeria, Ghana, Sierra Leone, and Gambia. So long as this fact remains, writers are perfectly justified in writing in English, although those who can, should write in the vernaculars.

What is more relevant than the parochial considerations that largely lay behind Obi Wali's arguments, is the cultural cleavage that has resulted from the existence of English as a second language used in commerce and industry, administration, education, and the production of written literature by a tiny (though growing) minority "elite" of the West African populations. The situation whereby no more than one-quarter of the people is developing a literary "minority" culture, based on the use of the English language and institutions that increasingly remove this minority from the culture of the vast majority of the people is obviously unhealthy. When creative writers, members of this "minority" culture, attempt, as they are constantly doing, to interpret the largely emasculated "majority" culture, sensitive people are bound to show some uneasiness. There is something a little depredatory about a man who has been brought up on the Bible, Shakespeare, and John Stuart Mill, who lives in a "senior service" apartment with the most modern amenities, owns a "pleasure" car, and earns a salary of more than two-thousand pounds a year—in short, a man firmly planted in mid-twentieth-century world culture and progress—sitting down to write a pretty little tale in praise of the dignity and glory of a peasant's life, the exquisite neighborliness and communality of the peasants, and their entrenched sense of security in spite of disease, ignorance, and material poverty. All this may, of course, be true, but there is always a sneaking suspicion that the writer is doing something opportunistic, like cashing in on an infirmity.

That the English language is being used as a satisfactory vehicle by creative writers in recreating and interpreting the traditional culture must not blind us to the truth that, because some of the people can and do use English as a second language and large numbers of others do not, English has become one of the major contributors to cultural change. Achebe, Nzekwu, Conton, and others may portray the African experience with sympathy and genuine insight, but the fact is that their English literary education has opened up for them a fresh channel of consciousness that their illiterate relations cannot avail themselves. The English language has become in some respect utterly subversive of the existence of a common culture and outlook in English-speaking West Africa. As the chief medium of transmission of world civilization, it has become an instrument for devaluating the "particular" West African cultures. On the positive side, however, it has also become the chief instrument for integrating vital elements both of world civilization and of the indigenous cultures of West Africa.

NOTES

1. Dennis Duerden and Cosmo Pieterse, eds., *African Writers Talking: A Collection of Interviews* (London, 1972), 130–31.

2. *Ibadan* 13 (November 1961).

3. C. K. Ogden and I. A. Richards, *The Meaning of Meaning* (London, 1923), 299–300.

4. Anne Fremantle, ed., *Mao Tse-Tung: An Anthology of His Writings* (London, 1971), 259.

5. Chinua Achebe, *Arrow of God* (London, 1966), 45–46; 55.

6. *The Voice*, (London, 1964), 126.

8. *Transition*, 3 (October 1963)

9. *The Concubine*, 78–79.

10. *The Palm-Wine Drinkard*, 47.

11. See Geoffrey Grigson, "An Epitaph for John Clare," *The Observer Weekend Review* (17 May 1964).

12. Chinua Achebe, *Things Fall Apart* (London, 1955), 14–15. Subsequent references are cited as *TFA* in the text.

13. See M. Fortes, *Oedipus and Job in West African Religion* (Cambridge, 1959), 19–25.

14. *Blade Among the Boys*, 46.

15. *The Concubine*, 102.

16. *Transition*, 10–13, 18 (1963); also *Nigeria Magazine* 78 (September 1963). The language controversy of the 1960s that engaged writers and many of their African readers was far from played out by the 1970s and 1980s. The problem has simply refused to go away. Ngugi wa Thiong'o has addressed the language question in a number of essays, including "Return to the Roots: National Language as the Basis of a Kenya National Literature and Culture" in *Writers in Politics* (London, 1981) and more extensively in his book, *Decolonizing the Mind: The Politics of Language in African Literature* (London, 1986). He not only supports Obi Wali's view that an authentic literature of Africa has to be written in African languages, but he has dismissed his earlier works in English as "Afro-Saxon" literature and the entire body of African writing in any of the European languages as "Afro-European" literature. He has committed himself to writing in his Gikuyu language. His works in that language include a play, *Ngaahika Ndeenda* (I Will Marry When I Choose), coauthored with Ngugi wa Mirii, and a novel, *Caitaani Mutharaba-ini* (*Devil on the Cross*). Whether African writers are going to follow Ngugi's example remains to be seen.

CHAPTER 4

Perceptions of Colonialism in West African Literature

Every colonized people—every people in whose soul an inferiority complex has been created by the death and burial of its local cultural originality, finds itself face to face with the language of the civilized nation; that is, with the culture of the mother country.

THE QUOTATION is from Fanon's *Peau Noir, Masques Blancs (Black Skin, White Masks)* [1] in which he explores the psychological effects of colonialism on colonized peoples, especially insofar as the problem is further complicated by considerations of color and race. The truth of the matter is that colonialism, which begins as the imposition of the will of a colonizing group on a formerly independent people for the often explicit, or sometimes implicit, intention of exploiting them economically, subsequently finds it necessary, especially if the colonizing group has a strong tradition of freedom, to defend its existence to internal critics of the system and so, inevitably, to the colonized. It attempts to do this by promising the latter a higher order of existence; by trying to convince them and to reassure domestic critics that, on balance, the gains of the colonized will far outweigh their losses; and by contending that, at any rate, they are being saved from the brutality of their old life and offered the blessings of a morally and technologically superior civilization. This psychologically potent propaganda has a way, as Fanon has observed, of working on the minds of the colonized, destroying the confidence of the colonized in their way of life, their institutions, and their creative ability within their own culture. Every anticolonial movement therefore necessarily includes an effort by intellectuals, writers, and artists to restore confidence in the native culture and tradition, to revive submerged mythologies, to resurrect dead languages, and to restore old habits of dress and behavior. In other words, such a movement involves an attempt to destroy the "inferiority complex" spoken of by Fanon, in order to release the energies formerly emasculated by colonialism and use them freely and uninhibitedly for postcolonial reconstruction. Conversely, there is a determined attempt to devalue or at least deemphasize, the culture of the colonizing group and to minimize the so-called gains postulated as validating reasons for colonialism. This phenomenon, which sociologists call cultural nationalism, is well documented in the nationalist movements in nineteenth-century Europe, Ireland, Latin America, and, more recently, in the colonized areas of Asia and Africa.

Historically, this period of militant anticolonial cultural assertion is often preceded by a period of some measure of acquiescence by the colonized people to the colonial myths of the colonizers—a period in which the intellectual posture of the colonial subjects is fully dominated by the ideas and insinuations of the proponents of the colonial civilizing mission. Both of these stages are clearly present in Africa and are amply documented in African literature written in English and French.

African writers' response to colonialism began with a guarded, if tacit, affirmation of the assumptions made for it. That colonialism conferred a higher order of social organization, a higher civilization, and a means of refining and upgrading the cultural life of the subject peoples was believed and sometimes overtly canvassed in the early works by the colonized intelligentsia that made its presence felt by the second half of the nineteenth century. In West Africa, from which the illustrations will be taken, a small core of this indigenous intelligentsia emerged in both the English- and French-speaking coastal towns of Freetown, Cape Coast, Lagos, and Senegal's Quatre Communes of Dakar, Gorée, Rufisque, and Saint Louis. Members of this black elite intelligentsia were formally educated in the Western sense and some of them had post-secondary-school education, while others had risen, especially in the English sector, to the professions of law, medicine, and the Christian ministry. They were well-read in European literatures and grounded in European philosophies. In spite of their high educational attainments, however, all but a few of them found themselves outside the European governing circles.

In English-speaking West Africa, the members of the black intelligentsia became increasingly aware of the ambiguity of their position. Many of them were either the children of manumitted and resettled ex-slaves in Freetown and Monrovia or later black immigrants from Brazil, Cuba, and the West Indies. Being educated in the European sense, they saw themselves as being in an advantageous position compared with the rest of the subjects, but they also saw themselves as black people and subjects or protected persons under an imperialist white government. The fact that, despite their education, the degree of mobility open to them within the power structure was limited brought their predicament emphatically home to them. The need to identify themselves as black people and oppressed people was therefore very strong, but the implications of such identification went much further than most of them would accept, since they were at the same time conscious of themselves in their privileged position as sharers in a "superior civilization." To repudiate colonialism totally might undermine the privileged position they occupied in relation to their unlettered, hinterland kindred. They were trapped in a many-sided dilemma in which they wished to identify with traditional life and culture but were instinctively repelled by a system they hardly understood. They recognized the ambivalence of their relationship with Western civilization but, at the same time, their deepest instincts of self-preservation told them that, vestigial though their hold on this civilization was, it represented their only substantial anchor. To renounce Western life and culture for the traditional way of life would amount to giving up something they already possessed for something that was only hypothetically theirs. It was tantamount to sacrificing an intellectually satisfying position for a persistent but largely emotional pressure. Overreacting to a threatening situation that confronted them with cultural ostracism, the coastal intelligentsia stigmatized all nationalizing and traditionalizing trends as "going native," or "going Fantee." To say in those days that a gentleman of the coastal intelligentsia had gone "Fantee" was to place on him the highest label of disapprobation.[2]

The early coastal intellectuals, however, were no cowards. They vigorously debated the cultural question in the newspapers and journals that flourished throughout the coastal towns. A few minor concessions were made to cultural nationalism. For example, possessors of the more exotic foreign names were ready to replace them with local ones. Even though until today such names as Craig, Campbell, da Silva, da Rocha, and Barbossa still survive as reminders of the foreign connections of the coastal families, it is quite obvious that there would have been more such names had there been no inspired campaign against them. It is true also that there was a reverse trend on the "names" question whereby some people anglicized their traditional names in order to appear "modern" and "civilized." But, on balance, the correspondent who wrote in the *Lagos Standard* on 25 March 1896 seems to have spoken for most of the people's general feeling when he said: "It may be true that there is nothing in a name, but there is something in it when viewed in connection with the history of a nation. It is that by which we distinguish one nation or individual from another. Every nation has its system of names."

After names, dress apparel came up for discussion among the coastal intelligentsia, the question being whether people should drape themselves in the dresses and costumes of the colonizers or go back to wearing indigenous dress. Opinion was radically divided between those who would jettison European manners of dress and, for them, in the words of the *Lagos Record* of March 1896, "the Europeanized African is a non-descript, a libel on his country, and a blot on civilization,"[3] and those for whom the advocates of the native dress were "hare-brained patriots [who] would need prate of a recurrence to primitive quasi-nudity" (editorial in *Lagos Observer*, 1882).

A more seriously inhibiting factor to their total identification with cultural nationalism was the philosophical preoccupation the coastal intelligentsia acquired from their Western education. Their constant reference to the words "civilization" and "race" in their polemics indicates that they were looking at the question mainly as an offshoot of the same concern in the metropolises of Europe. Their views were heavily influenced by the philosophical thoughts of Darwin, Spenser, and the philosophical evolutionists. Their writings suggest that they accepted the hierarchical definition of races and civilizations and felt that the African civilization was yet to evolve, with the aid of the European civilization, by absorbing European cultural models rather than by establishing an autonomous existence. In this respect, colonialism became for them a kind of evolutionist instrument for raising the qualitative levels of the human and cultural content of the continent. And without actually making common cause with the colonial administration, many of them saw themselves as "middlemen" and "brokers" for the new civilization. Indeed, one of them, John Craig, said as much to the Reverend Townsend in a letter in October 1865. "We have always considered ourselves as Middlemen between you and the Egbas," he wrote.

Besides the majority of the intelligentsia, there was a small minority of dedicated nationalists who were less uncertain of their position and more assertive of the claims of native rights and native heritage. The most prominent among them was Dr. Edward Wilmot Blyden, a West Indian immigrant from St. Thomas in the Virgin Islands who naturalized in Liberia and carried his turbulent intellectual campaigns all over West Africa and as far afield as the United States and London. Others included Dr. Africanus Horton of Sierra Leone, an M.D. of the University of Edinburgh, John Casely Hayford and Mensah Sabah of the then Gold Coast. They were convinced that Africans must begin to build modern states on African traditional foundations. In several learned works they argued cogently for the revival of the submerged cultures, histories, and institutions.

Dr. Blyden's giant figure dominated the late nineteenth century as he focused his enormous intellectual powers on such questions as the essential unity of the black race (composed of blacks of the diaspora in the Americas and the West Indies and those of the African continent), advocating what Thomas Hodgkin calls a Black Zionism. Interestingly enough, Blyden wrote a pamphlet on the *Jewish Question* in 1898. He saw the need for black nationalism and the necessity for black people to create modern states and linked this to the restoration of the racial pride of the blacks:

> An African nationality is our great need—We shall never receive the respect of other races until we establish a powerful nationality. We should not content ourselves living among other races, simply by their permission or their endurance—We must build up Negro states; we must establish and maintain the various institutions; we must make and administer laws, erect and preserve churches;—we must build ships and navigate them; we must ply the trades, instruct the schools, control the press and aid in shaping mankind.[4]

Projecting the African personality was a major concern of Blyden's. In fact, he first used the term "African Personality" in a lecture in Freetown in 1893. His views on this and related questions were crystallized in *African Life and Customs* where he enunciated ideas that were to be given great rhetorical and ideological force in the writings of the negritude poets and intellectuals of French expression. He argued eloquently in favor of the African social and economic system, emphasizing its socialistic, cooperative, and humanistic aspects and contrasting it with the European individualistic system that gave rise to "poverty, criminality and insanity."[7] He thundered against the Western-educated African middle class that was parasitically living off the cultural heritage of Europe:

> From the lessons he every day receives the Negro unconsciously imbibes the conviction that to be a great man he must be like the white man. He is not brought up—however he may desire it—to be companion, the equal of the white man, but his imitator, his ape, his parasite. To be himself in a country where everything ridicules him is to be nothing less, worse than nothing. To be as like the white man as possible—to copy his outward appearance, his peculiarities, his manners, the arrangement of his toilet, this is the aim of the Christian Negro—this is his aspiration. The only virtues which under such circumstances he develops are, of course, the parasitic ones.[5]

Among Blyden's prescriptions to meet the problem was the Africanization of the educational system to put an end to the "Europeanizing" trends. Speaking as President of Liberian College in 1881, he told the students and Congregation:

> All our traditions and experiences are connected with a foreign race. We have no poetry or philosophy but that of our taskmasters. . . . Now if we are to make an independent nation—a strong nation—we must listen to the songs of our unsophisticated brethren as they sing of their history—we must lend a ready ear to the ditties of the Kroomen who pull our boats, or the Possahs and Goleh men, who till our farms; we must read the compositions, rude as we may think them, of the Mandigoes and the Veys. . . . We shall in this way get back the strength of the race.[8]

Such profoundly good advice fell largely on deaf ears until more than fifty years later when negritude poets began to propagate identical views. Sadly enough, when such poets invoke the precursors of their movement, they are eager to name illustrious blacks like Du Bois, Marcus Garvey, and René Maran, but they forget Blyden who was closest to them in more ways than one. At the time Blyden carried on his campaign, the intellectual mood was against all such "nationalizing" tendencies. In fact, just a year after his nationalistic speech, the *Lagos Observer*, an inveterate articulator of the more resistant views to radical nationalism, came out in an editorial of 20 July 1882 with a scathing attack against these tendencies and in support of the dominant colonial myth:

> The words run glibly, [it commented polemically] but we confess that we do not understand what they mean. Perhaps some of the learned exponents of Wesleyanism at Lagos will enlighten us. It cannot mean that the acquisition of one of the noblest of modern languages, the language of Milton and

Shakespeare can have any such tendency for they teach it exclusively at their Seminaries. If it is not then the language, is it the costume? Is it the social and domestic habits? Is it the religion or, tell us, you who know, if know ye do, what denationalizing tendencies are they which you are going to discourage?

And the final damper was thrown on the idea of using African institutions to build an indigenous civilization by the *Observer* of 1 February 1883. Here a critic asserted: "The African can develop in his own African way; but what has he of himself to develop? What literature has he from which he could develop in his own line? To develop anything denotes a previous existence of such a thing, before development could ensue."

These stringent proponents for the primacy of European civilization and their challengers who vigorously argued for autonomy of the African native heritage sustained their debate, but on an abstract level. For, at that stage, the question was understandably handled as an intellectual exercise since the elite, as mentioned earlier, was insufficiently inducted into the native way of life. The vaguely felt need for cultural rehabilitation had to await the arrival of a new breed of intellectuals with roots in the hinterland before it could become a reality.

There was little truly creative writing in this early period of cultural nationalism. It should be observed, however, that the nineteenth-century intellectuals were fully alert to the demands of style and the immense possibilities of rhetoric for the development of argument or the exposition of ideas. Indeed, there is no reason why much of their writing cannot be seen as literature that is analogous to the eighteenth-century essays of Addison and Steele and their contemporaries.

The Black Victorians of West Africa composed their essays with great stylistic skill and architectonic finish; their thundering periods and balanced phraseology have far surpassed anything that has been produced by the writers of subsequent generations. The nearest thing to a creative work remains John Casely Hayford's *Ethiopia Unbound* (1911), which carried the cultural and nationalistic debates in a thinly fictionalized but highly discursive mold very much in the style of Johnson's *Rassellas* and many other eighteenth-century treatises.

When purely creative literature began to develop from the 1930s onward, it was to reflect the nineteenth-century evolutionary thinking noted earlier. Typical examples are some of the poems by the first generation of West African creative writers in English. Gladys Casely-Hayford, daughter of the great Africanist, wrote a poem that strongly reflected the evolutionist view, including the following suggestive lines:

> Oh Lord! as we pass onward, through evolution rise.
> May we retain our vision that truth may light our eyes.
> That joy and peace and laughter, be ours instead of tears.
> Till Africa gains strength and calm, progressing through the years.[7]

The Nigerian poet-politician, Denis Osadebay, writing a decade later, strikes an identical evolutionist note in the poem "Young Africa's Plea":

> Don't preserve my customs
> As some fine curios
> To suit some white historian's tastes.
> There's nothing artificial
> That bests the natural way
> In culture and ideal of life.
> Let me play with the whiteman's ways.
> Let me work with the whiteman's brains.
> Let my affairs themselves sort out.
> Then in sweet rebirth
> I'll rise a better man
> Not ashamed to face the world.[8]

These and similar poems reflect a state of innocence before the stormy awakening of the independence and nationalistic period. Many of Osadebay's countrymen reading his poems today would feel somewhat embarrassed by his childlike and uncritical eagerness to eat the poisoned apple, but those who were sufficiently grown up in the 1940s will recall the frenzied enthusiasm with which hinterland people all over West Africa struggled to obtain modern knowledge and skills, to acquire what, in the cliché of the day, was called "the golden fleece." Osadebay only versified a prevailing attitude among his contemporaries. This irrepressible drive for Western education he poignantly recaptures in these lines from "Young Africa's Resolve":

> On Library doors
> I'll knock aloud and gain entrance;
> Of the strength
> Of nations past and present I will read.
> I'll brush the dust from ancient scrolls,
> And drinking deep of the Pyrrean stream,
> Will go forward and do and dare.[9]

Osadebay became a lawyer and ultimately the premier of the Mid-Western Region in Nigeria's First Republic. Although his poems seemed to carry echoes of Alexander Pope and eighteenth-century English verse in expressions like "drinking deep of the Pyrrean [sic] stream" the sentiments were typical of the time, antedating the hot and feverish nationalism of the 1950s. As we survey the English-speaking West African scene during this period for works of vigorous protest against colonialism, we do so in vain: the dominant sentiment was, if anything, in favor of the blessings that were believed to accrue from colonialism.

In French-speaking West Africa of the same period, one is aware of similar attitudes among the intelligentsia, but in this case expressed more forthrightly in creative literature. The French colonial policy of assimilation had, by the nineteenth century, produced a small body of well-educated Africans in the favored Quatre Communes. The policy was meant to skim off from among the subject native population the most promising men capable of absorbing French civilization and to give them the best French education and full French citizenship in order to use them as cadres in the service of the French continental and colonial service. At least, so the theory of assimilation tended to be defined; and indeed by the 1920s, the Quatre Communes were sending deputies to the French Parliament.[10]

The policy, as may well be imagined, at first produced a pro-French black intelligentsia full of praise for French culture and colonial policy and critical of indigenous customs and traditions. One of these assimilated French Africans, Ahmadou Mpete Diagne of Senegal, wrote a juvenile reader in 1920 called *Les Trois Volontes de Malic*, which contains much propaganda in praise of the blessings of French colonialism and the culture of "nos ancestres les Gaulois" ("our ancestors, the Gauls"). Malic, the hero, is a great enthusiast of modern education. Having attained it and the skill of a blacksmith, he sets up a workshop in his village, much to the chagrin and horror of his caste-ridden neighbors and relatives. As a member of the village aristocracy, it is considered demeaning for him to use his hands for manual labor and to work with iron. But he perseveres and not only helps his village and neighbors to recognize the irrationality of the old order but brings them, by example, to see that there is dignity in labor. His bright-eyed, innocent view of French colonialism is well illustrated by his lecture to the "misguided" natives who resist progress and French civilization:

> Ce n'est plus le moment de parler d'origine et de caste. Les hommes ne se distinguent plus que par le travail, par l'intelligence et par leurs vertus. Nous sommes gouvernés par la France, nous appartenons à ce pays ou tous les hommes naissent egaux.[11]

> (This is no longer the time to speak of origin and race. People are now only distinguished by work, by intelligence, and by their virtues. We are governed by France; we belong to this country where all people are born equal.)

Diagne was probably taking the French colonial principle of the equality of all citizens too seriously, although, coming from the favoured Quatre Communes whose position accorded him better consideration than "les sujets," this is perfectly understandable. The glorification of France and her colonial mission of civilization is also a feature of Bakary Diallo's *Force Bonté*, which appeared six years later. Diallo's tale is an autobiographical exposition of the vast possibilities the French colonial empire offers to the tribal man in Africa. The hero, a (Fulani) shepherd boy from Futa Toro of Senegal, decides to give up the closed life of a cattleman for the adventurous life of the city. His new life takes him into the French army and war campaigns in Morocco and Europe. The emphasis in this book is on the blessings the French colonial presence brought to this part of Africa, including saving the

natives from intertribal squabbles, from revolts of serfs against landed pro-
prietors, from decimation of rural populations by marauding armies of mer-
cenaries, and the breakup of families by slave raiders. In other words, all the
horrors of a barbaric past have been charmed away by the civilizing French
presence. Indeed, Bakary Diallo relates his call to the new life in ecstatic and
religious terms:

> Le Dieu de la nature m'appelle. . . . Je lui reponds. Je pars, oui . . . je pars, lais-
> sant a sovanable coeur que j'aime. . . .[12]

> (The God of nature calls me. . . . I answer him. I am leaving; I depart, leaving
> behind as a remembrance this heart I love so much.)

For Diallo no less than for Diagne, France is destined with "la mission
capitale de la bonne entente humaine." Both accepted the colonial myth of
black inferiority, that the black man was a child needing the maternal care
of France. This so-called dependent complex, so well described by Manoni
in *Prospero and the Psychology of Colonialism*, is reflected by an incident in *Force-
Bonté* in which the hero, walking through Parc Monceau in Paris and, seeing
a pretty young woman feeding pigeons, draws an analogy between this scene
and colonialism: "That benign woman over there feeding pigeons is Mother
France; the birds are ourselves, the Blacks, who crave love and affection from
her."[13]

Both Diagne and Diallo are looking at the colonial situation with thoroughly colonized eyes. While recognizing the benefits of colonialism, they
are entirely ignorant of or oblivious to its veiled and sinister aspects, including
the fact that Mother France's beneficent gains are achieved at considerable
economic, political, and psychological costs to Africans. However, a few,
better-educated French-speaking Africans and Afro-Caribbeans were able,
even as early as this, to see through the ruse and to decipher the treachery,
and like the militant cultural nationalists of the nineteenth century in English-
speaking West Africa, to read the signs correctly. One of them, René Maran,
a French-speaking Afro-Caribbean who had attained the high office of District Commissioner, or Commandant in the French colonial hierarchy, wrote
a novel in 1920, regarded as the first true African novel. It was called *Batouala*.
In the preface to this novel, which deals with the tragic life of an African
prince of that name, trapped and betrayed by the colonialists, he thoroughly
denounces the idea of colonialsim as a mission of civilization and enlight-
enment. He sees it as merely a pretext for the exploitation and dehumanization
of the African peoples. The bitterness of his indictment is well illustrated by
this quotation from the preface: "Civilization: the European's pride and the
charnel-house of innocents. The Hindu poet Rabindranath Tagore, one day
in Tokyo, said what you are. You built your kingdom on corpses."[14] This
tone of castigation and militant rejection of the claims made for colonialism
by its apologists was to gather strength in the 1930s among French-speaking
African and Caribbean intellectuals, artists, and writers based in Paris. Racist

theories of black inferiority and barbarism, which the apologists for colonialism play on to support the necessity for a civilizing mission, were hotly contested and the exploitative and capitalist basis of colonialism was emphasized. The Malagasy poet Jacques Rabemananjara articulated this point of view in a paper he read at The First International Conference of Negro Writers and Artists:

> The Negro only became a barbarian the day the white man realized the advantages of this barbarism, the development of capitalism in the XIX century, and its expansion overseas had to have an excuse; the myth was born of the desire for moral elegance, and the fable of the civilizing mission continues to haunt the conscience of noble souls. For the barbarism of the Negro is an irreplaceable gold mine for certain modern Midases.[15]

The colonial myths were reversed. From being the carriers of civilization and superior morality, the colonialists were from then on to be regarded as the barbaric destroyers of a flourishing African civilization. Far from being the initiators of a superior moral order, they were portrayed as the harbingers of a squalid immorality, hard-grained with all the coarseness of materialism, perfidy, treachery, and—worst of all—a brutality that denied human status to its victims. This total reversal of attitude began with the African and Afro-Caribbean writers and artists, who expressed their revolt in journals by refusing to countenance any longer what they bitterly referred to as "the surrounding ignominy."[16] In 1932, Martiniquan students in Paris started a radical journal, *Légitime Défense*, in which they expressed their rejection of the Christian-capitalist assumptions of the colonial metropole in favor of communism and the artistic vision of surrealism, with surrealism offering them a poetic framework for expressing their radical dissent from the official culture, distorting it, dismembering and mutilating it, and creating over the rubble a new revolutionary identity for oppressed blacks. This militant journal created by Etienne Lero, René Nenil, and Jules Monnerot, among others, appeared only once. But it was soon succeeded, in 1934, by *L'Etudient Noir*, established by a group of African and Caribbean students, many of whom were later to become famous men. They included Aimé Césaire (Martinique), Léon Damas (French Guyana), Leonard Sainville, Aristide Mauges (West Indies), Léopold Sédar Senghor, Birago Diop, Ousmane Soce (Senegal). Even though many of them were professed Marxists, the platform of the paper was not officially Marxist but, rather, combative in fostering black nationalism and cultural interests and in attacking factors that undermined black solidarity and progress, factors such as tribalism and divisive ethnocentricism. The search for African roots was intensified, leading to the cultural ideological formulation known as negritude.

Many reasons have been advanced for this upsurge of militant nationalism, especially on the part of people who by their education (most were products of the prestigious Ecole Supérieur and the Sorbonne) stood to gain most from French official colonial policy. Among these factors must be mentioned the West's renewed interest in African culture since the beginning of the twentieth century, the works of historians and anthropologists (like Leo Frobenius) who were beginning to reveal the wealth and diversity of African civilizations, past and present, the enthusiasm inspired by great black American and New World thinkers, writers, and nationalists like W. E. B. Du Bois, Marcus Garvey, Claude McKay, and Langston Hughes, who were associated with the Negro Renaissance then sweeping through America, and finally the knowledge that by this time it had become obvious that the policy of real assimilation was a proven fraud—that France was not prepared to extend equality to her black citizens.

That the movement should develop in Paris when it did is no matter for great surprise. Paris had long been the center of boisterous anticolonial intellectual agitation, with men like André Gide making a valiant case for the colonial natives. It was also no accident that the major essay that launched the poetry of the new movement was by the young Marxist humanist Jean-Paul Sartre. His essay, characteristically titled *Orphée Noir*, was a prefatorial statement to Senghor's *Anthologie de la nouvelle poesie negre et malagache* (1948), which, apart from putting into sharp focus the significance of the new black voice, attempted to link the movement to the global pattern of Marxian dialectics and revolution. As for the distinctly primitivistic overtones of negritude, the involvement of Paris was also probably decisive, since this city, more than any other, had for some time been the center of philosophical primitivism, the city of Rousseau and the glorifiers of the "noble savage." Even French anti-Negro theoreticians of the late nineteenth century, like Count de Gobineau, couched their attacks largely in primitivistic terms.

Negritude at the outset meant many things to different people, until Senghor, its chief theoretician, began to build it into a full philosophical system and artistic ideology, and *Présence Africaine* (1947) became its mouthpiece and theoretical organ. One thing was certain from the beginning, negritude meant the ability of the black intellectuals to talk back to the racist theoreticians of the colonial policy of assimilation. More importantly, it enabled them to reverse the very arguments of the oppressor; all those arguments used to prove the cultural inferiority of blacks were taken by the negritude exponents who used them to show that African culture was not only different from Western culture but had elements that made it superior to Western culture. The best negritude poet of this belligerent assertiveness was Césaire who, in his *Cahier d'un retour au pays natal*, assailed the white world with accusations of brutality and inhumanity and, at the same time, as an act of total dissociation from the white man's cultural values, appropriated for himself those criticisms and accusations previously flung at the black man. "Look at the tadpoles of my prodigious ancestry hatched inside me," he wrote:

> Those who invented neither gunpowder nor compass
> those who tamed neither steam nor electricity
> those who explored neither sea nor sky

> but those who know the humblest corners of the country of suffering
> those whose only journeys were uprooting
> those who went to sleep on their knees
> those who were domesticated and christianized
> those who were innoculated with degeneration.[17]

In contrast to the white man's obsession with reason, calculation, success, and the desire to emasculate, control, and govern, the black man is, he said, unselfishly loving of all humanity, is simple in his intuitive and integrative nature, and exuberant in his expression of joy, with a sense of rhythm and spontaneity. In spite of all his sufferings, the black man is still a happy creature because of his nearness to nature and vital links with the source of his being. The white man, because he has cut himself off from these links, is doomed to unhappiness and tragedy. Césaire writes pityingly of the Western world:

> Listen to the white world
> appallingly weary from its immense effort
> the crack of its joints rebelling under the hardness of the stars
> listen to the proclaimed victories which trumpet their defeat
> listen to their grandiose alibis (stumbling so lamely)
> Pity for our conquerors, all-knowing and naive![18]

In 1938 when the *Cahier* appeared, Western civilization seemed at the brink of collapse, seriously threatened by fascism and nazism, among other "-isms."

Leopold Senghor's negritude, even though less rhetorically strident in its denunciation of the West than Césaire's *Cahier*, is equally critical of colonialism and the Western worship of reason, of what he refers to as the "Cartesianism" of the West. To this he opposes the intuitive humanism of the blacks.[19] In his poetry he emphasizes the mystical unity of the world as perceived by the black consciousness, a unity that derives from an integration with nature and communion with all being, that ennobles and reconciles. Senghor's poetry is studded with symbols of this integrative humanism of the blacks—the ancestors are constantly invoked through the symbolism of masks, the essential unity of man is suggested through totemic symbols, integration with nature is often expressed through natural images, and integration within African culture through cultural artefacts, especially drums and other musical instruments.

Besides Césaire and Senghor, who were the apostles of negritude, there are others, their disciples, who followed in their wake and more or less played the notes composed by the masters. The notes of violent anticolonialism chosen by Césaire were played by Senegalese David Diop, especially in *Le Temps du martyr*, the opening lines of which are full of strident accusations against the colonialists:

> The White man killed my father,
> My father was proud.
> The White man seduced my mother,
> My mother was beautiful.
> The White man burnt my brother beneath the noonday sun.[20]

David's brother Birago follows more in the line of Senghor, playing on the ancestral theme and the theme of mystical unity of the black world. In his poem "Souffles" he writes:

> Ecoute plus souvent
> les choses que les etres,
> la voix du feu s'entend,
> entends la voix de l'eau
> ecoute dans le vent
> le boisson en sanglots
> C'est le souffle des ancestres. . .[21]

> (Listen more to things
> Than to words that are said
> The water's voice sings
> And the flame cries
> And the wind that brings
> The woods to sighs
> Is the breathing of the dead.)

Militant self-assertion accompanied by militant denunciation not only formed the anchor of negritude poetry but were carried over to the cultural congresses at which black intellectuals and artists attempted to confront the colonial menace. The most influential of these congresses was The First International Conference of Negro Writers and Artists, which took place at the Sorbonne from 19-22 September 1956. It drew together black writers and artists from French- and English-speaking parts of Africa, the U.S.A., and the West Indies. Speaker after speaker denounced colonialism, analyzed it, and put forward suggestions for its overthrow. All were agreed that assimilation had done much to damage the black personality and to convert the African into a being without roots. Some of the New World participants, such as Richard Wright and Frantz Fanon, expressed irritation with this obsessive quest for roots and tried to direct the conference toward practical programs for overthrowing the oppressive system by modernizing and industrializing African life as an effective way to challenge the West. But such dissentient voices were easily drowned by theoretical denunciations of imperialism and assertions of the uniqueness of black civilizations, including the achievements of these civilizations in the past, and their contributions, in music and art especially, to modern Western civilization.

The sins of colonialism were forcefully epitomized by the Malagasy poet, Jacques Rabemananjara, in his paper "Europe and Ourselves." "By this we can judge the misdeeds of colonialism," he declared:

It arrives, it organizes, it labels. Savage, everything in the land of the Negroes is savage. Contempt for the individual, violation of treaties, lack of scruple in the choice of means and the use of methods. . . . But its monstrous character

lies in the diabolical art of perfidiously assassinating a culture, a native civilization whose normal development it fears, because that would ruin its argument
by destroying all basis for theory of generosity. This cunningly connived death
is then presented, not naturally, as the result of its intervention, but as the consequence of an endemic state affecting a poor people to whom it has obligingly
come to offer, or rather to impose, its care and teach the secrets of its reme-
dies.

The supreme cunning has actually been to get the cock and bull story swal-
lowed by millions of Europeans, the most logical race in the world. The incredible thing is this: we have ourselves fallen under the charm of the sympathetic
magic. The "inventors" are quite capable of assuming the voice of Mars as well
as the song of the sirens. The sorcery has worked so well that they have succeeded in the dazzling conjuring trick of innoculating us with contempt for
ourselves and making us forsake the values which ensured to our fathers the
dignity of their lives, and which enriched the source of their originality.[22]

The supreme sin of colonialism was therefore its devaluation of African
culture and alienation of educated blacks from their native traditions and
history. The negritude movement, taking up the challenge to restore black
originality, became of necessity a counteroffensive, launched by assimilated
intellectuals who were determined to recover the cultural initiative from the
colonial racists. It was a kind of intellectual freedom-fighting, a guerrilla
action in which these black intellecturals lay in ambush in conference halls
and in their poetry and prose, intent on dealing shattering blows to the
colonial monster. Senghor himself expressed these sentiments in less polemical
language when he explained that negritude was intended to combat the
"tabula rasa" theory behind assimilation. "We had to get rid of our borrowed
garments . . . those of assimilation . . . and affirm our existence, that is to say
our negritude." Aimé Césaire put it in his usual style: "The older generation
say 'Assimilation'; we the youth answer: 'Resurrection.' "[23]

Attacks on colonialism and the assimilationist policy behind it went beyond the original ideological mold of negritude, especially in the prose fictional works of Africans of French expression. These novelists used their art
to discredit the colonial system as well as the people who promoted it in
their direct line of duty or, indirectly, as conscious or unconscious collaborators. Colonial administrators, missionaries, and commercial men—all came
into the critical orbit of sharp-eyed satirists with their ridicule and satirical
jabs. The colonial world was x-rayed to expose its barrenness and decadence.
Modern towns, which are the best specimens of colonial innovation, were
stripped of their assumptions of sophistication and progress. All their hidden
sores and disfigurements were exposed: their slums, prostitution, unem-
ployment, crime, violence, and human degradations were spotlighted; the
old view that the colonial order brought greater security to the colonized
people was easily discredited in view of the major global wars of "civilized"
nations, which reverberated in the colonial outposts, the mass poverty of the
colonized, the diseases (some of which were introduced by the colonialists

themselves), the deaths, the hunger, and force labor. Exploitation, brutalilty, and perfidy as features of colonial life were all too often witnessed. The contrast between the serenity of pre-colonial life or village life, little touched by the colonial influence, and the insecurity and restlessness of life under the new order became a recurrent theme.

From 1947, and especially after the 1950s, the novel emerged as the dominant art form adopted by French-speaking African writers in their crusade to reestablish the authenticity of their traditional life and discredit the colonial system. Works ranged from those that recreated the traditional life, such as Camara Laye's *l'Enfant noir*, to those using the picaresque tradition to show how the false lights of the colonial world led characters astray from the integration of traditional life to the despair and disintegration of modern life engendered by colonialism. To this group belong Cheikh Hamidou Kane's *l'Aventure ambigue* (which is a storehouse of negritude in prose), Ousmane Soce's *Karim*, and Ferdinand Oyono's *Chemin d'Europe*. Several others satirized colonial officials, missionaries, and European traders. The colonial commandants were portrayed as violent and heartless tyrants, as in Oyono's *Une Vie de Boy* and *Le Vieux Negre et le medaille*. Ousmane Sembene's *Les Bouts de bois de Dieu*, and Mongo Beti's *Ville cruelle*. In some of the novels, misguided missionaries are shown foolishly uprooting traditional institutions without any hope of replacing them with something comprehensible and meaningful, as in Mongo Beti's *Le Pauvre Christ de Bomba* and *LeRoi Miracule*. "La Situation Coloniale," as French writers called it, dominated their consciousness, their attention, and their art up to colonial independence, and has, rather surprisingly, continued to form one of the major themes of post-independence African writing in French. Not much writing has appeared since the sixties but the little that has, in addition to focusing interest on individual problems of post-independence adjustment, deals with some aspects of it, the theme is far from played out.

In English-speaking West Africa, there was nothing approaching the same concentration on the colonial question. The cultural question was there, of course; so was the feeling that colonialism devalued and undermined traditional life and brought in changes, some of which were detrimental to the African. But in handling these themes there was always an effort towards objectivity and balanced judgment, a desire to see the question dispassionately, to weigh the evidence, to establish the positions, and to pin down the causes and effects. There was no attempt to blame all human disasters on some abstract monster called colonialism or on some sinister and monstrous humans called colonialists.

The problem was seen in terms of a clash of systems, a clash in which the colonial system, supported by superior coercive sanctions and more seductive appeals, wins over the other. The conflict, because it signified imperatives of fundamental differences, generated unhappiness and tragedy. But the note of acerbity and anger that was all too frequently present in French-

African writing was absent in writing by English-speaking authors. The idealization of the past, which was part of the attack on colonialism in French-African literature, was absent in all but a few works by English-speaking writers.

That is not to say that cultural nationalism was not a vital factor in African writing in English, especially before and leading up to the independence period. The English-speaking novelist Chinua Achebe put the case for a writer's use of his medium to further national awareness and revival of national faith and confidence in an essay called "The Role of the Writer in a New Nation," a kind of apologia for his own fictional interest in the past and an answer to those who felt a writer should concern himself with the present rather than with the past. After cataloguing some of the damaging and false views of blacks and their world contained in European writing on Africa, Achebe reaches the conclusion that a writer is obliged to join in the restoration of the past as a means of strengthening the present. The writer was, in his own words, to demonstrate

> that African peoples did not hear of culture for the first time from Europeans; that their societies were not mindless but frequently had a philosophy of great depth and value and beauty, that they had poetry and, above all, they had dignity. It is this dignity that many African peoples all but lost in the colonial period, and it is this that they must now regain. The worst thing that can happen to any people is the loss of their dignity and self-respect. . . . A writer who feels the need to right this wrong cannot escape the conclusion that the past needs to be recreated not only for the enlightenment of our detractors but even more for our own education.[24]

This does not read too differently from many of the negritude manifestos. But the difference appears if one compares Achebe's works, giving effect ot his theoretical formulation, to similar works by French-speaking Africans of the negritude persuasion. In *Things Fall Apart*, in which Achebe successfully recreates a traditional culture before the colonial attack on it, he attempts to do so without idealization or overt coloring. His Igbo peasants are real people, full of admirable qualities, as well as numerous faults. They are nothing like those saintly little phantoms of Hamidou Kane's *l'Aventure ambigue* or Camara Laye's *l'Enfant noir*. The Igbo society before the falling apart is portrayed with justice. It is a well-ordered society with a deep sense of religion, well-organized political and legal systems, rich traditions and colorful ceremonies, complex rhythms, and patterns of work and play woven into the regular rhythm of the seasons. But it is not a perfect society. It destroys twins and war hostages and discriminates against caste slaves.

Yet with all its imperfections, it is not a barbaric society, nor is it a society to which any reasonably man would feel ashamed to belong. Its people are peasants and humble, but they are not contemptible; they have a highly developed sense of personal worth and dignity and immense feeling for propriety of words and action. This society is assailed and broken up by

Christian missionaries and the colonial administration in a series of encounters and confrontations. The white colonialist, in his drive to set up the imperial order, walks over native institutions, tries to supplant them with his own, and shows no sympathy for the traditionalists when they fight for the life of their system.

Achebe tries to see the situation objectively. The missionaries and the colonial administrators were misguided, but what else could they have been? They were not natives and certainly did not understand the African way of life. They were, of course, ignorant, conceited, full of racial arrogance, and they generated a lot of suffering, but they were often given the benefit of at least being well meaning. The missionaries were eager to bring religion to those they wrongly believed to be in spiritual darkness. As for the administrative officers, their job was not to defend and protect native institutions but "to establish the empire" and "Pax Britannica." Achebe approaches a note of censure when, at the end of the story, the Commissioner sees Okonkwo's tragedy and suicide, most unfeelingly, as just one more incident in his projected anthropological work on "The Pacification of the Primitive Tribes of the Lower Niger":

> The Commissioner went away, taking three or four of the soldiers with him. In the many years in which he had toiled to bring civilization to different parts of Africa he had learnt a number of things. One of them was that a District Commissioner must never attend to such undignified details as cutting down a hanged man from the tree. Such attention would give the natives a poor opinion of him. In the book he planned to write he would stress that point. As he walked back to the court he thought about that book. Every day brought him some new material. The story of this man who had killed a messenger and hanged himself would make interesting reading. One could almost write a whole chapter on him. Perhaps not a whole chapter but a reasonable paragraph, at any rate. There was so much to include, and one must be firm in cutting out details. (*TFA*, 147-48)

In such a passage, Achebe's satire grows teeth and, very much in the manner of the French-African anticolonial novels of Ferdinand Oyono and Mongo Beti, bites deep into the flesh and marrow of the colonial system and its promoters. In *Arrow of God*, obtuse and insensitive colonial administrators are held up to ironic treatment as they ignorantly attempt to supplant a democratic, republican native order with puppet paramountcies. Young Oxbridge graduates, obsessed with their self-approving mission of empire and civilization, seize and imprison traditional rulers and inflict grave wounds on the traditional order. But they are not explored in the same detail as they are by French-speaking African writers. They are portrayed simply as catalysts of tragedy in the lives of their subjects.

Other West African writers of English expression see the colonial situation largely in terms of a crisis of choice confronting individuals in a confusing situation of clashing values. Present values are often contrasted with the values of the precolonial past, and there is no doubt at all that the weaknesses of the present are decried, accompanied by a feeling of regret at the loss of some of the past values. Criticism of the present is persistent and vocal—the scandal cannot be hidden—burgeoning crime, disgusting slums, pimps and prostitutes, unbridled materialism, futile hedonism and self-seeking, lack of individual self-discipline and social cohesion. Are these not the veritable products of the colonial order?

Yet it should be observed that these writers, while regarding colonialism as a historical nuisance, do not altogether discount its usefulness as a gateway into the present. They do not see it as an unmitigated evil as do their French counterparts. And they are unwilling to blur their vision by an uncritical and romantic attachment to the past so that they may look critically at the present, and participate fully in its drama, and direct its course.

Wole Soyinka struck the dominant note of English-speaking African writing in an independence play he called *A Dance of the Forests*. In it he showed that crime, self-seeking, and abuse of power are old as well as new. The artist's task in society should therefore be to function at all times as its conscience. English-speaking writers have sought to fulfill this task as the keepers of collective conscience in the here and now. They have managed to preserve a sense of proportion in their concern with the colonial situation. They are thus often critical of people, their own countrymen and women, and reluctant to identify all their frustrations with colonialism. This is perhaps understandable because English-speaking African intellectuals did not go through the trauma of deliberate assimilation that their French-speaking counterparts experienced.

Some English-speaking writers in West Africa, who give wide and enthusiastic treatment to the theme of colonialism, are popular writers who produce pamphlet literature based in the market town of Onitsha in eastern Nigeria. Onitsha market writing appeared in the late 1940s at the time of the nationalist movement. The pamphlet authors therefore devoted many of their works to the heroes of the struggle. There are works on Nnamdi Azikiwe of Nigeria, Jomo Kenyatta of Kenya, Kwame Nkrumah of Ghana, and Patrice Lumumba of the then Congo-Leopoldville. They are treated as folk heroes, vested with supernatural and apocryphal powers, while the colonial persecutors are thoroughly abused. The pamphlets are a storehouse of popular sentiments on the struggle. In these popular booklets, attacks on colonialism turn up in the most unlikely places and forms, as in this parody of Psalm 23 in Ogali A. Ogali's *Mr. Rabbit Is Dead*. It is called "Government":

> Government is my shepherd, I am in want.
> He maketh me to lie down in prison yard.
> He leadeth me beside hold of firms.
> He restoreth my doubts in the crown colony system . . .
> He leadeth me in the paths of helplessness,
> For the sake of his official redtapism.

> Yea, though I work [*sic*] through the shadow of perpetual economic
>   and political servitude,
> I fear all evil for it seems thou art against me.
> Thou preparest a reduction in my salary
> In the presence of my economics.
> Thou annointest my head with income tax.
> The politicians and profiteers, they frighten me.
> My expenses runneth over my income.
> Surely oppression and misery shall follow me
> All the days of Crown Colony system of administration.
> And I shall live in misery
> In my own God-given home for ever. Amen[25]

A study of these anticolonial popular pamphlets deserves attention for their language and content. For instance, the following words are put in the mouth of Patrice Lumumba, the saint and martyr par excellence of the popular authors: "We have been ruled and exploited by Belgium for donkey-long years, but now, I am sorry to say that the wind of change will in no time blow across this great nation of ours."[26]

The granting of formal independence to African countries by the imperialist powers between the late 1950s and the early 1960s has not dissolved the interest in colonialism. First, there is the offshoot of colonialism, manifesting itself in the new tactics of the ex-colonial powers, to hang on to some of the economic concessions enjoyed during the colonial period. This is often referred to by African nationalists as neocolonialism and is regarded as more insidious because it is more subtle than the old form of blunt domination and exploitation. In African writing by English-speaking authors, this new form of colonialism is seen as a sideline to the central themes of post-independence novels. In Wole Soyinka's *The Interpreters* (1965), corrupt politicians, acting in conspiracy with foreign companies and fake expatriated "experts," swindle and spoliate the new nation; in Okara's *The Voice* (1965), the faceless dictator in the story has a European security chief who helps him to smother opposition and to destroy the progressive nationalists. The new leaders in Ayi Kwei Armah's *The Beautyful Ones Are Not Yet Born* (1968) are the spiritual children of the departed colonialists who continue the exploitation of the common people on behalf of themselves and their principles. In Achebe's *A Man of the People* (1966), political corruption is stimulated by expatriate interests; foreign firms ply the corrupt black politicians with "ten-percent" bribes. However, in these novels the ultimate responsibility for the state of society rests on the new African rulers; white men, be they neocolonialists, mercantile thieves, or rougish contractors, merely take a peripheral, collaborative part.

In French-speaking West Africa, colonialism continues to excite writers to a far greater extent than in English-speaking West Africa. The reasons are not easy to define. One may hazard some guesses. In the first place, anticolonial militants of the negritude movement continue to dominate the political as well as the cultural scene in French-speaking African and Caribbean countries, combatants like Senghor (former president of Senegal) and Aimé Césaire in Martinique, for example. Perhaps, the temptation to go on playing old tunes has become irresistible. In English-speaking West Africa, the alliance between writers and politicians that developed during the nationalist struggle broke down soon after independence, and the writers have since become very critical of the politicians in their works. The French-African author-politicians find in anticolonialism a ready-to-hand scapegoat and a peg on which to hang their frustrations and failings. Moreover, *Présence Africaine*, which was established as the "intellectual clearinghouse" of negritude, has survived as the forum of negritude orthodoxy, even a decade after formal decolonization.

There are indications, however, the younger francophone African writers are shifting their viewpoint from the old approach of glorifying the past and censuring European colonialism for all the ills of the present. This shift has become more strenuously ideological and inward-looking since the revolutionary theses of Frantz Fanon became a major stimulant among African intellectuals. In four tautly argued works strung into a pathetically short life, Fanon proferred insights into the problems of colonialism that continue to excite much enthusiasm, especially among French-speaking Africans. These works, *Peau noire, masques blancs* (1959), *Les Damnes de la terre* (1961), and the collection of disparate essays published posthumously under the title *Towards the African Revolution* (1964), increasingly provide an ideological frame of reference for African writers. One of the most outstanding illustrations is the Malian writer Yambo Ouologuem's *Le Devoir de violence* (1968).

Although this novel has come under a cloud with the discovery that some of its passages have been closely based on some other works, this criticism has not extended to its treatment of the theme of colonialism, which manifests a refreshingly new approach. The central theses of this novel are that West African colonialism did not begin with the Western Europeans but with the Arabs, that the West African empires of the Middle Ages were slave empires, and that the African personality had suffered a serious emasculation long before the coming of European colonialism.

The story is set in medieval Nakem in Western Sudan (probably Mali), bordering the Sahara Desert and watered by the Yame River (Niger). The empire has been ruled since the Middle Ages by a Moslem dynasty—part Arab, part Jewish—the Saifs. Its life is explored in terms of its feudal brutality, blood lust, sadism, and the well-tried feudal techniques of oppression through religion, manipulation of supernatural beliefs and magic, along with underhand methods of stealthy poisonings and assassinations. The novel traces how this medieval empire maintained its power and political stranglehold on Africans (contemptuously referred to as the "niggertrash"), up to and beyond the establishment of the French colonial empire. The book's major contribution to the question of colonialism is its dramatization, of what has been called "internal" or "self-colonization," the exploitation and brutalization of the masses by their own people or by people who have lived with them for so long that they have become a part of the local life. Ouologuem is more scathingly critical of this form of colonial brutalization than of Western colonization. Here is a typical quotation from his novel:

> In that age of feudalism, large communities of slaves celebrated the justice of their overlords by forced labour and by looking on inert as multitudes of their brothers, smeared with the blood of butchered children and of disembowelled, expectant mothers, were immured alive. . . . That is what happened at Tillaberi-Bentia, at Granta, at Grosso, at Gogol Gosso, and in many places mentioned in the Tarik al-Fetach and Tarik al-Sudan of the Arab historians.[27]

Much of the actual brutalization of the native population results from rivalries, palace conspiracies, and coup d'états among the feudal nobles as they jostle one another for imperial control. In terrible and destructive wars, the common people prove contemptuously expendable, which more than explains the term "niggertrash." The picture is often explicitly drawn:

> Amidst all this turmoil, this dissolute life with its general bastardization, its vice and corruption, the Arab conquest, which had come several centuries earlier, settled over the land like a she-dog baring her white fangs in raucus laughter: more and more often, unfreed slaves and subjugated tribes were herded off to Mecca, Egypt, Ethiopia, the Red Sea, and America at prices as ridiculous as the flea-bitten dignity of the niggertrash." (*BV*, 18)

The Fanonian inspiration of this book is not in doubt, especially in its theory that colonial domination is sustained by coercive or implied violence, as graphically expressed by Bishop Henry, the one humane character in the novel:

> The crux of the matter is that violence, vibrant in its unconditional submission to the will to power, becomes a prophetic illumination, a manner of questioning and answering, a dialogue, a tension, an oscillation, which from murder to murder makes the possibilities respond to each other, complete or contradict each other. (*BV*, 173)

The principle derives from Frantz Fanon's thesis in *Les Damnes de la terre*. Indeed Ouologuem's "niggertrash" are just the same brutalized and dehumanized blacks that Fanon referred to as "les damnes," the victims of political oppression and violence. Ouologuem does not devote as much attention to the impact of French colonialism on the African personality as he does to the effects of Arab colonialism-cum-feudalism. Perhaps this is because he is reacting against those who have attributed all the black man's woes to the evils of Western colonialism and feels the necessity to tilt the argument well on the other side.

The Ghanaian novelist Ayi Kwei Armah sees colonialism as an evil that destroyed the dignity of Africans and undermined their sense of wholeness.

In *Two Thousand Seasons*, his fourth novel, Armah uncompromisingly attacks the colonialists for betraying the African natives, abusing their kindliness and hospitality and rendering them desolate. The Arabs are called "predators" and the Europeans "DESTROYERS." Between them, they colonized, oppressed, and dehumanized Africans. The language of attack is strident, reminiscent of the anticolonialist rhetoric of militant negritude.

The crimes of which the predators and the destroyers are accused are many, very grave, and often graphically sketched. Here, for example, is the image of the predators:

> [To them] force is goodness. Fraud they call intelligence. . . . In their communion there is no respect, for them woman is a thing, a thing deflated to fill each strutting, mediocre man with a spurious, weightless sense of worth. With their surroundings they know but one manner of relationship, the use of violence. Against other peoples they recommend to each other the practice of robbery, cheating, at best a smiling dishonesty. . . .
>
> They plant nothing. They know but one harvest: rape. The work of nature they leave to others: the careful planting, the patient nurturing. It is their vocation to fling themselves upon the cultivator and his fruit, to kill the one, to carry off the other. . . .[28]

Within this rhetoric of disapprobation are buried the usual stock accusations against feudalists and foreign conquerors. They make violence their instrument of policy, keeping men, women, and children down by sustained pressures through use of force and coercion. They contemn agricultural labor, which they relegate to slaves, serfs, and peasants. They are chauvinistic, using one set of morality and social values for their own group and another for the conquered peoples. They discriminate against women and despise gentleness. And yet, the economic basis of their drive to conquer and subdue is never in doubt. "Sharp-clawed desert beasts" is an expression that marks a high peak in Armah's rhetoric of abuse. The portrayal of the destroyers is no more attractive than that of the predators:

> The white men wish us to destroy our mountains, leaving ourselves wastes of barren sand. The white men wish us to wipe out our animals, leaving ourselves carcases rotting into white skeletons. The white men want us to take human beings, our sisters and our sons, and turn them into labouring things. The white men want us to take human beings, our daughters and our brothers, and turn them into slaves. The white men want us to obliterate our remembrance of our way, and in its place to follow their road, road of destruction, road of a stupid childish god. (*TTS*, 130–31)

The rhythms of language and action mark this novel out as a parabolic narrative. There is no great drive towards realistic particularization of character, setting, and language; much is generalized and broadly evoked through firmly set moral positions, attitudes, and categories of action. The action is organized around a number of consciously chosen symbols and images. The world of the novel is Manichaean and rigidly divided into the bad and the good, with the bad represented by the colonialists and the good by the African indigenes before they were devitalized by their conquerors.

Critics of this novel have tended to misapprehend and therefore misrepresent it by imposing on it the demands of fictional realism instead of reading it as an anticolonial parable. Armah can be a master of realistic particularity, as is evident in his three earlier novels, but he is also competent in handling his material on a generalized level of symbolic contrasts in the promotion of a thesis or the advancement of an argument. In *Two Thousand Seasons*, the parabolic inspiration shows clearly in the affirmed attributes of the autochthonous inhabitants before they are undermined and subverted by the corrosive presence of the predators and the destroyers. The claims for them are peasant and uncomplicated virtues and great generosity of spirit. Their old life is idealistically presented as "the way": "Our way is reciprocity. The way is wholeness. Our way is hospitable to guests. The way repels destroyers. Our way produces before it consumes. Our way creates. The way destroys only destruction." (*TTS*, 62)

Like Ouologuem, Armah's contribution to the theme of colonialism is his insistence that the historical phenomenon does not begin and end with the European incursion into Africa but equally includes the incursion of the Arabs into the region. Unlike Ouologuem, however, Armah's vision is animated by a more positive perception of the Africans. They are not the trashy, doomed creatures bound perpetually to the threshing mill of other people's violence, but noble beings temporarily suppressed but having a manifest potential for redemption. Indeed, Armah's last novel, *The Healers*, is another parable built strongly on the inevitability of this redemptive promise.

In conclusion, it should be emphasized that the colonial question is a major subject in the literature produced by West African writers using English and French, that the two recognizable postures of pro- and anticolonialism are present in both writings and that, whether overtly or implicitly, the subject continues to excite writers more than a decade after the formal granting of independence by the imperialist powers. But it should also be observed that the subject generates a certain militancy of outlook and violence of style in African writing in French that is absent in works by English-speaking authors, except for some of Okigbo's poems and Armah's novels. This in turn may be traced to certain stylistic traits in French and British literature. For example, if one compares poems by Baudelaire and the French imagists with those by Eliot and Yeats, one is likely to feel the differing stylistic pull and temper of the works, which must have influenced those who absorbed their models.

Form also dictates different textures to the works. Verse provides different facilities to the writer protesting against colonialism from prose, and each work represents both the possibilities as well as the limitations of the form adopted by the writer. In the final analysis, however, the main factor in determining response to colonialism in works by West Africans remains the cultural and economic policies of the colonizing powers. The French policy of assimilation, which overtly posited the superiority of the culture of the metropole and demanded that salvation for the colonized must come through emancipation through this culture, was more likely to arouse militant rejection than the British approach which, while not so much as remotely conceding equality to the cultures of the colonial subjects, was nevertheless content to transform the colonials as little as possible into Englishmen. Paradoxically, French policy, which implied that at least some of the subject people could become Frenchmen, elicited greater fury and feeling of outrage from African writers than the British attitude, which seemed to deny that the subjects had any such capacity to absorb the British way of life. Indeed, many British writers on Africa up to the end of the 1930s expended much energy and argument proving that Africans educated in the Western tradition lost their cultural roots and fell between the African and European cultural stools. The tendency in the past few years for writers to dwell more on the concrete failings of post-independence African leaders and only residually on the part played by colonial or neocolonial agents is becoming the pattern in the English-speaking part of West Africa; it remains to be seen whether their French-African counterparts will come to see the wisdom of a shift that will add vigor, presence, and authenticity to their writing.

NOTES

1. *Black Skin, White Masks* (New York, 1967), 18.

2. See M. J. C. Echeruo's *Victoria Lagos* (London, 1977), 35–49, for a perceptive discussion of the dilemmas of the black Victorian elite of Lagos.

3. Ibid.

4. Edward Wilmot Blyden, *Liberia's Offering* (New York, 1862), 74–76.

5. Quoted in Hollis Lynch, *Edward Wilmot Blyden: Pan-Negro Patriot* (New York, 1970), 72.

6. Edward Wilmot Blyden, *Christianity, Islam and the Negro Race* (Edinburgh, 1883), 77.

7. Frances Ademola, ed., *Reflections* (Lagos, 1965).

8. Dennis Osadebay, *Africa Sings*, 11.

9. Ibid., 13.

10. See Michael Crowther, *Senegal: A Study of French Assimilation Policy* (London, 1962), chaps. 2 and 3.

11. Ahmadu Mpaté Diagne, *Les Trois Volontés de Malic* (Paris, 1920), 27.

12. Bakary Diallo, *Force Bonté* (Paris, 1926), 22.

13. Ibid., 107–8.

14. René Maran, *Batouala* (London, 1973), 8.

15. Jacques Rabemananjara, "Europe and Ourselves," *Présence Africaine* 8-9-10 (June-November, 1956).

16. "the surrounding ignominy" cf. *Présence Africaine* 8-9-10 (June-Nov. 1956).

17. Aimé Césaire, *Cahier d'un retour au pays natal*, tr. John Berger and Anna Bostock (Harmondsworth, 1969), 110.

18. Ibid.

19. See Senghor's *Liberté I: Négritude et Humanisme* (Paris, 1964) and *Liberté III: Négritude et Civilisation de l'Universal* (Paris, 1977) which embody most of his discourses on negritude.

20. David Diop, *Hammer Blows* (London, 1976), 40–41.

21. John Reed and Clive Wake, eds., *A Book of African Verse* (London, 1964), 26.

22. *Présence Africaine* 8-9-10 (June-Nov., 1956), 26–27.

23. See article in *Présence Africaine* 8-9-10.

24. Chinua Achebe, "The Role of the Writer in a New Nation," *Nigeria Magazine* 81 (June 1964): 157.

25. Chinua Achebe, *Things Fall Apart* (London, 1959), 147–48.

26. Ogali A. Ogali, *Veronica My Daughter and Other Onitsha Plays and Stories* (Washington, D.C., 1980), 181.

27. Ibid.

28. Yambo Ouologuem, *Bound to Violence* (London, 1971), 4. Subsequent references to this work are cited as *BV* in the text.

29. Ayi Kwei Armah, *Two Thousand Seasons* (London, 1979), 62–63. Subsequent references to this work are cited as *TTS* in the text.

CHAPTER 5

Politics in the Early African Novel

THE PLACE of politics in West African creative fiction reflects the importance of the topic in the whole of Africa and, indeed, in former European colonies all over the world. There are good reasons for this. In the first place, politics has been given enormous importance by the nationalist struggle in Africa, especially since the 1940s when mass political parties were established by African nationalists. Since then, we have achieved political independence and native Africans have assumed responsibility for the government of their people. The growth of literacy and spread of the mass media have encouraged the dissemination of ideas and information about political events everywhere in the continent and in the world at large. The post-independence campaign against the threat of a real or hypothetical neocolonialism has kept interest in politics alive. The introduction of party politics or, where there are one-party systems, of populist movements, has fostered political awareness among most West Africans. The very novelty of organized politics, which is an inevitable concomitant of the modernizing process going on in Africa, fascinates the popular imagination, coupled with the fact that the first generation of post-independence politicians live in style, exercise great influence, and have made themselves into a clearly observable elite group. This draws attention to politicians and their profession in a way that is inconceivable in more technologically advanced countries. For the political scientist, West Africa has provided a fascinating opportunity to study the dynamics involved in the welding of traditional, kinship-oriented societies with different backgrounds and historical developments into nation-states.[1] The novelists dealing with contemporary West Africa cannot ignore a subject of such absorbing interest to the people.

The novelist is concerned essentially with values: the values by which human behavior is determined, and, more particularly, with the quality or ranking of these values and their adequacy or otherwise for ensuring human happiness and individual integration into society. We expect the novelist in exploring the values of society to contribute substantially to social and moral insight, to the vision of the good life. In a subject like politics, the concern with values inevitably leads the novelist into the sphere of ideologies, which largely determine political morality. As Irving Howe observes, "The political novel . . . is peculiarly a work of internal tensions. To be a novel at all, it must contain the usual representation of human behavior and feeling; yet it

93

must also absorb into its stream of movement the hard and perhaps insoluble pellets of modern ideology."[2] It should be noted, however, that apart from Ekwensi's *Beautiful Feathers*, Conton's *The African*, and Okara's *The Voice*, of the early African novels, politics as an interplay of ideas is not treated in any sustained way in the West African novels I am concerned with but, rather, as part of the panoramic sweep of social conflict resulting from cultural change.

I shall consider these three books in order to examine the political behavior of the characters, eliciting from them the social and cultural forces that condition such behavior—how, for instance, those who have a background of traditional political culture operate the machinery that was evolved in an industrial, urban, and "individualistic" civilization. The ideology of traditionalism seems to have no effective power in the political structure, and yet its persistence as a social reality is no less strong than the persistence of the traditional religion, economy, social attitudes, and other beliefs.

One of the results of European colonialism in Africa was the formation of nation-states that comprise a large number of ethnic groups that had existed as independent entities in the past. Some of them, like those in Yorubaland, had divine kings; others, like the Igbo, had a republican system of government; and yet others, like the Tiv, had an egalitarian system based on a well-balanced system of family relationships headed by oligarchs. These different groups, with their different political structures, were brought under single administration by the colonizing powers. Under an indirect rule policy, British administrative officials ruled the local populations through the traditional and indigenous authorities; where there was no local paramountcy, as in Igboland and among the Tiv, the administration created one.[3] This expedient was obviously very suitable for administering vast areas at the local government level with a small number of British administrators. At the national level, the administrative machinery was run exclusively by a bureaucracy under a resident governor. In spite of the indirect rule system, the structure of political power was altered irrevocably. The most immediate effect was that chiefs became civil servants and had to adjust the traditional pattern of relationship among themselves, their employers, and their subjects. They began to play an intermediary role that sometimes made them unpopular with the administration or their people—but more often than not with their people.

The change in political structure was profound, for it altered the basic political values of traditional society, even though the externalities of the system continued to exist.[4] It is impossible here to go into the political structure of all the traditional societies, but some general statements can be made. First, with a few exceptions, West African societies in precolonial days were homogeneous, and had political structures that reflected the structure of kinship relationship. The Yoruba king, the Ashanti chief, the Igbo *okpala*, or the Tiv elder was related by kinship ties, traced to a single ancestor, with the rest of the people in his community. Political power was always exercised for the benefit of the group. Elaborate checks and balances were worked into the system to prevent the emergence of dictatorship.[5] The nature of political action was democratic because it was representative (except in conquered states where power lay with a feudal oligarchy of alien conquerors). Authority was supernaturally sanctioned and upheld by consensual agreement. Flouting of the constitution by a would-be autocrat called down ancestral retribution or sparked civil war. Such threats were frequent enough to curb political extremism. But the kings amassed vast, illegal, nontraditional powers under the patronage of the colonial administration.

By making modern nation-states out of an agglomeration of traditional societies, the colonial powers had to introduce, for the purpose of uniformity as well as expedience, political and judicial institutions evolved in Europe. This caused far-reaching changes in the West African traditional societies. In politics, for instance, the mystical and supernatural values once associated with political office have been weakened by the secular nature of the introduced Western institutions, and so has the charisma attaching to the monarchy, the chiefs, and old age. Ritual, religious, and moral sanctions and taboos, Christianity, the emergence of the educated commoner, the introduction of modern economic values and technology, urbanization, and the imposition of an alien political ideology—all these have undermined the traditional political system that was based on reciprocal rights and obligations. In spite of the changes in traditional politics, however, behavior based on the old values persisted under the indirect rule system and has become more pronounced since independence in the former British colonies.

The political dominance of the colonizing powers in West Africa was challenged by the West African intelligentsia from the late nineteenth century, but the really massive opposition to colonialism began after the war of 1939–45 and was led by those who had absorbed the main European ideologies through Western education. Since 1957, when colonial Gold Coast became independent Ghana, all the West African colonies, including Portuguese Guinea, have become independent nations. Most of these countries have also been through political crises resulting from the alienation of the masses from their rulers and leading, in a number of cases, to military takeovers from civilian administration. Of the four former British colonies, three—Nigeria, Ghana, and Sierra Leone—have had military takeovers; of the nine former French colonies, five have been taken over by the military.

Most of the novelists are severely critical of politicians. Politics and politicians are not treated idealistically in the novels under discussion. It is said that politics is a dirty game and that politicians are corrupted by power. Since the time of Machiavelli, the politician has been seen as a half-whimsical and half-dangerous animal by the intellectual, something to be despised and feared at the same time. Thomas Uzzell is right when he says that in prose fiction heroes and villains have vanished but, instead, "The villain today . . . is politics."[6] And yet, what is so surprising about the alienation of the writer from politics and the politician in West Africa is that only a few years ago the people who now hold political responsibility (some of them intellectuals) were involved in a common endeavor with other intellectuals (including writers) to get rid of the colonialists. Now the writers satirize politicians mercilessly in their books. It cannot be entirely because the writers are "allowing some sense of personal failure to affect and colour excessively their views and their relations with other people."[7] Rather, we may see the real reason in the writer's perception of his role in society, as a kind of custodian of the moral conscience of society, whose duty it is to keep an alert and critical eye on societal values and to hold a mirror up to society to let it see when it is in danger of going wrong. In West Africa it is likely that something *is* wrong, not necessarily with writers, but with politics and politicians.

Two things should be emphasized about politics and politicians in West Africa. First, there is the problem of operating the democratic machinery; and second, there is the problem of human nature. Let me begin with the first problem. It has been said before but it is worth saying again: the great dilemma of African politics arises from the nature of African cultural change. It is the dilemma of how political sentiments arising from traditionalism can be reconciled with and perhaps accommodated to the sentiments necessary to run a modern nation-state. In the West, the evolution of the modern nation-state has proceeded side by side with the decay of traditionalism, culminating in the situation in which "the absolute individual faced the absolute state."[8] The process took hundreds of years and moved pari passu with change in society by slow evolution through "tribal," "feudal," and "industrial" stages. In West Africa, in contrast, Western institutions have been forced on the kinship-oriented traditional societies and "feudal" emirates. The result is that, although the externals of a democratic structure are set up in these countries, the spirit in which it should operate is not always there. For example, how can feudal rulers, who for generations have been used to ruling by "divine right," fit into a democratic framework, which implies that "politicians are subordinate to the public, in whom are vested the fundamental rights of free criticism, opposition and dismissal"?[9] The situation has been aptly summarized by Edward Shils:

> The constituent societies on which the new states rest are, taken separately, not civil societies, and, taken together, they certainly do not form a single civic society. . . .
>
> They lack the affirmative attitude towards rulers, persons, and actions that is necessary for consensus. They are constellations of kinship groups, castes, tribes, feudalities—even smaller territorial societies—but they are not civil societies. . . . The interaction among different sectors is tenuous. Parties are very often communal, sectional, and tribal. Civil associations tend to be tribal; trade unions tend to be creations and instruments of the political parties. Publications are local in circulations; there is no system of mass communications effectively covering the country. The whole infrastructure is fragile.[10]

The new states are committed to working out a kind of synthesis between the old and the new, between traditional African political values and the values necessary to sustain a modern nation-state aspiring to technological development. Some African nationalists (like Nkrumah, Senghor, Nyerere, and Touré) see the solution in the creation of one-party states that can be mobilized to develop a feeling of oneness among the different peoples of each country. Others see the solution in giving different ethnic components the opportunity for limited self-government within a decentralized state.

The technical aspect of the problem—that is, the actual decision-making and discussion of the theories involved—is a purely political one, which belongs to politicians and political scientists, and not to creative writers. The writers are concerned with the values those who operate the political machinery bring to bear on their actions and decisions, especially as these actions and decisions affect the happiness of people. Even when they criticize politicians and politics, it is not always because "young intellectuals tend to find their political outlet in opposing whichever party may be in power,"[11] but because the politicians have not lived up to the standard of political morality or because they are bad men for whom politics offers one more outlet for their viciousness.

This brings me to the second aspect of politics, what I have called the problem of human nature. Even a passably satisfactory system is liable to be perverted by the moral weaknesses of those who operate it. This goes for political institutions. A politician is liable to be tempted by money, prestige, and power. In the fluctuating political situation of West Africa, the temptation is stronger than in countries with a long-established code of political conduct. The political upheavals that have taken place in independent African countries so soon after the departure of the colonial powers are partly caused by some of the politicians not living up to the expectations of the people (or at least the articulate middle class of traders, artisans, secondary school and university graduates) who put them in power. In some countries, politicians have corruptly enriched themselves; in others, they have neutralized the democratic process, imprisoned or persecuted the opposition, and stifled criticism; and, in others, the political machinery has been emasculated by politicians and dictatorships and have replaced democratic process. Greed for power may lead politicians to imperil the very existence of the young nation states by furthering sectional ethnic solidarities and using them to foster their political ambitions. Creative writers as an important section of the modern body of intellectuals in West Africa are therefore understandably critical of them.

The writers deal with various aspects of politics and political behavior. Through them, we can see the practices they censure and the values they promote to ensure social integration and the happiness of the people. Not being politicians, they rely on their intuition to shape their attitudes to the political problems of society. And they do so by describing the political situation in terms of the men and women who inhabit society. "By the incidents he chooses, the characters he selects and his attitudes towards them," writes Somerset Maugham, "the author offers you a criticism of life."[12] It is best to begin with Ekwensi because he is an outspoken and early critic of politics and politicians in Africa.

Some of the politicians in Ekwensi's novel like Uncle Taiwo and Fred Namme (*Jagua Nana*) are involved in local government, others like the partisans of the Self-Government Now Party and the Realization Party (*People of the City*) in national politics, and yet others like Wilson Iyari (*Beautiful Feathers*) in postcolonial and pan-African politics. They are all professional politicians. With the exception of Wilson, who is a pharmacist as well as a politician, their full-time occupation is politics. They are therefore a product of that modern specialization and division of labor that result from the influence of the West on the African way of life. Each of them is in some way a cog in the wheel of what Weber calls "machine politics,"[13] the management of politics by professionals and the party machine. They are supposed to operate within a framework of "mass democracy." The system they work is political democracy.

Implicit in this system, as inherited from the West, is the acceptance of the primacy of the individual. The individual is the target of party political propaganda. He has the prerogative of making and unmaking governments by the free exercise of his franchise. This, in theory at any rate, makes the individual the real holder of political power in the state since, with his vote, he says who shall exercise governmental control on his behalf. The affirmation of the primacy of the individual is because he has the ultimate sanction and can exert pressure through it on his rulers to do well. The exercise of the vote could be extended to the entire area of action, beliefs, and attitudes in the democratic state. It runs through the value system of the democratic countries of the West.[14] The obvious corollary of political individualism is the freedom of the individual to choose between different political parties seeking his vote, and, in return, his political choice. Another corollary is that the process of soliciting support by rival parties should interfere as little as possible with the individual in his exercise of his right to vote. And when the electorate has decided which political party shall become the government, then the party or parties that are not chosen must accept the voters' verdict. In other words, political democracy involves free elections and also respect for the results of elections.

In West Africa, especially in the former British colonies, the democratic system was set up before independence was granted. The first democratic election was held, but since then, the values of democracy have been slowly undermined.

Ekwensi, like many intellectuals in West Africa, is a believer in democracy. He is deeply outraged when he sees the values of democracy being systematically destroyed by self-seeking politicians. He therefore marks them out for attack. He portrays them as greedy, egocentric, and corrupt, and often implies or says outright that they are in politics not for the opportunity to serve their fellowmen, but for what they can get out of it. He employs in his two earliest novels a whole range of satirical weapons against them, from invective to ridicule and caricature. He singles out unmitigated self-centeredness as the mainspring of much of the oppressive viciousness, cynicism, and extremism that characterize the political behavior of his characters. Each of them is shown to be pursuing unswervingly a course of self-aggrandizement or self-glorification, whether by way of political power through ministerial or local government appointment, the adulation of the masses, or the glamor of an ill-digested ideology. He castigates this vulgar self-seeking in his characters. Uncle Taiwo is bumptious, shamelessly sensual, and a thug; Wilson Iyari is an exhibitionist and a demagogue; the Minister of Consolation is a buffoon and a narcissist. The later Ekwensi (the Ekwensi of *Beautiful Feathers* who, as director of the Federal Information Service, had become very much part of the establishment) shows marked restraint in his criticism of politicians and an unmistakable respect and even affection for the then prime minister of Nigeria.

Ekwensi does not stop at satirizing politicians, he also criticizes the ways in which they run political institutions. Their campaign methods do not ensure respect for politics or for politicians. Their agents seek votes by bribery, intimidation, and violence. The spirit of democracy is shown to be annulled by the general intolerance of political opponents, mob action, the recruitment of private bodyguards, promotion of illegal violence through what has been called "thuggery" (the word gained currency in Nigeria during the first general election in 1951), and the use of every conceivable unfair means to thwart political opponents. Political rivals regard each other as "enemies." They wage unceasing feuds (sometimes bloody feuds) to destroy each other. Uncle Taiwo in *Jagua Nana* advocates the destruction of his political opponents, actually referring to them as enemies—"Spare no foe!" is his battle cry—and when young Freddie, his rival candidate at the local election, is murdered by his thugs, Uncle Taiwo gloats without remorse, "I tol' him politics not game for gentlemen."[15]

Recent commentators on African politics have noted the absence of organized opposition within traditional societies, and Harrison Church has recorded that the word *opposition* is absent in most African languages.[16] We have noted the consensual nature of the traditional political system, which tends to support this view. Where people lived in a community and were interrelated by blood or marriage, or common economic interests and religion, there was little scope and, in fact, little need for the deep ideological cleavages that form the basis of the modern multi-party system. Everyone was involved directly or indirectly in the life of the community and in the well-being and health of society. Political offices and officials were supernaturally protected and social homogeneity reduced the areas of fundamental disagreement among individuals or groups. This was obviously most true of the traditional societies without chiefs and kings that depended more on internal structure, ritual and religious sanctions, taboos, witchcraft, and magic for the regulation of the social and political relations, and least true of the domination kingdoms. In all, however, group solidarity was very strong, and authority was supernaturally sanctioned and upheld by consensual agreement.[17] Intolerance of political opponents may therefore be a manifestation of the feuding spirit, which, in the past, characterized the relationship of those who were not related by ties of kinship. If so, it is feud without its traditional checks. However the phenomenon cannot be regarded as deriving entirely either from traditional political values or from Western democratic values, but from the absence of clearly defined values: it is a product of human imperfection in a society where fluctuations can be taken advantage of. There is no doubt that behind aberrant political behavior is someone who stands to gain in terms of power, prestige, or money, and who subverts legality as the quickest way to attain his end. It is this flagrant disregard for political morality and cynical exploitation of the weakness and newness of the democratic machinery by the politicians that Ekwensi attacks.

The theme of politics is not explored in a sustained way in *People of the City* and *Jagua Nana*. In the first, politics, like sex and materialism, is just another aspect of corrupt city life. The election of the first mayor of Lagos provides the opportunity for comment on politicians and their evil ways, including their corruption of voters. In *Jagua Nana*, the comment on politicians becomes more caustic and shrill. Even though Jagua's life dominates the story, a substantial part of it is devoted to politics and politicians. To give the interest sharp focus, the man who has been most closely associated with Jagua is involved in it. We cannot miss Ekwensi's bitter indictment of politics and politicians behind Jagua's words as she warns her young and inexperienced lover, who wants to go into politics because "I wan' money quick-quick; an' politics is de only hope," of the danger and risks involved:

> "Politics not for you, Freddie. You got education. You got culture. You're a gentleman an' proud. Politics be game for dog. And in dis Lagos, is a rough game. De roughest game in de whole worl'. Is smelly an' dirty an' you too clean an' sweet. I speakin' frank to you, Freddie. I don' want you inside at all. I hear rumour dat O.P.2. wan' to kill one man from your party. . . ." (*JN*, 137)

Freddie ignores the warning and is killed soon afterwards by the O.P.2.

The theme receives more concentrated attention in *Beautiful Feathers*. In fact, politics is the main concern of the novel. Apart from the stock criticisms already mentioned, other aspects of the political life of Nigeria are touched upon—national politics and pan-African politics. The main focus is pan-African politics. Wilson Iyari is a radical politician who believes in pan-African solidarity and runs the "Nigeria Movement for African and Malagasy Solidarity" to ginger up the Nigerian government, which is dragging its feet on the issue. Ironically, he is helped by Kwame, a political refugee from Ghana.

A huge demonstration is organized, and the police break it up but not until some of the demonstrators have broken into a bicycle-shop and ridden away on some of the bicycles. The prime minister summons Wilson later and makes him leader of the delegation to a pan-African conference in Dakar. Nothing but disillusionment follows. Once in Dakar, Wilson discovers how varied Africa is and how starry-eyed the idea he had labored for. Everything in Dakar is so French; even the girls look as if they "had just stepped out of Champs-Elysée and were on their way to cocktail party with the President." [18] His first shock is the language problem. The first French delegate he tries to converse with shrugs his shoulder with a "Non comprends pas" and walks off. But the real big shock is yet to come. At a hunt organized for delegates, an animal is killed and the African delegates fall to arguing as to who should have what part of the beast. While they are busy quarrelling among themselves, the Europeans who accompanied them as observers and gun-carriers run away with the booty. Wilson is shot and wounded.

All this, including the parable of the hunt, is a terrible oversimplification of the question of pan-African politics, but it is largely true in the outline. The novel is dedicated by Ekwensi to the late Sir Abubakar Tafawa Balewa and President Senghor, and it is not difficult to see that Ekwensi's sympathies in pan-African politics lie with the conservatives and gradualists and not with the radicals. The real interest in the novel, however, is its insight into the inner life of public men, the hidden realities behind the public gestures. While he is working fanatically for pan-African solidarity, Wilson's domestic life collpases, and his aggrieved wife runs away.

The novel is of considerable interest for the light it throws on the behavior of the urban mob, that vast unassimilated product of an immature democracy. The town, because of its greater opportunities for employment and numerous other attractions, has drawn, in ever-increasing numbers, ill-educated and sometimes illiterate young people from the villages in search of work. This body is constantly being increased by elementary school leavers. Because there are fewer jobs than there are people seeking them, many of these townspeople are unemployed or badly paid. This has resulted in the emergence of an incipient urban proletariat. This drifting urban mass is often very poorly individuated and very easily forms into a mob—irrational, impulsive, violent, and a prey to emotional manipulation by a demagogue.

The emergence of the mob is undoubtedly one of the results of social change and clearly contrasts with the old social order in which there were no disorderly crowds and no impulsive rioting, where there was organized warfare and institutionalized self-help. It is obviously a product of urban anonymity and the absence of familial control of individual behavior, which was a potent moral sanction in traditional society.

In *Beautiful Feathers*, Ekwensi brings out in broad relief this unstable nature of the mob during the pan-African demonstration. What starts off as a peaceful demonstration ends in rioting and looting. His attitude to the mob is tolerant. He accepts the existence of mobs and political demonstration. Both Wilson Iyari, the leader of the demonstration, and the Nigerian prime minister behave with dignity, restraint, and a sense of judgment.

If the mob itself is poorly individuated and unstable, the tolerance of its existence and the possibility of its mobilization to produce political pressure are auguries of the respect for public opinion that is an essential feature of modern democracy. Also, the volatile mob of an infant democracy is a better type of humanity than the grim-faced, silent, and sinister crowd of the totalitarian world of *The Voice*.

Ekwensi's *Beautiful Feathers* unmistakably reflects the vestigial values of traditional politics in present-day national politics of newly independent African countries, especially in his portrayal of the relationship between constituents and their elected representatives. Here we find the Minister of Consolation invaded by an army of constituents, some waving envelopes containing applications for jobs, others helping themselves to the minister's food and drink, and all behaving in a way that suggests that the minister has an obligation to look after their needs. For the minister, it is a matter of grinning and bearing it, for, ragged as his hosts are, his politician's instinct tells him that he is beholden to their goodwill if he is to be returned to parliament during the next election. "They vote me into power," observes the minister ruefully, "so I mus' respect them." (*BF*, 76)

Two traditional assumptions are at work here. First is the assumption that the more prosperous and successful members of the community have a duty to help and sustain the less successful and the needy; and second is what Max Gluckman noted in respect to the Zulu Chief, that the ruler (who is often the wealthiest member of the community) can enhance his position and buy goodwill by a show of munificence. The constituents, sharing these traditional assumptions, have not dissociated the role of the minister as a clansman from his role as a political functionary of the nation-state.

This failure to dissociate the traditional obligations of individuals from their roles in the new social context, where relations should be defined largely by contract and on a legalistic and formal basis, pervades every sector of national life and is behind much of the nepotism and corruption that is so prevalent. The kinsmen, clansmen, and townsmen of a man in a responsible position expect him in the spirit of traditionalism to advance their causes or treat them with special favor. The politician accepts this traditional blackmail, for it is in his own interest.

Though being invaded by his constituents must have seemed a great nuisance, in some respects the minister is thrilled by it, for it gives him a sense of power. This spirit in which democracy is operating as a result of this peculiar mixture of traditional and modern political values is reflected in the minister's Perennial Secretary's ironic exegesis of the function of the Ministry of Consolation. Founded as "a sympathetic gesture, a kind of Universal Aunt," it runs an orphanage in which most of the children come from the minister's constituency and only a few from other parts of the country. An institution set up to serve national needs has been turned to constituency (and therefore, in the West African context, ethnic and traditional) account.

We need to bear in mind the wide gulf separating the theoretical ideals of modern democracy from the actual operation of democratic institutions to understand the apparent "doing down" of politicians by Ekwensi. By education and intellectual orientation he is a democrat because he is an individualist. He is one of the most urbanized of Nigerians, having been born and brought up entirely in the towns. It is when he comes to compare the democratic ideals with the travesties that characterize actual political practice that he takes out his frustrations on the politicians. What fascinates him about the ascetic personage of his prime minister is his level-headedness and the tolerance he shows even to the young demagogue and rabble rouser Wilson Iyari. Obviously, Ekwensi tends to sentimentalize the prime minister, but the fact remains that what impresses him is the democratic outlook of the man, coupled with his devastating realism, which sharply contrasts with the reckless idealism of the demagogue.

The most antipolitical West African novel is Gabriel Okara's *The Voice*. Its dominant theme is the corrupting effect of dictatorship. Its atmosphere is dark with evil and brooding fear. One might say that it reflects the mood of frightened disillusionment in which contemporary African intellectuals have watched the high democratic expectations of the nationalist period give way to crushing dictatorships in different parts of Africa. Chief Izongo, the villain of the novel, is a post-independence dictator in the village where the hero, Okolo (obviously the mouthpiece of the author), opens his messianic campaign. There is also the "faceless" dictator, Big One, who rules over the adjoining town.

That autocrats like those in Okara's story are able to entrench themselves after the departure of the colonial administration is not accidental in the opinion of some political commentators, who relate the process directly to the administrative machinery the new rulers have inherited from the previous ones. The broad political policies of the various colonial powers in Africa have been described by Thomas Hodgkin as "French Cartesianism," "British Empiricism," and "Belgian Platonism."[19] These policies show marked differences, yet all the colonial powers ran their colonies on the Weberian principle of "the monopolization of the means of domination and administration based on the creation of a centrally directed and permanent system of taxation, the creation of a centrally directed and permanent military force in the hands of a central, governmental authority, monopolization of legal enactments and the legitimate use of force by the central authority; and the organization of a rationally oriented officialdom, whose exercise of administrative functions is dependent upon the central authority."[20] In spite of the administrative expedient of mobilizing the existing traditional political framework and using the traditional chiefs and creating artificial ones where there were none before (the basis of the so-called empiricism of the British colonial policy in tropical Africa), the British colonial administration in West Africa, like all other imperial regimes, was an oligarchic dictatorship which, despite some benevolent aspects, imposed the will of the ruling group on the ruled and operated in the interest of the "mother country" and the ruling group. In effect, it was an executive directed bureaucratic dictatorship with, as Kofi Busia observes, no tradition of party government or official opposition.[21] The "wind of change" that swept it away from African countries in the late 1950s and the early 1960s also swept in the new men, the new African political elite, who inherited its political and administrative machinery. It is not surprising that the new order is dictatorial, since the inherited machinery had been fashioned under an essentially dictatorial regime.

We must distinguish, however, between the amenability of governmental machinery to authoritarian control and the actual installation of an authoritarian regime. Not all postcolonial regimes in Africa have become authoritarian. Indeed, there is a good reason why they need not be. The strongest argument in the nationalist attack on colonialism was its unrepresentative and authoritarian nature, an argument African nationalists used to prick the consciences of the colonialists themselves. However, a perverted and ambitious politician like Chief Izongo, who takes a gloomy view of human nature and is contemptuous of the common people, can easily impose authoritarian rule in his country and finds the postcolonial administration machinery a ready-made vehicle. This view has been proved, by the recent army coups d'état in Nigeria and Ghana, not to be altogether right. The military, like the civil service, was the instrument of government in the colonial days; but the army has since acted independently in each case and removed the politicians. The army, after all, contains intellectuals who, like writers and other intellectuals, are just as concerned as politicians about the state of society and political morality.

Okara portrays authoritarianism as corrupting and destructive of human dignity. All Chief Izongo's counselors, including the pompous Abadi, who has studied in England, America, and Germany and is very proud of "my M.A., Ph.D.," are stooges, and so is the white official who, as security chief in the service of the Big One, supervises the concentration camp where political opponents are interned. They speak the language of opportunism. They have pawned their consciences and annihilated their own individuality. There is no creative individuality in the domains of the autocrats, and the only person with an individuality and a moral conscience as well as a creative potential is marked out and destroyed. Yet it is not quite correct to say that Okolo is the only person with an individuality. The dictator of his village, like every dictator, is an extreme egoist; it is his belief in himself as superman that drives him to destroy the individuality of his subjects and makes the possibility of the emergence of any other individualist haunt him with a deep pathological fear.

Okara explores the cruelty of dictatorship with an almost uncanny doggedness. All the tricks and subterfuges used by a dictatorship to trap and break resistant victims are in full display here, often revealed with engaging subtlety and through powerful poetical images and symbols. Violence and bribery, threats and intimidation, imprisonment and psychological cruelty, surveillance, fear, and propaganda are all used to keep the people down. The violence is real, as Okolo finds out to his cost when he takes up the moral agitation that brings him into conflict with the dictatorial establishment. In the village of Amatu, Chief Izongo keeps the people in line by violence and intimidation alternating with gifts and bribes, a well-tried ploy. His treatment of Okolo is typical of his use of terror to crush opposition. As soon as Okolo's moral questioning, his quest for *It*, becomes an open criticism of the corrupt status quo, Izongo sees him as a threat to his power and moves against him. He attempts to isolate and destroy him. First, he uses propaganda to isolate Okolo by declaring him insane; when that fails he unleashes his terrorism. He has him arrested after a nightmarish chase in which he is manhandled by a mob. The passage describing this chase aptly recaptures the fantastic terrors that become the lot of a rebel against a dictatorship. When sheer physical terror fails to break Okolo's will, Izongo finds it convenient to banish him from the village on pain of death.

What Chief Izongo wants of his subjects is blind, unquestioning allegiance. He cannot tolerate dissent or criticism, and even when Okolo, as a compromise, offers to keep his personal views to himself without proselytizing openly, Izongo will have none of that; nothing will satisfy him until he has reduced Okolo to a doormat, like the rest of the people. So he says to Okolo: "Keeping your thoughts in your inside alone will not do. . . . Your hands will only be untied if you agree to be one of us."[22] He exacts blind conformity. He is not content to control the physical life of the people, he must also dominate their thoughts and feelings.

Izongo's use of "us" in the expression "if you agree to be one of us" is a deliberate misrepresentation of the realities of his society. The impression he is desperately trying to create, like every dictator, is that his personal views are those of the people. He projects himself as a popular leader who presides over a system beneficial to everyone and to which everyone should give support. The dissenter is therefore a misguided, antisocial enemy of the people. When he demands that Okolo become "one of us," he is invoking this hypothetical collective political mystique binding together the general aspirations of everyone in the community and asking, with a show of reasonableness, that this errant son of the community throw away his disruptive individualism and enter into the corporate destiny.

Izongo's chief stooge and apologist, Counselor Abadi, collaborates with him to sell this fiction of corporate aspiration, and to project the lie that Izongo is a democratic leader. Their speeches are filled with "democratic" claptrap. Izongo says, for example, that "on an important matter like this [that is, dealing with a dissenter] there should be no different voice. All the voices must be one as we have 'collective responsibility.' " (*V*, 42) He refers to the counselors who are mere puppets as "the representatives of the people." (*V*, 42) Abadi's acquaintanceship with "democratic" clichés is quite impressive. "We are in a democracy and everyone has the right to express any opinion. But we have to think what our leader has done for us." (*V*, 38) "What our leader has done for us," reminds the counselors of their dependence. Abadi spelt the matter out more fully earlier: "What could you have been without our leader?" he asked unabashed. "Some of the Elders shook their heads, others nodded in agreement and yet others tried to do both, resulting in a confusion of heads bobbing and swaying from side to side like the heads of puppets." (*V*, 37) Later, after Counselor Abadi has scolded them for showing "bare-faced ingratitude" to "our most honourable leader," "a leader and chief the like of which we've not seen or heard of in Amatu, nay, in the whole country," (*V*, 42) and after the chief himself has capped the rebuke with his own sharp threat ("Anyone who raises not his hand I know is not one of us"), (*V*, 42) the counselors are prepared to "toe the party line." When the question is put to them, "Hands flew up with the precision of drilling soldiers even before Chief Izongo went half way through his questioning words. Some raised both hands, and one who thought his hands went up before any other waved them so as to catch Chief Izongo's eyes." (*V*, 42)

This is not democracy but puppetry sustained by fear and intimidation, with the ultimate sanctions of violence and bribery in the background. The democratic front is a facade behind which the dictatorship mutilates individualities in the name of collective well-being. The people crawl around, enslaved by fear. They talk in whispers and visit one another at night because of the rigid system of surveillance. We find the messengers on their way to arrest Okolo suddenly oppressed by the fear that what they say to one another in conversation might be used against them by the dictator. One of the messengers suddenly "throws his eyes back and front, left and right and speaks with lowered voice" to the other companions: "Speak of this thing no more. The ears of Amatu are open. If this the ear of Izongo enters, we will fall from our jobs. You know this yourself." (*V*, 12) Fear is reality here, and so is the feeling of insecurity promoted by the wakeful vigilance of the dictator's spies who keep the population under constant surveillance.

Surveillance is even more efficient in Sologa of the faceless dictator, "Big One." The agents, characteristically named "listeners," stand at street corners, appear in public places, and filter into private accommodations with their ears trained in all directions and their eyes "looking at no one but looking at everyone like portraits hanging on a wall." (*V*, 94) Comical as these robotlike beings may appear at first, they are not amusing in action, as when one of them arrests Okolo and drags him to the chief security officer of the Big One. These people seem to read even the mirror thoughts of their victims. On the night of Okolo's arrival in the town, he no sooner sets foot on dry land than two security men detach themselves from the darkness (described as a "black black night like the back of a cooking pot") to announce to Okolo that they were sent to meet him and take him where he would find *It*. Subsequently, they drag him through the darkness and fling him into a dungeon containing human skeletons.

Things are grimmer in the domain of the Big One, but this is not immediately apparent because of the refinement of his methods. The psychological attack on dissenters is more sinister but more secretively operated. There are dungeons, like the one into which Okolo is thrown, but they are kept out of sight and receive their victims under cover of night. There is also a concentration camp to which "hardened" cases are sent on the charge that they are "mental" and the concentration camp is an asylum. Everything is smoothly and unobtrusively handled, as smooth as the spruce appearance and demeanor of the expatriate security chief who says, when Okolo asks him whether he believes in truth and honesty: "Look, my lad, these things simply don't exist in real life, if you want to get anywhere, if you want to make good. But mind you, I am not saying I do not believe in them. All I am saying is, you have to be judicious. No one will thank you, especially one who is in authority, for telling him by implication that you are, morally, a better person. You've got to be discreet. You just put on the act and 'Open, Sesame!' As simple as that." (*V* 101–2) The deep corruption is hidden under the smooth surfaces of friendly discretion and reasonableness. And yet the mutilation of man is further advanced in Sologa than in Amatu because of the technical superiority of the machine of oppression in the town.

Again, the personal differences between the two dictators probably give a distorted picture of life in the two places. Izongo is a crude dictator, almost a buffoon. He wields power with a heavy hand. His methods are blunt-edged when compared with those of the Big One. For instance, there is something theatrical about the way he treats his counselors, as when he stops in the middle of a loud guffaw to yell at them, "Laugh." He becomes truly sinister towards the end, after Okolo defies his orders and returns to Amatu. What stings him into action is that he notices that his authority is slipping, people are beginning to have second thoughts and the monolithic conformism he had labored so hard to erect is cracking before his eyes. Even his best supporter and "yes man," Counselor Abadi, begins to drag his feet and, rather belatedly, is trying to apply the brakes to a situation that is irreversibly plunging down the tragic precipice. When faced with the full challenge to his autocratic authority, the steel in Izongo comes out and the man of ruthless power and decisive action replaces the melodramatic villain and blusterer. He sweeps out at the head of his counselors (Abadi alone stays away) and takes personal control of the actual execution of Okolo and Tuere by tying them to the rudderless canoe in which they later drown in the whirlpool. The Big One, on the other hand, remains strictly anonymous. There is no physical trace of him anywhere, not even in posters and portraits in public places, no proud head graces coins, no official motorcade and police sirens mark his passage through the streets. There is no overt display of violence in his territory, no crowds stamping and panting after a victim, as in Amatu. And yet, one is aware that something has died in this nightmare city, something vital and purposeful, and that the inscrutable dictator is responsible for this death. He seems to sit at the wellspring of social life, pouring into it a poison that saps the moral vitality of anyone who drinks there. Whereas the inhabitants of Izongo's village are corroded by physical fear, those of the domain of the Big One are soaked in decadence and paralyzed by psychological fear.

The most outstanding feature of dictatorship is the abdication of personal responsibility. To buy personal safety, most people are content to follow unquestioningly the course marked out by the autocrats, and always at the cost of truth and justice they still hazily descry. Elder Tebeowei, who visits Okolo at night to try to divert him from his messianic course, appeals to him to abandon his quest and conform:

> "I see in my inside that your spoken words are true and straight. But you see it in your inside that we have no power to do anything. The spirit is powerful. So it is they who get the spirit that are powerful, and the people believe with their insides whatever they are told. Everything in this world has changed. The world is no longer straight. So if a person turns his palms down I also turn mine down. If he turns them up, opens them and shows them to the eye of the sky, I also turn mine up and show them to the eye of the sky. So turn this over in your inside and do as we do so that you will have a sweet inside like us." (*V* 46–47)

The same seductive conformism and submergence of individuality is urged on Okolo by the owner of the eating house in Sologa: "The people who have the sweetest insides are the think-nothing people and we here try to be like them. Like logs in the river we float and go wither the current commands and nothing enters our insides to turn the sweetness into bitterness. So, my man, here stay and be one of us." (*V*, 95) One of Izongo's messengers epitomizes this negation of individual personality and abdication of responsibility when he tell his companions: "If the world turns this way I take it; if it turns another way I take it. Any way the world turns I take it with my hands. I like sleep and my wife and my one son, so I do not think." (*V*, 12)

Okolo's crime is that he thinks and transforms his thinking into words, questioning words. Thinking and questioning distinguish him from the "think-nothing," pliable citizens and mark him out as a danger to the autocrats. Both the dictator of the village and that of the town object to Okolo's articulate individuality, especially his tendency to question the existing order and assumptions and to imply the existence of a purposeful way to creative living. Questioning is one way of answering oppression, because implicit in the question is a certain defiance, a refusal to acquiesce in what is. For, the moment people cease to think for themselves and ask questions, they cease to be worthy of freedom and are ready to be enslaved.

Okolo's real crime, in the estimation of his enemies, is only partly the substance of his moral campaign, which, when it has been unwrapped from the poetical suggestion in which it is contained, only amounts to a few moral abstractions. Their chief concern is the dangerous precedent of his openly expressing his dissent and his questioning of the social order established by the dictators. Characteristically, when Okolo asks Izongo why his hands have been tied, Izongo scolds him for "always asking questions." (*V*, 36) One of those who arrest him at Sologa also "advises" him not to ask questions: "Do not try to know the bottom of things." (*V*, 84) As the expatriate security chief says to him: "My instructions are that you are to be taken to the asylum. You are not wanted here. You have given too much trouble already to Sologa. You are to be confined here in a room until you are taken to the asylum." (*V*, 99) All Okolo has done since his arrival has been to ask a few people if they "have got it" and to want to see the Big One in order to ask him the same question, but that is enough to show him to be a dangerous revolutionary. Finally, Izongo drowns him as the only effective way of removing his influence "forever," of silencing his questioning voice once and for all.

A warning against dictatorship seems particularly pertinent in West Africa now that cultural confusion has left room for a cunning egoist to impose his will on entire peoples, either as a messianic retriever of the African heritage, or as a reformist Caesar (the warning is dramatically articulated in Wole Soyinka's *Kongi's Harvest*), or as a charismatic leader. We have seen that the traditional political system hedged by secular and religious sanctions was proof against the emergence of a dictator (with the probable exception of Chaka Zulu). The secularization of modern society, the decay of the spirit of traditionalism and social homogeneity, and, of course, the indeterminate nature of democratic institutions as they are being worked out, all make the emergence of dictators a distinct possibility.

William Conton's approach to politics and his general attitude differ considerably from those of Ekwensi and Okara. Conton in *The African* is registering responses to the West African cultural situation. One of the things he deals with is politics—nationalist politics and pan-African politics linked to the question of apartheid. The latter he discusses through his hero's encounter with the white South African girl Greta in the Lake District and through a series of conversations culminating in the statement that "racial hatred is wicked, whoever shows it and against whomsoever it is directed."[23] His mission to the Republic of South Africa to avenge the murder of this girl is melodramatic. What is of more interest to us here, however, is his attitude to national politics.

Unlike the other two writers, he is not interested in the workings of the democratic system in West Africa, but in the application of traditional African political values to modern politics. This aspect of his idealization of the African heritage is also noticeable in his attitude to the African family system, collective security, and so on. This attitude marks him out as conservative and backward-looking.

Conton's hero's entire venture into nationalist politics expresses the values

associated with traditional life. Thus, Kisimi Kamara, a British-educated graduate, gives up Christianity (regarded as a nontraditional religion) and joins
Islam (more identified with traditionalism) when he becomes a politician.
He also becomes a polygamist, not because he likes it, but because "in my
new role as politician, the whole of my success would depend on knowing
what gestures had to be made, and at what time." (*A*, 115) He invites his
boyhood friend Samuel, a southerner, to join him and organize his party
because (being himself from the north) they could together mobilize ethnic
solidarities against their more bourgeois opponents, who rely on their intellectual superiority and the patronage of the colonial administration. Kisimi
sweeps the hinterland chiefs and their people into his party, so the Creole
elite of the colony find their gentility and bourgeois arrogance of little avail
in the ensuing encounter. This is what actually happened in Sierra Leone
when the privileged Freetown elite found political dominance slipping from
their hands into those of the relatively less well-educated, and much despised
protectorate men.

The important aspect about Conton's treatment of the theme of politics
is his implied endorsement of the use of ethnic solidarity in national politics,
which African intellectuals tend increasingly to regard as the real obstacle to
progress and modernization of the continent to fit the realities of the mid-
twentieth century.

◆

Concern for political morality is constantly linked with economic morality. The drive for political power, especially within the context of socio-
economic underdevelopment, necessarily accompanies the quest for material
success and social prestige; acquisition of political power is often a means to
exercise control over economic policy and advance social status. West African
writers, therefore, cognizant of the means-end relationship between politics
and the economic aspirations of their characters, approach both political and
economic problems as aspects of the same broad spectrum of contemporary
life. A discussion of the theme of politics inevitably leads to a discussion of
the economy and the values which individuals bring to its operation.

Every character in the West African novel does something for a living.
In fact, it could be said that they divide their time between making money
and spending it. Some of them are civil servants, journalists, pharmacists,
artisans, houseboys, and housewives; others follow such questionable professions as prostitution and crime. Desire for money is an obsession. They need
to satisfy their drives and appetites and to buy modern consumer goods. To
most of them, possession of money and prestige goods is the height of
achievement. They equate the acquisition of money and possessions with
progress. The novelists, on the other hand, agree that possession of these
things does not in itself ensure happiness or a sense of fulfillment. They show
that the obsession with money and material things and making them the

object of life can only deprave the individual and destroy his sense of civic responsibility. Even though the writers do not usually say so, they are probably aware of the tremendous strain and anxiety individuals suffer in success-oriented industrialized societies and attempt to protect their own society from them by attacking the materialistic determination of progress. A Nigerian psychiatrist, Dr. S. O. Lambo, connected the growing incidence of mental sickness to increased industrialization. Again, materialism may and often does lead to self-seeking, greed, and corruption. Writers therefore roundly condemn it and use their tales to illustrate how their characters are ruined by their pursuit of it.

Even on a topic like this, where the writers reveal identical attitudes, their approaches to the theme differ considerably. In some of the novels, the theme is well integrated into the plot. In some, it is expressed through the author's direct intrusive remarks or asides. In others, the authors' ideas are put into the mouth of one of the characters. Again, the temperaments of the different writers emerge in the heat and indignation or the gentle subtlety of language they use in attacking the evils of materialism.

In William Conton's discursive novel, the evil of materialism is diagnosed, and its cause stated. When his hero-narrator, Kisimi Kamara, returns from his studies in Britain to Songhai, he complains that "during my absence, my country too had been swallowing pills—large and indigestible doses of materialism of Western Civilization." (*A*, 115) He sees the symptoms as "the lust for quick power, for quick riches; the unconcern as to what methods were employed in the process" (*A*, 115) and attributes the cause to "a deliberate policy of abandoning almost abruptly a way of life which our forebears had pursued contentedly for many centuries, and adopting that of a distant northern people." (*A*, 99–100) This is negritude writ large, the arrogation to old Africa of all the peasant virtues of primitive simplicity, deep spirituality (as opposed to the vulgar materialism of the "distant northern people") and saintly altruism. The attitude is obviously overly simple, although it is consistent with the author's intention to vindicate African culture vis-à-vis Western civilization.

But Conton is too honest to imagine that simplicity is all. After watching a crowd of happy villagers dancing, his hero observes: "I would look around for the sufferers from rickets or beri-beri or malnutrition, seldom absent from a company like that; and I would remind myself that, as the bodies of the few were wasted by disease, so the minds of the many around me were undeveloped, and cut off from access to a rich heritage of human thought and achievement. If they were happy, they were happy by default; it was the happiness of the ignorant, the smile of the baby in sleep." (*A*, 123–24) There is obviously an ambivalence here or even a contradiction, which characterizes the attitude of African intellectuals toward the simple traditional virtues of old Africa and the need for progress and modernization.

In Okara's *The Voice*, the theme of materialism is not treated independently of the main theme of political corruption and dictatorship. This conveys the general loss of cultural direction and sense of moral purpose once autocrats have dethroned democracy and enthroned their will. In the village, Chief Izongo uses gifts of money to smother the conscience of his subjects. In the town, everybody is bent on making money and living pleasurably. The police take bribes. There is one law for the rich, another for the poor. One of Okara's characters sums up the position: "Everybody's inside is now filled with money, cars and concrete houses and money is being scattered all around." (*A*, 48–49) The degree of moral decay in the corrupt society is symbolized by the epicurean club of the town of Sologa. The absolute abandonment of moral responsibility is reflected in the slogans painted on the walls of the club. One of them reads: "Even the whiteman's Jesus failed to make the world fine. So let the spoilt world spoil." (*A*, 93)

Achebe shows an admiration for some of the white man's things—his Bible, his literacy, his machinery, and material culture—but he is obviously dismayed by their destructive impact on the moral life of modern Africans. The main import of *No Longer at Ease* is that the hero's idealism about helping in the task of building his country with honesty and diligence is choked to death by the weedy reality of actual Nigerian life, the reality of mixed and confused values, of human greed and callous mutual exploitation. Obi's problem is complex. He is sent to England to get a university education by his "family" union, the Umuofia Progressive Union, based in Lagos. He returns to become secretary to the scholarship board. As a "senior service" man, he has to live in the style of the newly developing car-owning middle class; he has to maintain his family and pay school fees for a younger brother in the grammar school. He also has to refund, in installments, the money spent on his education in England. All this is too much to meet on a monthly salary of £60. He disastrously quarrels with the union, which could have lightened his financial burden by deferring his monthly payments until convenient, and is compelled to face all the obligations simultaneously. He falls into debt and, after resisting briefly the temptation to take bribes, which his job abundantly offers, succumbs and is arrested and disgraced.

Obviously, Obi's disaster is partly of his own making, but also partly the making of a materialistic society. Achebe demonstrates where the new materialism is driving people by showing how easily public men are corrupted. The female scholarship candidates who would pawn their virginity for an award show how far people will go to gratify their desire for success in the new society.

The most sustained criticism of modern materialism and economic individualism is to be found in Ekwensi's urban novels. For Ekwensi, the spirit of the new materialism is embodied in the obsessive drive for money. About Sango, the main character in *People of the City*, he writes: "His motto has become money, money, money. . . . We saw the treachery, intrigue and show of power involved."[24] Ekwensi sees everybody as tainted by the desire to grab as much money as he can. All his characters show this. He typifies it in the mammonism of extortionate landlords like Bejide and the sharp Syrian trader Zamil and the unscrupulous speculators Tade and Burkle, the timber dealers. In *Jagua Nana*, Ekwensi's rogues' gallery includes "criminals, senior service men, contractors, thieves, detectives, cheats, the rabble, the scum of the country's grasping hands," and he blames the "headlong rush to 'civilization' and all the falsehood it implied" on the state of moral decadence in the towns. (*JN*, 128)

In *People of the City* and *Jagua Nana*, Ekwensi does not look for the underlying cause of the obsessive materialism and undisciplined individualism of his characters. He is content, like some other novelists, to blame all the self-seeking and corruption on Western civilization. In *Beautiful Feathers*, he shows more insight into social problems. He sees the heart of the problem as the absence of a coordinated body of moral values that would provide guidance for individual action. His hero states the situation with rare clarity of moral perception in one of his few moments of self-awareness: "In the old days the African had a bond with the Ultimate Being. Then came 'civilization' that took away the older religion and substituted something new and unstable. Now that which the white man had substituted was gone. There was nothing . . . the New Black Man . . . was alone. Alone." (BF, 62) This is a cry from the heart, which recognizes that desirable though "civilization" may be, its price is very high.

Although the tone in which the novelists criticize the materialism of the present day tends to be moralistic, the problem is largely sociological. They make the right diagnosis when they attribute the cause of all this unhappiness and social corruption to the emergence of economic individualism that accompanied Western contact. Economic individualism is the social basis of modern technological civilization. West African countries are launched on a course of modernization and industrialization. None of the novelists has actually rejected in principle the modernization of Africa's material culture or the raising of the standard of living of the people in new African states. What they deplore is the depravation that the working of modern economic institutions has had on the African personality. The institutions are not necessarily evil, for there is much truth in Durkheim's observation that civilization is morally indifferent. The trouble is that old values are dying, or only surviving residually, and new and stable values are not replacing them fast enough. The result has been the existence of a moral vacuum, or a conflict of values that leaves most people morally confused, downright immoral, or blissfully amoral, in their everyday life and relationships.

Because the scope of their social analysis is restricted to small portions of the vast area of social experience, novelists tend to make their statements on the basis of a narrow social exploration. To equate materialism with corruption and criminal self-seeking is to distort the picture; to imply that there was no materialism in the traditional African societies until it was introduced through Western colonialism is even more inaccurate. As Achebe has shown, there is an element of the individualist in the character of Okonkwo, and the individualist in him asserts itself more clearly in the economic sphere. His standing in Umuofia derives largely from his economic success. He is an efficient farmer with a well-stocked barn, three wives (for whom he must have paid bride-price), and titles (which he could only have acquired by paying the recognized price in agricultural and other stock). These are the status symbols of Okonkwo's society. There were very few truly egalitarian traditional African societies. Even among the Tiv, one of the most egalitarian West African peoples, the social principle of equality could not prevent the emergence of individuals who, by initiative and drive, proved "more equal" than the rest.

But there are differences between the economic situation now and in the past. In precolonial African society, the material needs of individuals were few and satisfied by self-help or with the help of their families. The taboos against antisocial behavior, the clear definition and ritualization of the bonds of social relationship, and the existence of clear-cut rights and obligations in every relationship weakened the tendency towards criminal egocentricity and the ruthless and illegal exploitation of one man by another. The operation of the traditional spirit in economic matters, especially the use of wealth to achieve status and power within the traditional society, ensured its creative channelling. The acquisition of wealth, though an essential reality of traditional society, also served the interests of the community.

The change from a subsistence to a cash economy, the decline of familial control of the individual's conduct, the replacement of social unity and the sense of tradition with social heterogeneity and extreme individualism, especially in the towns, the introduction of new consumer goods such as, radios, refrigerators, bicycles—and cars in place of the limited personal requirements of traditional society—all these, which are the results of modern development, have increased the day-to-day material needs of individuals while weakening social control and the collective surveillance that in traditional society inhibited unbridled self-seeking and extreme individualism.

In the West, too, the development of economic individualism, closely associated with the division of labor and economic specialization, was also attended by a weakening of community life and familial control of the individual and led to the development of new relationships based on contract and social solidarity (in place of the old community solidarity). But enough time has passed to allow for the growth of civil and professional codes of behavior, time during which such codes of behavior have permeated the collective and social conscience of Western societies. They are taken for granted by Westerners. Every type of relationship, be it economic, social, or political, evokes some defined response that is generally recognized. In other words, a state of greater social equilibrium has been reached in Western societies, which embody the distinctive ethos of an industrial system. In essential aspects, they differ from the traditional societies of Africa, which embody the ethos of an agrarian system.

Each system has developed its own type of social behavior, attitudes, and values. The superimposition of the industrial system of the West on the agrarian system of Africa has created a situation of ethical flux in which behavior not normal in either context is possible. Durkheim describes this state of social disequilibrium and ethical flux: "The normal state cannot be determined in a state of disturbance—when the moral conscience of nations is not yet adapted to the changes which had been produced in the milieu, changes which partake of the past which holds it from behind and the necessities of the present, keep it from becoming fixed. Then there appear rules of conduct whose moral character is indecisive, because they are in the midst of acquiring or losing it without having definitely acquired or lost it."[25] This describes the situation of present-day West Africa.

So it becomes easier to understand much of the social conduct criticized by the novelists, especially the conduct attributed to the introduction of Western materialism. We can understand why Obiajulu Okonkwo or Patrick Ikenga, who are legitimately pursuing their careers and receive their normal salaries contractually arrived at, resort to the immoral practice of bribe-taking to satisfy their economic aspirations. We may understand why the satisfaction of economic necessity sometimes takes the debasing form of prostitution, pimping, violence, and crime. The case of prostitutes is particularly interesting. They are found in all the new urban centers of West Africa as well as in villages adjoining them. They are therefore a product of the large influx of people from the villages into towns. There are, in those new settlements, more men than women, most of whom are unmarried or have left their wives behind in their villages. Unattached women in such places would be tempted, especially if they have no education and skills, to minister to the men; and some, by so doing, secure much higher living standards than those who patronize them.

Behind all this is an absence of stable moral and social values so firmly fixed in the individual consciousness that the individual recoils from actions that are reprehended by the social conscience. These activities may even be legislated against, but if the ethical base of legislation is not firmly "rooted" in individual social morality, then the individual will not scruple to break the law if he can get away with it. Bribery and corruption are illegal, but the individual who looks on his work only as a means of acquiring material satisfaction and not as a contractual situation, will not hesitate, when the opportunity arises to make illegal extra money in the execution of his function. The absence of a developed sense of civil obligation, or its existence only in a rudimentary state, implies that there are no very strong incentives compelling any individual to respect the civil code of behavior. Antisocial tendencies reflect his lack of identification with the spirit in which modern industrial laws have evolved.

The development of industrial capitalism in the West, especially in Britain, has been associated by Max Weber, in *The Protestant Ethic and the Rise of Capitalism*, with the disciplining effect of Protestantism, especially its Calvinistic arm. The assimilation of work to religious virtue, the extolling of thrift and diligence, all that developed from the religious asceticism of Calvinism in England, became secularized, was extended to the capitalist economic enterprise, and helped to form individual attitudes to material possessions and enjoyment. When the Western capitalist system of free labor is introduced in places where the background of Calvinist asceticism is absent, as in West Africa, then an undisciplined and vulgarized attitude to wealth and material possessions results. Money is wanted solely for the gratification of pleasure and for the purchase of prestige-conferring goods.

The West African novelists attack the vulgarity displayed in the soulless scramble for lucre, the lack of discipline, and the megalomania shown by many West Africans in their pursuit of money and material wealth, their espousal of shortcuts to prosperity, their lack of thrift, and their improvident self-indulgence. There is obviously a streak of puritanism in this attack on materialism and the plutocracy of such social groups as politicians, landlords, traders, and the great mass of social parasites that infests the towns. It is not the puritanism of a Westernized bourgeoisie steeped in the social virtues and refinements of civilized Europe, but the puritanism of an African humanism based on personal sympathy, on the assumption that it is morally indefensible for a few people to accumulate wealth and dissipate it on soul-destroying pleasures while the great mass of the people live in squalor, poverty, and degradation. The criticism of individuals always implies a criticism of society.

This is why there is often in the West African urban novel an incongruous juxtaposition of the wildly rich and the miserably poor, of the self-indulgent voluptuaries and the criminal poor—a juxtaposition meant to touch the conscience of the reader and elicit horror and revulsion against the vulgar self-indulgence of the rich as well as against the cynicism, degradation, and recklessness of the poor. It is a puritanism rooted in respect for human dignity, which sees in sensuality as well as in stark indigence the two evils most destructive of this dignity. But though the criminal poor are criticized, it is the self-indulgent rich who are the real villains.

It is easy to see that the novelists are using African traditional values to judge the economic life of their characters, for, while they acknowledge economic individualism as the basis of the modern economy, they are liable to quarrel with the use of wealth purely for the satisfaction of individual lusts. The novelists are themselves a product of economic individualism, the division of labor and specialization. They are all hard-working people whose personal initiative and industry have brought them to the higher levels of the socio-economic pyramid. They belong to the "affluent" and coveted "senior service" class. In their criticisms what they are really inveighing against is greed and avarice, which drives many people to employ illegal means to amass wealth, and the hedonism and plutocracy that characterize their attitude to wealth—the craze for flashy women, for "pleasure" cars, "posh" mansions, and lavish cocktail parties.

The politicians embody the worst aspects of hedonism and plutocracy because they have the money and the power and influence to make money, and they are regarded as pace-setters by most people in society. Even Achebe, the most gentle of the novelists, emphasizes the vulgar materialism of the politicians in his description of the Honorable Sam Okoli, Minister of State and his uncritical adulation of the white man's material culture. Feeling self-satisfied about possessing a giant radiogram, he exclaims to his guests on one occasion: "White man done go far. We just de shout for nothing."[26] It is this type of worship of material possessions that the novelists so mercilessly satirize.

The attack on materialism is one of the oldest lines of West African intellectual protest. It goes back to the nineteenth century. Not only is the tone of the criticism similar, the language is also very close. This is an extract from an address by Edward W. Blyden to the Common Council and Citizens of Monrovia in 1857:

> We have been in too much haste to be rich. Relinquishing the pursuit of those attributes that would fit us for the faithful discharge of our peculiar duties as men, as Liberians, as an infant nation, we have used every possible measure to enhance our pecuniary importance; and in our precipitate efforts at wealth, we have not been careful as to what means we have employed. The desire to be rich, or to appear rich, pervades all classes. . . . Another cause of our adversity may be seen in the unjustifiable extravagance in which we indulge; in that luxury of expenditure for houses, for dress, for furniture, for food, constantly made the subject of reprehensive remark by thinking foreigners. We are in a fearful error with regard to our country, if we suppose that we are truly prosperous. Our prosperity is not real; it is false; it is fictitious. The prosperity of a nation is real when the springs of that prosperity are contained within itself, in the hands of its citizens; when it depends on its existence upon its own resources; when it is independent. But this is not the case in Liberia; we are, as a nation, upheld by foreigners. We are entirely dependent upon foreigners for schools, for churches, for preachers, for teachers.[27]

If Blyden and his contemporaries were to return to West Africa today, they would recognize many of the failings they preached against more than a century ago, some of them immensely reinforced by costly expanding opportunities. They would also recognize the West African writers as those who have inherited their moral and cultural leadership, who have become the keepers of the conscience of society and of posterity.

West African novelists see in the decay of traditional values the main cause of the corruption and unhappiness of the modern period. Ekwensi uses the breakdown of the domestic relationship as an index of social disruption arising from the weakening of the collectively shared moral vision, a by-product of the individualism of the towns. "Lagos," he writes in his disenchantment, "was rapidly becoming Nigeria's divorce centre. It was the mark of its outward sophistication that nowhere did a happy marriage really exist. . . . That was independence!" (*BF*, 41)

Undoubtedly, present-day problems of marriage have their roots in social and cultural change. The traditionally determined code of marital relationship, for instance, the sexual division of labor, which left a woman economically dependent on the husband, is being replaced, in the towns at any rate, by the modern economic system that opens economic opportunities to women as well as to men and increases the economic and social independence of the women, an independence that implies greater freedom of action than hitherto. Implicit in this independence are the breakup of the old marital code and greater sexual laxity, which lead to more divorces.[28] Again, the weakening of familial control over people in towns and the economic independence of young people have also destroyed the matchmaking rights of families and their corresponding power to intervene as a stabilizing influence on marriage.

The marriage of Wilson to Yaniya is a two-person contract based on romantic attraction. Its near-complete disaster is Ekwensi's disapproving comment on the new social order as it operates in the sphere of marriage. Ekwensi is not alone in this opinion about "modern-style" marriage. There is truth in Austin Shelton's assertion that Obiajulu Okonkwo in Achebe's *No Longer at Ease* and Peter Obiesie in Nzekwu's *Wand of Noble Wood* (one may add Patrick Ikenga in Nzekwu's *Blade Among the Boys*) all come to grief when they flout the voice of family and tradition in their marriages. Domestic instability and the failure of romantic attachment to sustain the serious vocation of marriage are ways the novelists choose to contrast (implicitly no doubt) the traditional against present-day values, to the obvious disadvantage of the latter.

On the other hand, there is unequivocal condemnation of the opportunities of exploitation of sentiments derived from traditional concepts of social relationship. Ekwensi sees in the shameful monetary exploitation of Wilson by his unscrupulous brother-in-law, Brother Jacob, mere parasitism and a travesty of the reciprocal rights and obligations of the traditional marriage relationship. Much of the suffering of individuals is due to the survival of familial obligations they are no longer able to meet under the new economic conditions. The need to care for his ailing mother and see his brother through grammar school increases Obi Okonkwo's financial burden, just as "the insatiable demands of the lineage" impoverish Patrick Ikenga; in the end both accept bribes as a way out of their difficulties. Moreover, we sense a sly exploitation and insidious vampirism in the way some stay-at-homes insist on a share of the wealth of kinsmen who have worked hard and got on in the towns. (French Africans refer to these ruthless exploiters in the name of tradition as human parasites, *les parasites humaines*, and many a novelist has made them a target of attack.)[29] The philosophy of "what belongs to one belongs to one's kindred"[30] rings a little hollow when it is realized that what belongs to one may have been garnered in town through self-discipline and self-deprivation, while the kindred at home enjoyed the idyllic pleasures and relative self-sufficiency of the village.

Cultural change is the greatest single reality of modern Africa; no novelist can fail to take account of it in his writing. It is part of his duty as a creative artist to provide an insight into society; and as he has to deal with a society in transition, his peculiar insight may even influence the direction of change. If West African novelists attack the extreme self-centeredness and self-seeking of modern West Africans, it is not that they are advocating a return to the traditional life of Okonkwo's Umuofia. This is clearly impossible in the socially heterogeneous nation-states of West Africa. What they are saying is that the solid traditional values that formed the basis of traditional life and are universal among traditional Africans—human sympathy, respect for life and human dignity, and for legality—should form the cornerstones of the value-system of modern Africa. There is nothing incompatible between this value-system and technological progress. By implication, the novelists emphasize that the only valid foundation for modern Africa is to build on such universal African values and not on travesties of European values. In the attitudes of the writers generally, yearning for a better society from which greed and selfishness will be absent, where men will be free to express themselves, and where all will move toward an ideal state in which African tradition and modernity will be in harmonious fusion.[31]

NOTES

1. See W. Arthur Lewis, *Politics in West Africa* (London, 1965), 12–17 and Thomas Hodgkin, *Nationalism in Colonial Africa* (London, 1956), especially chapter 5.

2. Irving Howe, *Politics and the Novel* (London, 1961), 20.

3. See Margery Perham's study on Lugard and indirect rule in Nigeria in *Native Administration in Nigeria* (London, 1937).

4. See Peter C. Lloyd, "The Political Structure of African Kingdoms: An Exploratory Model," *Political Systems and the Distribution of Power* (London, 1968), 61.

5. See J. H. Beattie, "Checks on the Abuse of Political Power in Some African States: A Preliminary Framework for Analysis," *Sociologus* 9 (1959): 98–113.

6. *The Technique of the Novel* (New York, 1964), 143.

7. H. Coombes, *Literature and Criticism* (Harmondsworth, 1963), 90.

8. Lewis, *Politics in West Africa*, 63.

9. Edward Shils, "On the Comparative Study of the New States," in *Old Societies and New States*, ed. Clifford Geertz (London, 1963), 22.

10. Ibid.

11. Ibid.

12. Somerset Maugham, *The Art of Fiction: An Introduction to Ten Novels and Their Authors* (New York, 1977).

13. See Reinhard Bendix, *Max Weber: An Intellectual Portrait* (London, 1960).

14. Shepherd B. Clough, *Basic Values of Western Civilization* (New York, 1960), 36.

15. Cyprian Ekwensi, *Jagua Nana* (London, 1961), 161. Subsequent references to this work are cited as *JN* in the text.

16. *Environment and Policies in West Africa* (London, 1963), 92.

17. See Meyer Fortes and E. E. Evans-Pritchard, eds., *African Political Systems* (London, 1940), 5–23.

18. Cyprian Ekwensi, *Beautiful Feathers* (London, 1971), 128. Subsequent references are cited as *BF* in the text.

19. *Nationalism in Colonial Africa*, 29–59.

20. Bendix, *Max Weber*, 380.

21. *The Challenge of Africa* (New York, 1962), 66.

22. Gabriel Okara, *The Voice* (London, 1964), 43. Subsequent references to this work are cited as *V* in the text.

23. William Canton, *The African* (London, 1960), 64. Subsequent references are cited as *A* in the text.

24. Cyprian Ekwensi, *People of the City* (London, 1963), 140.

25. Emile Durkheim, *The Division of Labor in Society*, tr. G. Simpson (New York, 1933), 434.

26. Chinua Achebe, *No Longer at Ease* (London, 1960), 68.

27. See Henry S. Wilson, ed., *Origins of West African Nationalism* (London, 1969), 79.

28. See D. McCall, "Trade and the Role of Wife in a Modern African Town," in *Social Change in Modern Africa*, ed. Aiden Southall (London, 1961), 287–99.

29. See Michael Crowther, *Pagans and Politicians* (London, 1959), 65–66.

30. Nkem Nwankwo, *Danda* (London, 1964), 8.

31. Edward Shils, *The Intellectual Between Tradition and Modernity: The Indian Situation* (The Hague, 1961), 108.

CHAPTER 6

Post-Independence Disillusionment

From THE 1940s, when the nationalist movement got under way in Africa, people were made to believe that political independence would usher in the millennium, solve all social problems, and create a fuller life for everyone. So much was promised and so little was to be realized—or indeed was realizable, given the deficient vision and the immensity of the difficulties— that disillusionment was bound to set in. From the late 1950s, formal independence was conceded by some of the imperialist powers. In the wake of the euphoria that came with independence, better prospects were held out to the masses, and more promises were made. Post-independence economic plans were based on broad egalitarian precepts, which were often an extension of the nationalist rhetoric of the independence struggle. They included commitment to equal opportunities and greater equality in the standard of living and development of opportunities in education, health, and employment.

These promises fired the imaginations of the different sections of the African population, especially the urban-dwellers who stood directly to gain from the transfer of power to the local people. But when it came to "keeping faith" with the people and fulfilling the promises, it became clear that a gulf separated fulfillment from hope. Within a few years of independence, the hopes had collapsed and disillusionment had set in. Political independence was not a panacea. A new black power elite stepped into the place vacated by the former imperialists. The lot of the common people did not improve as fast as they were led to expect; in some cases, the burden of life became heavier on the poor. The peasantry was becoming pauperized because agricultural lands were dying from exhaustion; a rapidly increasing population was working the arable lands to death; and without new methods of husbandry there was no hope of soil revival. Young semiliterates were deserting the dying villages and drifting into the towns to swell the thousands of unemployed people in the slums and shanty-towns. The new political class proved unequal to the challenge of nation-building and incapable of providing moral and civic leadership. The political machinery set up at independence broke down and there were instabilities attended by coups and counter-coups, with extensive violence. Between 1960 and 1968 alone, there were twenty-five unconstitutional changes of government in Africa, of which eighteen were military coups and others were military-inspired.[1]

The result of all this has been the alienation of the intellectuals, especially

121

writers and artists, from politicians and the bureaucratic class that run the post-independence political and administrative machinery. Faced with the new realities of power and politics in Africa, writers have had to reappraise their role in society. The preoccupation with the past had to give way to concern with the pressing problems of the present.

This reversal of direction has been accompanied by feelings of guilt and self-reproach. Some writers now think their interest in the past was diversionary and a waste of resources that could have been more fruitfully expended on the present. It is even being said that preoccupation with the past provided a cover for post-independence elites to carry on irresponsibly and corruptly.

This view is strongly held by Wole Soyinka and formed the core of his paper presented at the African-Scandinavian Writers Conference in Stockholm in 1967 on the theme of "The Writer in Modern Africa." Here is part of the essay:

> In the movement towards chaos in Africa, the writer did not anticipate. The understanding language of the outside world, "birth pains," that near-fatal euphemism for death throes, absolved him from responsibility. He was content to turn his eyes backwards in time and prospect in archaic fields for forgotten gems which would dazzle and distract the present. But never inwards, never truly into the present, never into the obvious symptoms of the niggling, warning, predictable present, from which alone lay the salvation of ideas.[2]

Soyinka spoke elsewhere in the same paper of "the lack of vital relevance between the literary concerns of writers and the pattern of reality that has overwhelmed even the writers themselves in the majority of modern African states,"[3] and later he accused them of an inability to respond with vision to the disturbing and disastrous events taking place before them:

> The stage at which we find ourselves is a stage of disillusionment, and it is this which prompts an honest examination of what has been the failure of the African writer, as a writer. And this is not to say that, if the African writer had truly responded to the political moment of his society, he would not still be faced with disillusionment. For the situation in Africa is the same as in the rest of the world; it is not one of the tragedies which come out of isolated human failures, but the very collapse of humanity. Nevertheless the African writer has done nothing to vindicate his existence, nothing to indicate that he is even aware that this awful collapse has taken place. For he has been generally without vision.[4]

"The very collapse of humanity" is a grandiose phrase. It sounds more imposing than practically relevant. But the general accusation of lack of vision is well grounded if it implies that the writer should arm himself with a skepticism that would make him, in the midst of popular enthusiasm, a sobering influence, a spokesman for more durable values. Soyinka had defined the task of the writer in the modern African setting more perceptively at the UNESCO Conference on "Colonialism and the Artist's Milieu" in Dar-es-

Salaam. He said then that "the writer is the visionary of his people, he recognizes past and present not for the purpose of enshrinement but for the local creative glimpses and statement of the ideal future. He anticipates; he warns. It is not always enough for the writer to be involved in the direct political struggle of today, he often cannot help but envisage and seek to protect the future which is the declared aim of the contemporary struggle."[5]

Given the gravity of events in Africa since independence, the collapse of optimism is understandable, as well as the feeling of guilt and self-reproach among writers that more was not done to warn and admonish. But one must allow for the historical and personal pressures operating on writers and influencing them to articulate current aspirations. Their perception of the problems of their societies during the struggle for political independence was dominated by nationalist assertiveness. At a time when the nationalist movement called on the corporate energies of the colonized people, the writer had to throw in his lot with the people; he had, as Soyinka expressed it, to submit "his integrity to the monolithic stresses of the time."[6] As a creative member of his community, his function was to use his art to advance the "cause," and this took the form of a cultural nationalism by which he tried to help his people regain their lost dignity by recreating and interpreting for them their cultural heritage.

The breakdown of this solidarity has been vitalizing to African creative writing. It has, for instance, infused in writers a certain radicalism as well as a sharpening of their social instincts. This is evident in the three novels that form the basis of this chapter: Soyinka's *The Interpreters* (1965), Achebe's *A Man of the People* (1966), and Ayi Kwei Armah's *The Beautyful Ones Are Not Yet Born* (1968).

The most outstanding feature of these novels is the uncompromising way their authors attack the post-independence elite of Africa. Its members are accused of expropriating from the masses the fruits of independence, and, more specifically, of being venal, corrupt, irresponsible, hypocritical, and without vision and common sense. The failure of independence is regarded as evidence of the failure of the elite to justify themselves to the masses and validate their claim to leadership. The novelists see the post-independence leaders as betraying the pledges they made in the nationalist days to create just, egalitarian, and contented new states out of the colonial societies. The writers attack the elite most sharply for creating a standard of living for themselves out of proportion to the national level of economic production, and in fact scandalously higher than that of the rest of society. Most of the social criticism can be traced to this major accusation, that the elite have used their privileged political and administrative position to appropriate the meager national resources to the near-exclusion of everyone else. David B. Abernathy has tried to find an explanation for this situation: "The government had committed itself to bring about greater equality, yet it was the government officials themselves who were far above the masses in education, income, social status and political power; hence the officials would be the first to suffer losses from any levelling reforms they might institute. This conflict of interest proved difficult, if not impossible, to resolve."[7]

Although the three novels would appear to be different, Armah, Soyinka, and Achebe adopt comparable approaches in their novels. Each sees his subject from behind the mask of a persona or personae. Armah's main persona is the Man, but the Naked Man also conveys some of his other views, the extreme pessimistic ones, which may not synchronize with the consistent image of the Man. Soyinka operates behind his young "interpreters," artists and intellectuals—Sagoe, Sekoni, Kola, Bandele, and Egbo; while Achebe uses Odili as a mouthpiece. The use of personae allows the writers to explore the questions in all their complexity and to pronounce on them with detachment. The persona is a much more "mobile" personality than the one-dimensional, first-person narrator. Because the persona can represent the author as well as have an independent existence, it is easier for his viewpoint to shift at different stages of the narrative. Moreover, and this is one of the advantages of this narrative approach, the author can, when he so desires, dissociate himself entirely from his persona. He can look critically at the persona while the persona himself is looking critically at a specific personal or social evidence. The result is a multiplicity of attitudes that provide a more complex account than the simple, uncomplicated authorial-narration. Psychological truth is advanced and the social picture is given more dimensions. The novelists can employ satirical techniques by contrasting viewpoints in this way. Invective, expression of moral outrage, or indignation are given "distance," and can be played off against each other: when they come directly from the writer they tend to seem simple in their directness. The process itself, of seeing things through other eyes, has a sobering effect.

Soyinka's "interpreters" are very diverse. They are active physically and intellectually and they explore their subjects through action and experience; they are fully participant and comment on social life through their actions as well as by their words. Achebe's Odili is a radical idealist who, like the "interpreters," clarifies issues through his action and comment, while Armah's the Man is a contemplative idealist who thinks much and acts little. He keeps the even tenor of his surface life while inwardly, imaginatively, and intellectually, he is immensely alive, almost catlike, in his grasp of the nuances of corruption and decay.

The first target of the novels is the tendency for the post-independence elite to "eat up" the meager national resources of the new states. They are portrayed as having used their position of dominance, not to husband national resources, not to step up production and disburse it equitably, but to develop "great appetites" and devour this wealth almost exclusively. For the members of the elite, the new state is a large and dainty cake to be shared and eaten. The novels borrow these images of "eating" and "sharing" from the politicians who talk of the "sharing of the national cake." The crises in the political and social life of the new states are reducible to the struggles by the elite to decide who should have what portion of the "national cake." The masses are often left out of the calculation; although when the crises heat up for the elite, they often mobilize the support of the masses and sometimes use them as a shield or reduce them to "cannon fodder."

Achebe's *A Man of the People*, which deals mainly with the power struggle among the elite, is thematically structured round images of "eating" and "sharing." The politics of Chief Nanga and Chief Koko is "eating" politics. Everywhere in the novel, in the parliament, among the people, during political campaigns, the theme is the same: national politics is a frantic struggle for a share of the "national cake." If the nation is not being "eaten," it is being fought over. "Eating-and-sharing" has become an all-pervasive symbol for the absence of health and constructiveness in the body politic; it yields an appropriate metaphor for exploring the corruption and the framework of the avarice and hedonism of the political class.

In the thick of the conflict between the intellectuals in the parliament and the corrupt philistines, the latter accused the former of being "snobbish intellectuals . . . [who] sell their mothers for a mess of pottage."[8] When Nanga appeals to Odili to leave his schoolmastering in the hinterland and come down to the capital city and join a government department as a civil servant, his reason is expressed in the language of "national cake" politics: "Our people," says Nanga, "must press for their fair share of the national cake." (*MP*, 13) Odili cannot avoid the eating image. He cannot see why "some people's belly is like the earth. It is never so full that it will not take another corpse." (*MP*, 97) Even the names of the two old parties typify the eating tendencies among the politicians. One of them is the People's Organization Party (POP) and the other the Progressive Alliance Party (PAP); the one reminds us of popcorn, and the other of a popular gruel eaten for breakfast in West African cities. One of the most sustained metaphors of eating is to be found in the section of the novel that deals with the launching of Odili's party, the Common People's Convention, formed by young radicals to wrest power from the corrupt older parties. In one short passage alone, there are six references to eating, (*MP*, 139–40) but the crowning image of "eating" politics is in the memorable valediction spoken by Odili about the fall of the politicians and the general state of affairs they have created:

> For I do honestly believe that in the fat-dripping, gummy, eat-and-let-eat
> regime just ended—a regime which inspired the common saying that a man
> could only be sure of what he had put away safely in his gut or, in language
> ever more suited to the times: "you chop, me self I chop, palaver finish", a
> regime in which you saw a fellow cursed in the morning for stealing a blind
> man's stock and later in the evening saw him again mounting the altar of the
> new shrine in the presence of all the people to whisper into the ear of the chief
> celebrant—in such a regime, I say, you died a good death if your life had in-
> spired someone to come forward and shoot your murderer in the chest—with-
> out asking to be paid. (*MP*, 167)

In *A Man of the People*, the politicians are the most inveterate "eaters," but the habit has permeated the rest of the population. For example, Nanga's father-in-law is an avaricious "eater" for whom a prospective son-in-law is an object of exploitation. He explains that the time before one's daughter's marriage is the time to enjoy an in-law, not when he has claimed his wife and gone away. "Our people say: if you fail to take away a strong man's sword when he is on the ground, will you do it when he gets up . . . ? No, my daughter. Leave me and my in-law. He will bring and bring and bring and I will eat until I am tired. And thanks to the Man above he does not lack what to bring." (*MP*, 103) The philosophy of "eating while you may" spreads like a dangerous fungus across the face of national life, destroying and disfiguring it and even threatening to kill the host altogether. Temporary reprieve only came with a military takeover.

"Eating" and "sharing" images also feature prominently in *The Beautyful Ones Are Not Yet Born* and *The Interpreters*. The hectic scramble for national resources goes on in these two novels too. The politicians, as well as lesser citizens are staunch believers in taking what one can out of the general coffers. *The Beautyful Ones Are Not Yet Born* opens with a bus conductor trying to steal money from passengers' fares. Confronted with an apparently open-eyed watcher (who turns out to be a sleeping passenger), he retorts, "You see, we can share."[9] It is all sharing and eating. When the Man attempts to dissociate himself from the shoddy boat deal between Koomson and his mother-in-law, his wife remonstrates with him: "Why are you trying to cut yourself apart from what goes for all of us? . . . you will be eating it with us when it is ripe." (*BNYB*, 50) Armah sees the fatal social disease in his country as this "eating" propensity. Nothing sums it up better than the crude, semi-literate daubing on the wall of a latrine: "SOCIALISM—CHOP MAKE I CHOP CONTREY BROKE." (*BNYB*, 124) In *The Interpreters*, Soyinka's eyes see the many ways in which the elite invent occasions to indulge their appetites. One of his "interpreters" seizes on the funeral of Sir Derinola to comment wryly on the interminable orgies and parties of the elite: "The hearse . . . was smothered in wreaths and the mourners carried the extras on their arms. 'Thank God,' said Sagoe, 'for our orgiastic funerals.' If he ever freelanced he knew where to go on lean days. Wedding also, yes, and child-naming, and engagements, cocktail parties, but a funeral with its night-long waking, its outing, its forty days turning over of the body, its memorial service only a few weeks later, its second turning over of the body, its sudden irrational remembrance feasts—a man could spend his entire life just feeding on a dead man. And many did."[10] The elite go to great lengths to invent excuses for celebrations and indulge their love of ostentation.

Soyinka and Armah, however, do not stop at describing the eating propensities of the elite; they dwell on the physical corruption that comes with overeating. The elite, glutted with the spoils of the society and given to hedonistic overindulgence, are made to pay a high price in physical and physiological decay and corruption. Soyinka and Armah have given a new dimension to West African fiction by creating in it what may be aptly called the literature of disgust. For example, the partyman Koomson's moral and political corruption becomes a terrible physical reality when, on the day of the military coup, he is trapped and cowed in a darkened room. As his confidence deserts him, and his fear of being seized by the new regime paralyzes him, he begins to disintegrate and decay physically:

> His mouth had the stench of rotten menstrual blood. The Man held his breath until the new smell had gone down in the mixture with the liquid atmosphere of the Party's man's farts filling the room. At the same time Koomson's insides gave a growl longer than usual, an inner fart of personal, corrupt thunder which in its fullness sounded as if it had rolled down all the way from the eating throat thundering through the belly and the guts, to end in further silent pollution of the air already thick with flatulent fear. (*BNYB*, 191–92)

Already the decadence that comes from overindulgence had been indignantly observed by the Man when he shook hands with the corrupt partyman:

> Koomson . . . looked obviously larger than the chair he was occupying. The Man, when he shook hands, was amazed at the flabby softness of the hand. Ideological hands, the hands of revolutionaries leading their people into bold sacrifices, should these hands not have become even tougher than they were when their owner was hauling loads along the wharf? And yet these were the socialists of Africa, fat, perfumed, soft with the ancestral softness of chiefs who have sold their people and are celestially happy with the fruits of the trade. (*BNYB*, 153–54)

Soyinka's Managing Director in *The Interpreters* is part of the same picture of corrupted and decaying human mass created from years of intemperate eating up of the country's limited resources: "The carcass of the Managing Director swelled, spurted greasy globules of the skin in extreme stages of putrefaction and burst in an unintelligible stream through the ruptured throat." (*I*, 79) Both novels are full of images of throat and belly and of filth and decay arising from intemperate eating. References to bodily secretions, excretions, and defecation abound in these novels too, with words like mucus, shit, sweat, urine, lavatory, smears, phlegm, grime, and saliva. Indeed, one of Soyinka's "interpreters" invents a "lavatorial" philosophy he calls "voidancy." According to him, "Next to death . . . shit is the most vernacular atmosphere of our beloved country." (*I*, 108) Blunt speaking, calling things by their proper names, is these writers' device for dealing with the wholesale corruption that has overwhelmed their societies. The tradition goes deep both in written literature and in the oral cultures of West Africa. It traces its line in Western literature back to the classical satirists through the medieval scatological preachers, Chaucer, Swift, to the British "kitchen-sink" dramatists of our own time. Plain speaking is also an element of traditional language, especially in satirical songs and personal altercations. Achebe's rural novels contain very impressive examples of robust rustic bluntness, especially in moments of heated exchanges, as when the priest of Idemili sends an insulting message to Ezeulu and when the police officer sent to arrest Ezeulu encounters the active challenge of Ezeulu's son. As for satirical bluntness, anyone reading *Igbo Traditional Verse* by Romanus Egudu and Donatus Nwoga, *Orin Ibeji* (Songs in praise of twins) by Val Olayemi, *Song of Lawino* by Okot p'Bitek, and other African works in the vernaculars, cannot but be impressed by the absence of bourgeois squeamishness. Chaucer's earthiness is, in this respect, the nearest thing to rustic bluntness in Africa.

The African writers' verbal bluntness derives from oral and literary traditions, or, to put it differently, African writers out to attack social abuses find ready to hand in the African oral tradition a method they can pick up, polish, and elaborate through the literary medium to produce a powerful neo-African literary mode. And this is what many of them do. In *The Beautyful Ones Are Not Yet Born*, *The Interpreters*, and, to some extent, *A Man of the People*, this bluntness powerfully focuses attention on the social vices being attacked. It is therefore a very effective method of satire.

Scatology has other uses in these works. It is adopted by the writers in order to prick the vast bubble of false respectability blown up by the African elite. Dirt and filth become dialectical instruments for attacking false gentility, philistinism masquerading as civilization, and hedonism and voluptuousness disguised as good living. The elite have set up a front, which obscures their own pretentiousness, hollowness, and lack of vision, as well as the abject poverty and the indescribable squalor of the lives of the common people and the peasantry. Scatology is a way of answering the elite's claim to have brought progress to the masses and justified the fight for national independence. The writers attempt, through scatological language, to show that the elite have succeeded in inflicting on the masses more disabling disasters than the departed imperialists, that they have strengthened and refined old methods of oppression, forged new chains to bind the masses, and infused their souls with spiritual disease more damaging than the physical manacles of imperialism. In the midst of so much dirt, filth, squalor, want, and disease, the elite attempt desperately to carve out a snug little pocket of cleanliness, health, self-sufficiency, and prosperity for their members; but the filth and squalor find them out, and everything is drowned in what Armah calls "victorious filth." (*BNYB*, 15)

The novelists' most developed satirical instrument is contrast. Each of them contrasts the state of magnificence in which the elite live and the desperate poverty of the rest of the people. In these three novels, the contrast is, in addition, between the spick-and-span plushness of the elite's world and the squalid, filthy world of the poor. Very often, these worlds exist in uneasy juxtaposition. Soyinka makes the office of the *Independent Viewpoint* an illustration of these contrasts. Sagoe's visit to the two toilets—one for the junior staff and the other for the senior staff—is an epitome of the contrasting worlds of the elite and the common people. In the one, "[The] cistern was caked and unflushed, and its walls matched the radio station's in suspicious smears," (*I*, 76) while in the other, after Sagoe has pushed in the Engaged bolt, "Immediately, a light wraith of scented breeze fanned him about the neck and filled the luxurious furnishing of the ante-room. It was an automatic purifier device imported by the Managing Director on his seventh Economic Mission to Sweden." (*I*, 82) The board-room bears testimony to the spirit in which the nation is run, almost exclusively in the interests of the elite. (*I*, 75) The filth that covers the rest of the society now and again spills over and spoils this comfort, as when a night-cart carrying human waste and a trailer collide in the middle of the highway and render the road unusable to everyone. The moral is explicit. Self-seeking and concupiscence render the elite insensitive to the plight of the rest of the society, but this insensitivity and neglect of the common people generate their own dynamic which, in the end, engulfs everyone in a national catastrophe.

Images of filth, squalor, and decay are also used to describe the literal physical reality. The persistent hacking at the fact of physical ugliness and filth is of a piece with the novelists' indictment of the society as a whole and the elite who lead it in particular. The inference is often obvious: you cannot produce good men out of squalor and physical dirt. The evocation of dirt and decay is thus a double-edged metaphor. On the one side, it symbolizes the spiritual filth and decay that result from moral corruption; on the other, it symbolizes the general social blindness and ineptitude that prevent the proper organization, development, and progress of the society. The inability to maintain physical cleanliness through a proper disposal of refuse indicates the failure of the elite to operate the modern state efficiently.

A very good example is the attempt by the Kumasi City Council to maintain urban cleanliness. A campaign has been mounted with some success and "big shots" have been pressed into radio appeals, but what follows is an anti-climax. Only a few boxes are supplied "though there was a lot said about the large amount of money paid for them." (*BNYB*, 8–9) In other words, someone has used the opportunity for personal gain and sabotaged a worthwhile public project. Next, the few boxes supplied are not emptied periodically as they ought to be. The small boxes are soon filled and people continue to throw their waste, not inside but around them. "People still used them, and they overflowed with banana peels and mango seeds and thoroughly sucked-out oranges and the chaff of sugarcane and most of all the thick wrapping from a hundred balls of *kenkey*. People did not have to go up to the boxes any more. From a distance they aimed their rubbish at the growing heap, and a good amount of juicy offal hit the face and sides of the box before finding a final resting place upon the heap. As yet the box was still visible above it all, though the writing upon it could no longer be read." (*BNYB*, 8–9) The writing that could no longer be read: "K.C.C. RECEPTACLE FOR DISPOSAL OF WASTE" was printed in blue, and "KEEP YOUR COUNTRY CLEAN BY KEEPING YOUR CITY CLEAN," was emblazoned in lucent red. At the time of the campaign, "the letters had [had] . . . their brief brightness," but now they have irrecoverably faded away. Corruption and official irresponsibility combine to destroy a praiseworthy social project. The failure is an acid comment on the way the post-independence elite are attempting to run the independent states. The effect on the masses is equally profound, for the elite infect the common people with their failings.

It is not hard to see why corruption should have assumed such grave proportions in the post-independence period. Educated West Africans felt frustrated during the colonial period because the colonial regime offered them restricted opportunities to enter lucrative public service or engage in commercial or industrial competition against the ruling interests. For them, therefore, the struggle was essentially to oust the colonial ruling class in order to replace it with an indigenous ruling class drawn from the educated middle class. Independence was seen first and foremost as a transfer of economic control and patronage from a foreign power elite to an indigenous one. The creation of mass parties gave the superficial impression of a populist-based political philosophy and organization; in reality, the dominant ideological orientation remained elitist. If one needs any evidence for this, it is clearly available in the fact that the new independence regimes carried over the colonial structure of administration, privileges, and perquisites with as little modification as possible.

The results are far-reaching. The educated middle class, which has inherited the privileges of the colonists, is promoting inequality in the new states; its living standards are inflated relative to those of the workers and peasants; this generates resentment among the less privileged and this, in turn, gives rise to instability. A number of corollaries follow: the elite's high standard of living has a damaging effect on national life by destroying the morale of the masses, and it puts the elite themselves on the defensive, in that they are constantly having to defend their privileges against the pressure of the underprivileged, especially as social alignments are beginning to be defined in terms of "the haves" and "the have-nots." This exacerbates existing conflicts and contradictions. Again, because the middle classes have accepted the principle of unequal distribution of wealth implicit in the colonial structure, they have tended to take up also the capitalist ideology that supports inequality; their members are instinctively averse to egalitarian social systems. The dilemma of the elite is easy to see. The urge toward the development of a capitalist class is strong, yet the absence of an indigenous source of capital is a constant worry. The meagerness of resources means that it is not easy to take substantial slices away from public resources without being noticed. The absence of a strong indigenous bourgeois class with a capitalist tradition and capital of its own is also a major factor, since anyone aspiring to capitalist accumulation will sooner or later run up against the general anticapitalist tendencies of the population. Given this contradictory situation, the elite's behavior is understandably inconsistent. Sometimes, in their attempts to gain the best of all possible worlds, they preach socialism and practice capitalist tenets, and sometimes they evade any ideological or intellectual position at all, hoping that the situation will resolve itself.

The writers recognize both the dilemma and the ways adopted by the elite to get round it. But they do not approve. Ayi Kwei Armah, for example, indicts the Ghanaian elite for preaching socialism and living capitalism. The Nigerian Soyinka and Achebe, in whose country the ruling elite have not taken up a public position one way or another, attack the unbridled acquisitiveness of the elite that has brought the new state to grief. Behind these criticisms is the writers' conviction that only a socialist organization of the new states will put them on a proper road to progress. They are therefore uncompromising in their attack on privilege and the tendency toward property accumulation by those in leadership of the new states.

The writers satirize the corrupt methods used by many people to amass wealth. It is a doleful tale of embezzlement of public funds, appropriation of public resources, diversion of public facilities to private use, and the use of bribery and corruption for personal enrichment. A corrupt society is full of thieves, big and small, professional and amateur. In the three novels, embezzlement of public resources by the post-independence rulers of the African states is the central focus of the writers' attack; the biggest public officials, according to them, are the biggest thieves.

In *The Beautyful Ones Are Not Yet Born*, Armah's the Man, watching with dismay the audacity with which public officials appropriate public resources for their personal ends, declares that "stealing is a national game" and dismisses the change of government resulting from the February 1966 military coup in Ghana as just "a change of embezzlers," no more. (*BNYB*, 191)

Leading the line of embezzlers is the corrupt politician. His Excellency Joseph Koomson, Minister Plenipotentiary, Member of the Presidential Commission, Hero of Socialist Labor. With a cluster of titles that would do honor to a Gilbertian comic emperor, Koomson is a master of the art of corruption, who exploits his public office to enrich himself and destroy the promise of independence and trample down socialism. The most glaring example of Koomson's dishonesty is when, in spite of his ministerial appointment, he borrows state credit under aliases to invest in fishing boats:

> I had asked Oyo's mother who would pay for the boats, and with a great deal of pride she said the Minister would. Which minister? Koomson, of course. Only she called him brother Joe. Brother! Aach, so. I said I didn't know Koomson had enough money to buy even one boat. Those things cost thousands and thousands of cedis. My mother-in-law asked me very patiently whether I did not know also that Brother Joe had influence. She called it infruence. I had taken a piece of paper to calculate Koomson's total salary since he joined the Party. Now I dropped the paper and said, "Oh, I see." And again with this patience of hers my mother-in-law asked me what I had seen at last. So I got angry enough to tell her I had seen corruption, public theft.
> (*BNYB*, 67)

Koomson, of course, soon proves the old lady right; he is a staunch believer in the omnipotence of power, in the everlasting possibilities of "influence." His motto is: "Everything is possible, it depends on the person," (*BNYB*, 175) that is, on who you are and where you stand in the structure of influence and power. Compare the statement in *A Man of the People* that "A common saying in the country after Independence was that it didn't matter *what* you knew but *who* you knew." (*BNYB*, 19) Finding money for the boats is no insurmountable obstacle. In fact, he says boastfully, "The money is not the difficult thing. After all, the Commercial Bank is ours, and we can do anything." (*BNYB*, 160) The Commercial Bank, formed originally to liberalize credit for the people, has become the property of the politicians and a means of serving their greed. Koomson gets the State Furniture Corporation to furnish his house free because, as his shallow wife reminds us, "Joe is like this with the Manager." (*BNYB*, 174) Koomson uses his "influence" to make a scholarship available for his empty-headed sister-in-law to study dressmaking in England and is even expected to make hard-to-come-by foreign exchange available to her to buy a Jaguar car because "she says she has fallen in love with a Jaguar, and she's going to kill herself if she can't have it." (*BNYB*, 175) Koomson cannot quite reconcile himself to the view that cabinet ministers should not involve themselves in business. This he regards as a "nuisance" and one of the effects of "this foolish socialism that will spoil everybody's peace," (*BNYB*, 159) as if ministers in capitalist states are not bound by the same rule. Of course, he gets round the problem by finding "somebody to . . . er, lend us the name" and cooperate with him in "a kind of partnership." (*BNYB*, 161)

In the midst of all the corruption, self-seeking, and public embezzlement going on in *The Beautyful Ones Are Not Yet Born*, the ghost of socialism, like the ghost of Banquo at Macbeth's banquet, glides in and out of the consciences of the elite, disturbing their inner peace, jolting their serenity, and ruffling their moral assurance. Even the insensitivity of Koomson is threatened by the formal, socialist expectations that represent a certain constraint on evil-doers. Koomson finds these expectations inconvenient: "Now take this boat business, for instance," he cries at one stage, "there is a lot of money to be made in it, but start something, and fools will start shouting slogans at you." And elsewhere, "They say we are socialist ministers, so we shouldn't do these things." (*BNYB*, 160) Armah's disillusionment is not with socialism as such but with the travesty of it, the negation of its promises, and, more specifically, with political leaders and bureaucratic bourgeois who pretend to be socialists while their actions belie their pretenses. Armah's disappointment is with the elite who have betrayed independence and infused the masses with cynicism:

> "How long will Africa be cursed with its leaders?" he asked. There were men dying from loss of hope, and others were finding gaudy ways to enjoy power they did not have. We were ready here for big and beautiful things, but what we had was our own black men hugging new paunches scrambling to ask the

white man to welcome them unto our backs. These men who were to lead us out of our despair, they came like men already grown fat and cynical with the eating of centuries of power they had never struggled for, old before they had even been born into power, and ready only for the grave. (*BNYB*, 94)

Perhaps Armah shows naïveté by putting so much trust in the heady nationalistic rhetoric and the orchestrated shouts of "Freedom!" But he is right to deplore the opportunistic part the elites have played in the post-independence disaster. Like the school dropout and ex-docker Koomson, these people passed through the ideological school without letting the ideology pass through them:

Everybody says with the wave of the hand, "Oh, you know, the ideological thing. Winneba?" True. That is where the shit of the country is going nowadays, believing nothing, but saying they believe everything that needs to be believed, so long as the big jobs and the big money follow. Men who know nothing about politics have grown hot with ideology, thinking of the money that will come. The civil servant who hates socialism is there, singing hosanna. The poet is there, serving power and waiting to fill his coming paunch with crumbs. He will no doubt jump to go and fit his tongue into new arses when new men spring up to shit on us. Everybody who wants speed goes there, and the only thing demanded of them is that they be good at fawning. (*BNYB*, 175)

Armah tells us that there is something wrong with a regime that is so easily exploitable through opportunism. The dissembling game succeeds so well because an adequate structural framework, self-correcting and principle-oriented, has yet to be evolved. Huge ideological gaps exist through which the antisocialist groups twist, turn, and manoeuvre until they are ready to smash up the machinery. Armah's bitterness is hardly concealed in his scathing criticism of the political and bureaucratic class in Ghana. No one escapes his indignation, from the president to the lowest fawning and scraping little man. But it is obvious that he pities the common people who are the victims.

Soyinka's satire against corruption has no overt indignation, but it is barbed with wit and irony. His main targets include public thieves, hypocrites, apostates, snobs, cunning leaders, and overcredulous followers. Like Armah, he shows up the public men who use their position and political patronage to enrich themselves and further their interests. His strategy is developed around the board of the *Independent Viewpoint* which is taken as the nation in miniature. The board members are selected according to obvious criteria, chief of which is compensation for political loyalty. They are referred to as "Compensation Members," and Sagoe tries to match them with each "compensation" aspect: "Lost election, missed nominations, thug recruitment, financial backing, Ministerial in-lawfulness, Ministerial porcing, general arse-licking, Ministerial concubinage. . . ." (*I*, 77) But this general berating of public men is less effective than the satirization of specific individuals. The unnamed Managing Director, for example, represents official pomposity and irresponsibility. He floats round the world on interminable economic missions, accumulating rubbish instead of promoting the progress of the press over which he presides. His ineffectuality is symbolized by the crude and useless radiogram that takes up so much space in the boardroom:

> Like two halves of a broad bean, the pachydermous radiogram and the Managing Director. And his attempt to disown his twin brother proved futile, in spite of the delicate china set from which they all, except Chief Winsala, sipped tea. The Director had picked up the set in the tenth economic mission to American China; he donated it to the Board remarking, "You know, Shanghai Chek has exactly this kind of cup and saucer." (*I*, 78)

As bad, if not worse, are the chairman of the board, Sir Derinola, a retired judge permanently identified by his *abatiaja* cloth-cap, and Chief Winsala, a gross, spirit-swilling buffoon. Soyinka makes a deft scene of the attempt by Chief Winsala to extract a bribe from Sagoe at the Hotel Excelsior, while Sir Derinola hides in his car outside waiting for his own share of the "kola." Chief Winsala tried, through a mixture of half-veiled threats and bonhomie, to get Sagoe to pay him fifty pounds for the job for which he has been interviewed by a board. Winsala's first, and quite unexpected, problem is establishing his identity, to a Sagoe deliberately and mischievously pretending not to know him. But Winsala rides the difficulty by assumed heartiness: "Let me refresh your memory. You were our interviewee the day before yesterday morning. . . . I am a member of the Board to which you came to answer our advertisement. . . . By the way, I take schnapps." (*I*, 83) Winsala goes on to make a number of weighty observations including: "Degree is two for penny. . . No more degree passport." . . . "The job is there, but you have to secure it." . . ."When the Sanitary Inspector looks under the bed he's looking for kola, not tanwiji [mosquito larva]." (*I*, 84–85) Of course, he gets no bribe and goes through a mortifying experience at the hands of the bartenders when he cannot pay for his drinks. Sagoe, meanwhile, has slipped away under pretense of going to find the bribe. Sagoe in the end saves him by paying for the drinks, but his discovery of the meanness and corruption of the chief and the black knight who is reputed to be a pillar of integrity proves an embarrassment to him. "He [Sagoe] was the guilty one who had trespassed on secrets that should never be exposed." (*I*, 86) He has seen these great men in their moral nakedness and the impression is so strong that, later, in a state of feverish reverie, he actually imagines Sir Derinola emerging naked and maudlin out of Dehinwa's cupboard.

More sinister than the corruption itself are the hypocrisy and cynicism that refuse to recognize its reality and continue to whitewash it. So Sir Derin goes to his grave in a blaze of glory, with the orator lavishing much flatulent, rhetorical panegyric on him at the graveside, crowned with such lofty sentiments as "his life [is] our inspiration, his idealism our hopes, the survival of his spirit in our midst the hope for a future Nigeria, for moral irredentism and national rejuvenescence. . . ." (*I*, 113) The last bit sounds like a malediction of Nigeria. Corruption has eaten so far into the fabric of society that the power of moral discrimination seems even to have died. How can it be otherwise when the organs of mass communication are under the control of corrupt officialdom? Nwabuzor, the hypercynical editor of the *Independent Viewpoint*, brings the matter home to Sagoe after his article exposing official scandal has been censored by the hierarchy of his newspaper: "Shut your mouth, I shut mine." (*I*, 95) The morally sensitive organs of public decency have been blunted by official corruption helped by middle-class cupidity and opportunism. Nwabuzor's "but look, man, journalism here is just a business like any other. You do what your employer tells you," (*I*, 95) may sound like a piece of realistic common sense, but not in a situation of appalling immorality and social disintegration. If the press cannot be a force for moral guidance and for exposing immorality, and if the journalist cannot do more than please his employer, the situation is hopeless.

The novelists criticize the elite for complacently creating a life-style for themselves different from the rest of the people. They are shown scrambling to take over the roles, posts, and privileges of the former white colonial administrators and to absorb the white man's manners and habits. These "black-white" men (also referred to by Armah as "golf-course" blacks) are the pet abomination of the novelists because their uncritical imitation of the white man is symptomatic of the loss of the idealism which, in popular imagination at any rate, animated the struggle for independence. They are easy targets for these catlike satirists, who keep their eyes skinned for the absurd and the incongruous in contemporary life. But the "black oyibos" (Soyinka's term for them) are attacked for more substantial reasons. Ridiculous they are, but the novelists also see them as dangerous. Their hankering after European bourgeois elegance is regarded as a deep-seated craving by the class to remove itself from the rest of the people and perpetuate its status as a permanent ruling class, showing its European bourgeois symbols as aspects of its equipment for leadership. The purpose of these symbols is to mystify the masses, to overawe them, and to compel them to look up to the black bourgeoisie. More important, the situation is regarded by the writers as a reflection of the overall lack of sensitivity, which asserts itself most strongly in the elite's inability to understand or identify with the yearnings of the masses, to evolve original and constructive ideas for the building of the new states, and to give direction and meaning to independence. The more the elite cut themselves off from the rank and file, the less they are able to provide adequate leadership. The most serious criticism of the black bourgeoisie is that they absorb the externals of the bourgeois culture while missing its inner qualities: they absorb bourgeois "form" without bourgeois "content," as someone aptly put it. Western bourgeois culture evolved organically out of the historical development of Western society. In Africa, the bourgeois class is largely an adventitious growth. Its impact is therefore largely gestural and diversionary because it diverts effort away from the development and strengthening of a mass culture that would be more organically based in the African people and society.

That the bitterest attacker of the "black imitators" is Ayi Kwei Armah is not surprising because coastal Ghana (as well as coastal Sierra Leone, Libera, and Gambia) has for a long time had a highly Westernized black bourgeoisie who take their cultural model and attitudes from Europeans. The coming of independence would not immediately change these people. Indeed, independence makes available to this class the means of expressing its new status through easier espousal of Western status-symbols. Here, for example, Armah captures a group of "golf-course" blacks in one of their ridiculous postures:

> Five white men and three women came down the road. Hidden in the group, in stiff white uniform, were two Ghanaian men in prosperous-looking bellies. Four little boys struggled behind them all, carrying their bags and sticks. As they went past, one of the black men laughed in a forced Senior Service way and, smiling into the face of one of the white men, kept saying, "Jolly good shot, Jimmy. Jolly good." He was trying to speak like a white man, and the sound that came out of his mouth reminded the listener of a constipated man, straining in his first minute on top of the lavatory seat. The white man grimaced and made a reply in steward boy English: "Ha, too good eh?" The black men both laughed out loud, and the one who had spoken put both hands to his paunch. (*BNYB*, 146–47)

Other symbols remind us that nothing has changed with independence. There are the usual prams pushed by little black baby-minders. The difference is that the babies are not white but "black as coal." The black bourgeoisie have found homes in the former all-white suburban reservation, but even here the desire to be "white" is unmistakable. The evidence is provided by "names of black men with white souls and names trying mightily to be white." "In the forest of white men's names, there were the signs that said almost aloud: here lives a black imitator. Hills-Hayford . . . Plange Bannerman . . . Attoh-White . . . Kuntu-Blankson. Others that must have been keeping the white neighbors laughing even harder in their homes. Acromond . . . what Ghanaian name could that have been in the beginning, before its Civil Servant owner rushed to civilize it, giving it something like the sound of a master name? Grantson . . . more and more incredible they were getting. There was someone calling himself Fentengson in this wide world, and also a man called Binful." (*BNYB*, 146–47)

Soyinka also satirizes the "black oyibo" for aspiring to the manners and cultural habits of white men. But they invariably emerge as caricatures. Professor Oguazor is a regular comic butt, with his affected manner and English gentleman's accent. He is almost grotesque in his odious preoccupation with "Merals," especially in his fiery denunciation of "meral terpitude" in the university after a young student has become pregnant. "The college cannot afford to have its name dragged down by the meral terpitude of irresponsible young men. The younger generation is too merally corrupt," (*I*, 250) he pontificates. The morally conscious professor has not himself been a model of discretion all his life; indeed, he had had a daughter by his housemaid and had her "tucked away in private school in Islington." (*I*, 149) Faseyi, another of the phony "black-white" academics, is a snob and social-climber, obsessed with etiquette and ridiculously insistent on formality of dress, including "white gloves for the lady." The lady is his English wife, luckily, a sensible woman who has no time for such silliness.

More crippling to the black bourgeoisie are the demands which bourgeois life makes on its adherents. To keep up appearances costs money, and in desperately underdeveloped states the cost cannot easily be met without committing some kind of injustice to someone or some group of people in the society. The economic equation must be such that those who maintain bourgeois standards do so at the expense of those whose fortunes must be depressed. Since this class has no independent wealth of its own, it can only sustain its high standard of living by taking more from the common pool than is justly due to it, and this gives rise to an endemic state of crises and instabilities in the new states. Because most of the available resources are government-controlled, the distribution of these resources is vested in politicians or those who have replaced them as government, and that explains why most members of the elite in the new states are attracted to politics and why the political struggle is so murderous, why anyone in power never wants to let go of the reins. The line that separates a man from great wealth and power and great poverty and obscurity can be very thin indeed, and can be crossed amazingly easily by the loss of an election. A politician is tempted to cling to power at all costs. Also, the temptation to "make it" while you can is overwhelming. The prospect of a sudden reversal must be one of the nightmares haunting public men in Africa.

A vicious cycle exists here. Everyone is eager to receive his "fair share" of the national cake. Those in power are aware that in order to have more than others they must continue as the sharers, that is, they must retain political control. But they are also aware that there are many outside sharpening their knives and eager to get in and cut their own slice. So, while he is at it, the politician tries to cut as much as he can for the rainy day. Those outside become more and more frantic as those within batten on the national cake. They may try to stop them through constitutional means, but this may not always be possible when those in power neutralize this machinery or those outside are too impatient to go through its processes. The situation generates instability: plots and counterplots, coups and countercoups, most of which may not bring fundamental change except to replace one set of the "eating bourgeoisie" with another set. There is considerable bitterness and some truth in the words of one of Armah's characters after the first Ghanaian coup that it was only a matter of "new people, new style, old dance" and that soon "another group of bellies will be bursting with the country's riches." (*BNYB*, 185) Achebe's Odili sums the matter up admirably in *A Man of the People*:

> The first thing critics tell you about our ministers' official residences is that each has seven bedrooms and seven bathrooms, one for every day of the week. All I can say is that on that first night there was no room in my mind for criticism. I was simply hypnotized by the luxury of the great suite assigned to me. When I lay down in the double bed that seemed to ride on a cushion of air, and switched on that reading lamp and saw all the beautiful furniture anew from the lying down position and looked beyond the door to the gleaming bathroom and the towels as large as a *lappa* I had to confess that if I were at that moment made a minister I would be most anxious to remain one for ever. . . . We ignore man's basic nature if we say, as some critics do, that because a man like Nanga had risen overnight from poverty and insignificance to his present opulence he could be persuaded without much trouble to give it up again and return to his original state.
>
> A man who just came in from the rain and dried his body and put on dry clothes is more reluctant to go out again than another who has been indoors all the time. The trouble with our new nation—as I saw it then lying on that bed—was that none of us had been indoors long enough to be able to say 'To hell with it.' We had all been in the rain together until yesterday. Then a handful of us—the smart and the lucky and hardly ever the best—had scrambled for the one shelter our former rulers left and had taken it over and barricaded themselves in. (*MP*, 41–42)

When they create a different world for themselves, the elite lose sight of the problems of ordinary people. How could the Koomsons, the Nangas, and the Oguazors really understand the crushing poverty of the masses? Esconced in ministerial mansions and suburban villas or in the artificial coziness of a professional mansion in the sedate little world of the academics, how could these people really understand the plight of Armah's the Man and the Naked Man, and the other unfortunate people trapped in the permanent maze of poverty and insecurity, those "living dead" about whom Armah writes so harrowingly and sadly:

> the increasing numbers who had decided they were so deep in despair that there was nothing worse to fear in life. These were the men who had finally, and so early, so surprisingly early, seen enough of something in their own lives and in the lives around them to convince them of the final futility of efforts to break the mean monthly cycle of debt and borrowing, borrowing and debt. . . . But perhaps the living dead could take some solace in the half-thought that there were so many others dead in life with them. So many, so frighteningly many, that maybe in the end even the efforts one made not to join them resulted only in another, more frustrating kind of living death. (*BNYB*, 25)

One bourgeois tendency the writers criticize is the desire of the black elite to perpetuate themselves by giving their children superior educational opportunities. There are quality schools, the so-called Corona and Santa

Maria schools for the children of the black bourgeoisie who can pay the high fees demanded, and bad and indifferent schools for the children of the poor. Armah sees the practice as an indication of an inferiority complex and another symptom of the desire of the elite to become like the white man. Koomson's daughter, absurdly named "Princess," is a product of such a school, and so are Nanga's children, though Nanga sensibly insists on taking the children to the village so that they will not lose the traditional culture altogether and, more importantly, so that the village influence will cancel out the more objectionable gloss of the elite school. Mrs. Nanga does not want her children to "become English people." (*MP*, 43) Children trained in these special schools have advantages. According to Barbara B. Lloyd, "Children of the educated elite are taller, heavier, healthier, and begin schooling earlier and with more skills than the products of illiterate or traditional Yoruba homes. These are the most obvious results of superior housing, diet, medical care— in fact, of privilege." [11]

The novelists also accuse the elite, especially the political elite, of being anti-intellectual. Toward the end of the passage in *A Man of the People* in which Achebe attempts to diagnose the main cause of the political malaise in Africa, he speaks of the post-independence politician's tendency, after barricading himself in the ministerial mansion, to persuade everyone else through loudspeakers that "all argument should cease and the whole people (should) speak with one voice and that any more dissent and argument outside the door of the shelter would subvert and bring down the whole house." (*MP*, 42) There is one segment of the population that by training and historical orientation is not content to stop all argument and speak "with one voice," a group which, by tradition, is more likely to speak in a babel of tongues than "with one voice." This is the intellectual class. Even if it were only for speaking with a different voice from that of the post-independence politicians, this class would have rendered itself abhorrent to the politicians. But there are more substantial reasons why intellectuals are not beloved by the politicians, especially when things are not going as well as they should. The intellectual class in Africa is rooted in a world culture and feels most poignantly the possibilities and promises of a new society; it is also acutely aware of lost opportunities and the dimming of visions. Moreover, the intellectual class has developed a way of looking at the world that includes constant striving toward the ideal and the elevated. The spiritual dimension is antithetical to the materialistic obsession of the politicians. Intellectuals are bound, in their quest for the ideal, to come into conflict with politicians whose actions are governed largely by expediency. Laurens Van Der Post sums up the intellectual position of the African writers as the projectors of ideal values in this way:

In view of the ominous breakdown in the religious machinery in Africa, writers, both in Africa and of Africa, have a tremendous responsibility laid upon them. Art to me is the technique of presenting unrealized and hidden values to people potentially capable of appreciating and understanding those values. It is a means by which men can penetrate places in their minds and souls they had never reached before. Writing especially can be a kind of magic mirror which holds up to man and society the neglected and unrealized aspects of himself and his age.[12]

Because writers and other intellectuals represent a force hostile to the aspirations of the peddlers of corrupt conformism, they are often attacked by corrupt regimes. Achebe speaks in *A Man of the People* of "the . . . general anti-intellectual feeling in the country." (*MP*, 29) As corruption swamped the post-independence states, and intellectuals of all types became increasingly strident in their criticisms, the political class became more and more bitterly opposed to intellectualism. All over West Africa, there developed a distinctive opposition to intellectuals by politicians and, to a lesser extent, the bureaucratic and commercial elite. Political parties used a few intellectuals, of course, but these were mere hostages of the political machine and constantly at war with the party bureaucracy, which more often than not was manifestly anti-intellectual.

In the novels, anti-intellectualism, philistinism, and corruption go together. The characters most thoroughly corrupt tend also to be the most anti-intellectual. Chief Nanga, who is supposed to be a minister of culture, does not even know the few writers of his country. At a Writers' Society book exhibition he is to open as the minister in charge of cultural affairs, he is more concerned with the proprieties of dress and address than with culture and literature. He shamelessly acknowledges that he has never heard of his country's most famous novel, yet he is anxious to announce his impending honorary doctorate from an American university for his services to culture. Not surprisingly, when Odili surveys the cultural minister's library, all that it contains are a decorative set of an American encyclopedia, cheap pulp romances, *She*, and *The Return of She* by Rider Haggard, a few books by Marie Corelli and Bertha Clay, and the all-purpose *Speeches: How to Make Them*. (*MP*, 45)

Anti-intellectualism takes different forms in the novels, from Koomson's caviling at the intellectuals, through Nanga's vulgar jokes at the expense of good education, to deliberate obstruction of competently qualified professionals. In *A Man of the People*, anti-intellectualism assumes frighteningly dangerous proportions during the political crisis at the beginning of the novel. The minister of finance, "a first-rate economist with a Ph.D. in Public Finance," has advised cutting the price of coffee in answer to a prevailing slump in the coffee market. The prime minister, who is facing an election, will not hear of this; instead, he causes the National Bank to print fifteen million pounds more money. Then he dismisses the minister of finance and two-thirds of the cabinet that support him. He next mounts his anti-intellectual campaign because the "Miscreant Gang" (the name invented for the dismissed

men) "were all university people and highly educated professional men."
(*MP*, 4) The ground is prepared for Nanga and people like him who shout
their way to prominence on the high tide of demagogic anti-intellectualism.
The editor of the party newspaper sets the tone of the campaign:

> "Let us now and for all time extract from our body-politic as a dentist extracts
> a stinking tooth all those decadent stooges versed in text-book economics and
> aping the white man's mannerisms and way of speaking. We are proud to be
> Africans. Our true leaders are not those intoxicated with their Oxford,
> Cambridge or Harvard degrees but those who speak the language of the peo-
> ple. Away with the damnable and expensive university education which only
> alienates an African from his rich and ancient culture and puts him above his
> people. . . ." (*MP*, 4)

Although the attack is couched in pseudonationalistic terms, the intention is
to silence the voice of enlightened dissent and of sanity. The prime minister
caps this incitement with a "solemn" declaration in parliament: "From today
we must watch and guard our hard-won freedom jealously. Never again must
we entrust our destiny and the destiny of Africa to the hybrid class of Western-
educated and snobbish intellectuals who will not hesitate to sell their mothers
for a mess of pottage. . . ." (*MP*, 6) In other words, the intellectuals have
become traitors because they would rather the country experienced economic
austerity than senseless inflation. Nanga later speaks disparagingly of African
specialists who will not allow him to build a road to his constituency for his
buses because the technical problems need first to be studied. He denounces
this as "dillying and dallying" and abuses the specialist, referring to him as
"one small boy . . . we all helped to promote last year." (*MP*, 48) He expresses
his preference for a white "expert" who is likely to prove more obliging and
less obstructive.

In *The Interpreters*, the corrupt disparage university education, but the
most striking feature is the deliberate frustration of intellectuals. Sekoni, the
engineer, comes home from overseas studies well qualified, enthusiastic, and
patriotic, only to find official prejudice standing in the way of his using his
knowledge usefully. He is initially reduced to signing bicycle vouchers, ap-
proving leave applications and duty rosters, and interviewing third-class clerks.
When Sekoni protests that his professional knowledge is being wasted, he is
stigmatized as "one of the keen ones" and sent to work on the "Ijoha Project"
for producing cheap electrical power. Now in his proper element, Sekoni
builds an experimental power station. The chairman suborns an expatriate
"expert" and has the project discredited:

> To Ijoha Sekoni went, "where you may work with your hands until your back
> blisters" and Sekoni built a small experimental power station. And the Chair-
> man chuckled and said, "I knew he was our man. Get me the expat. expert."
> Hot from his last lucrative "evaluation," came the expatriate expert. Expatriate,
> therefore impartial.

"Constitute yourself into a one-man commission of enquiry and probe the construction of our power station at Ijoha which was built without estimates approved expenditure."

"Is it unsafe for operation?" and he winked, a truly expert expat. expert's wink.

"That's the safe idea. You put it in technical language." And the expatriate expert came to Ijoha, saw and condemned. And the Chairman read the report and said, "that expert never fails one," salivating on the epithets, a wasteful expenditure, highly dangerous conditions, unsuitable materials, unsafe for operation. (*I*, 27–28)

"Bring me the Write-off file," chortled the chairman. (*I*, 27–28) Sekoni is broken and hounded into a mental hospital while the expatriate expert collects his reward of ten thousand pounds, eight for "injuries sustained in the course of duty" and two as "lump sum compensation for the termination of his contract." (*I*, 94) As in *A Man of the People*, the expatriate becomes a collaborator of the corrupt African leadership to frustrate the course of African progress.

In *The Beautyful Ones Are Not Yet Born*, anti-intellectualism takes the form of active resistance to the theoreticians of socialist ideology. A school of political orientation set up by the political party to wean the political and bureaucratic elite from their old ways fails because of the built-in resistance of the elite. The change requires intellectual commitment to a body of ideas that would constitute the framework of political action. But the elite refuse to make this commitment because such a commitment calls for drastic changes in attitudes to property, status, and civic responsibility. There is a wide gap between crypto-capitalism and socialism; the elite refuse to make the leap and reduce the whole program to a joke. The bourgeois intellectual, the bureaucratic elite, and the philistine politician make common cause to defeat the social experiment. Armah recaptures this brand of anti-intellectualism in the cleavage between the party theoreticians and the political and bureaucratic elite whom they set out to convert. The scene in which an "ideological" professor attempts without success to convert an audience to socialism is described hilariously. The story is aptly put in the mouth of Koomson, the corrupt partyman:

Some people think being a Minister is all good-time. Heh, heh, sometimes I wish I had been a business-man instead. One day they brought a man to give the Ministers and the Parliamentarians and the Party activists a lecture. That was during the Winneba days.

The man had many degrees, and he was very boring. In the first place he was dressed like a poor man. . . And for a long time he spoke to us about economics. They say he was telling us how to make poor countries rich. Something called stages of growth. I have tried to find out what he really said, but it seemed I wasn't the only one who slept that day. I woke up when I heard some clapping. The others also woke up, and we clapped and said, "yeah yeah." (*BNYB*, 155–56)

The attorney general, "drunk as usual," treats the audience to what he calls "a vote of thanks" but what turns out to be a mug's lecture on "the stages of booze." These, according to him, are:

Stage One   — The Mood Jocose
Stage Two   — The Mood Morose
Stage Three — The Mood Bellicose
Stage Four — The Mood Lachrymose
Stage Five — The Mood Comatose

Quite predictably, the attorney general falls down after the last stage, to the amusement of everyone except the professor who packs his bags and leaves the country to its jokers.

The attack on anti-intellectualism is aimed at something symptomatic. But intellectual commitment is an essential part of charting the course of action and giving a sense of purpose to national life. Ideas rule the world, for they serve as a focus for human energies and a guide to human actions. To run a state without commitment to any body of ideas and principles would be as ineffectual as trying to navigate without a chart. But commitment to ideas and principles is inconvenient to the indolent and the corrupt. The corrupt find that ideas and principles are a measure by which the actions of public offices are judged. The indolent would prefer to do without them because ideas and principles make demands on the will, intelligence, and judgment. Those who, in the cultural evolution of the continent, are most capable of calling its leaders to account are the intellectuals, the writers, the artists, and the professionals and executives of the mass media. Political leaders attempt to buy them out and steamroll them to toe "the party line" or, failing that, attempt to silence and constrain them by imprisonment, detention, and terror.

In *A Man of the People*, Dr. Makinde and the intellectuals of the People's Organization Party are thrown out of the party and denounced to the people as traitors, decadent stooges, ingrates, and enemies of the people. The Professor in *The Beautyful Ones Are Not Yet Born* is driven out by the ridicule of the comedians and the corrupt; while Sekoni and the other "interpreters" in *The Interpreters* are reduced to being outsiders in a state to which they have so much to contribute. The effect is to enthrone mediocrity, opportunism, and ineffectuality in states that desperately need to use the best in human resources and require efficiency and speed in the implementation of national goals.

What is the position of the broad masses in the post-independence drama as presented in these novels? In the first place, the novelists see the masses without sentimentality. In the corruption created by the elite, the masses are both victims and cynical collaborators. Their initial innocence and naïveté is always assumed, and so is the cynicism that results from their lack of trust in the new bringers of ideals and hopes. Their naïveté shows most clearly in their belief in politicians' promises, and their cynicism in their repudiation of all idealism altogether, a feeling that all public promises are mere verbiage, and that one set of politicians is as bad as another. And it would seem that the writers are angriest with the political and bureaucratic elite for so destroying the optimism of the masses and innoculating them with the virus of cynicism.

In *The Interpreters*, Soyinka sees the masses as victims of the inequalities entrenched in the social structure. The elite are in control of the political and administrative machinery. And they manipulate this machinery to their own advantage and often to the detriment of the common people. In this novel there is a practical illustration when, Barabbas, the small thief, is chased and beaten by a mob, while big thieves like the managing director, the manager of *Independent Viewpoint*, and other public functionaries despoil the country with impunity. Soyinka gives poignancy to this social inequity in his exhortation to the fleeing thief: "Run, Barabbas, run, all underdog sympathetic. Run you little thief or the bigger thieves will pass a law against your existence as a menace to society." (*I*, 114) But in the same breath, Soyinka remarks upon the brutality, gullibility, and irrationality of the mob that throws stones and sticks at the little thief and then hails the big public thief grown rich on the spoils of the country's economic resources: ". . . Run, Barabbas from the same crowd which will reform tomorrow and cheer the larger thief returning from his twentieth Economic Mission and pluck his train from the mud, dog-wise, in their teeth." (*I*, 114)

The mob can become brutal and heavy-handed when dealing with its victims. Its ruthlessness is often reserved for its own class: "Like the casual barbarism of such a crowd, their treachery against those who were momentarily below them in daily debasement . . . Like sand-elves in Ogboju Ode, the mob materialized with every step and every sting of a stone or the passing-breath of a near-miss made him begin to wish for a merciful release." (*I*, 115)

This view of the mob has nothing in common with the Coriolanus-like, aristocratic contempt for the common people, the "hydra-headed mob," but is rooted in precise observation of human nature. The poor can be violent and oppressive just like everyone else; but because of their own lack of power, they become tyrannical when they sense they have some advantage over others. The "daily debasement" of the poor drives their violence and oppressiveness inward, against their own kind, especially those at temporary disadvantage, like Barabbas.

In *A Man of the People*, Achebe emphasizes this brutality and cynicism. Once they form into a mob, the people become willing tools in the hands of demagogues. Their amenability to manipulation is not always a result of ignorance and innocence but is often a cynical determination to play their part in compounding the national confusion. They act according to the pressure of the moment. They have come to believe that corruption is the normal mode of national life, that there is no altruism in social life, only calculated self-interest, and all public officers are thieves and villains. Odili's father's view of public life, we are told, is that "the mainspring of political action was personal gain," and Odili hastens to add that this view "was much more in line with the general feeling in the country than the high-minded thinking of fellows like Max and I." (*MP*, 126) They see their main interest as trying to find and sustain positions of vantage in the corrupt structure. Their reactions are determined by opportunism.

We first see the mob howling its execrations at the disgraced "intellectual" ministers from the parliamentary gallery. In the conflict between his party, the Common People's Convention, and Chief Nanga's party, Odili is cha-grined to find the common people he is trying to save supporting Nanga and his corrupt crew. He is even beaten senseless by Nanga's mob. The fact is that the common people are skeptical of all politicians because they have been deceived for so long that they have come to distrust the good intentions of all would-be messiahs. In the crude logic of the benighted time through which they are living, the people would rather trust Nanga and the devil they know than the angels that they do not know.

The common people's skepticism emerges forcefully after Max, the theo-retician of Odili's radical party, has tried to project the two older parties as vultures "fighting over what remained of the carcass" of the depreciating national resources. The people should take their guns (the opportunity offered by the impending election) and shoot down the predators. To which a mem-ber of the audience answers that "there were three vultures. . . . The third and youngest was called C. P. C." (Max's party). (*MP*, 125) When the politicians overreach themselves and plunge the country into chaos, it is not the people who step in to save the situation but the military.

Achebe is perhaps exaggerating the cynicism. And, certainly, he does attribute more political awareness to the common people than they can be expected to possess. The people are no fools, but they are not in full possession of the facts, have no conception of national goals (the elite themselves do not seem to have clear-cut ideas of these goals), and their response cannot therefore be grounded on rationally considered judgments, in fact, cannot be more than a conditioned response. The elite control the machinery of national life, manipulate and juggle it, make available as much information as they consider expedient and withhold what they want, and, in the end, elicit whatever response they want from the people.

After the launching of the Common People's Convention by Max and Odili in his village, an old man makes reply on behalf of the community. (*MP*, 125) It soon becomes clear that the old man is regurgitating much that was fed to the village. He speaks in the familiar rhythms of traditional rhetoric and makes recognizable references to a sense of community solidarity, yet he is reacting in the terms of modern politics foisted upon the villages by the new political elite. The language of "eating" is alien to traditional politics and would hardly have been understood by the people in Okonkwo's

Umuofia, or even those of Ezeulu's Umuaro. They would have had a better criterion for civil leadership than the fact that a candidate could simply increase the communal share of a national good. And even if one accepted to present national politics as a process of sharing among different communities, it would be clear that the substantial truths of modern politics had not been communicated.

In view of the total dependence of the common people upon the leadership of the educated elite, it is hard to admit the accusation of complicity and cynicism against them. They have been allowed so little participation in the working of the modern institutions, and so little inside knowledge, that justice demands that they be given the benefit of the doubt. The only image that appears to fit them is that of victim. The educated elite seem to have run away with things, only resorting to the people when they needed validation of their authority. They operate a system little understood by the people, often in a language alien to a vast majority of them. They mystify the people with the new concepts and ideas of government, keep them ignorant as long as it suits them, and then rush back to them with passionate harangues when they need the support of the people in their competition for power with other members of their class. The elite have not succeeded in making the idea of the new nationhood a reality to the masses.

Frantz Fanon, in *The Wretched of the Earth*, emphasized the collaborative relationship that should exist between leaders and followers in the new nations:

> The duty of those at the head of the movement is to have the masses behind them. Allegiance presupposes awareness and understanding of the mission which has to be fulfilled; in short, an intellectual position, however embryonic. We must not voodoo the people, nor dissolve them in emotion and confusion. Only those underdeveloped countries led by revolutionary elites who have come up from the people can today allow the entry of the masses upon the scene of history.[13]

Fanon warns against the formation of a bourgeois privileged class, which he sees as more inhibiting than foreign domination, because, once privileges are created and people have tasted them, it will be difficult to persuade them to let them go for the sake of higher national goals. Fanon's warning is unequivocal:

> We must repeat, it is absolutely necessary to oppose vigorously and definitely the birth of a national bourgeoisie and a privileged caste. To educate the masses politically is to make the nation a reality to each citizen. It is to make the history of the nation part of the personal experience of each of its citizens.[14]

Obviously, this ideal has eluded most of the newly independent states. The politics of the "national cake" is not a way of making the nation "a reality" to its citizens.

In their criticisms of the new elite, the writers show attitudes shared with Fanon. Even before they became active Fanonists, their observation of the social and political scene of post-independence Africa led them to the conclusion that the greatest threat to orderly development was the nature of the modern African elite and the style of post-independence political leadership. Fanon confirmed views formed from observation and gave ideological support to fears and anxieties already felt.

It is clear from Achebe's writing since the end of Nigeria's civil war that he is beginning to see the common people in a new light. He shows in a collection of poems, *Beware Soul Brother*, many of which deal with wartime experiences, and a collection of short stories, *Girls At War*, that the common people can show heroism, and that their power of endurance and ability to revive after a major disaster are among their most admirable qualities. In poem after poem and story after story, he conveys that his impression of the common people is not that of cynical collaborators in evil and corruption but of a hard-pressed and vulnerable people finding their way out of terrifying group and individual disasters through patience, resignation, and, above all, compassion.

Armah sees the common people as first duped by their would-be redeemers and then betrayed through the cupidity and selfishness of the political and bureaucratic elite. But with time they too become part of the national image of wholesale and unmitigated corruption. They accept with cynical abandon the fact of corruption as the crucial reality of existence and they strive to outdo one another in leaping over the moral barriers to reach the gleam of success. But there is always an implied or overt criticism of the elite who have brought the nation to such a sordid state and blighted the earlier promising hopes. Certainly, the dice are loaded against the common people when their interests and those of the elite clash, because the elite are in control. An example is the commission of enquiry to rid Ghana of corruption. The affair is manipulated in such a manner that the big culprits escape and the little "dispensable" fry are sacrificed. We are told that "the net had been made in the special Ghanaian way that allowed the really big corrupt people to pass through it. A net to catch only the small, dispensable fellows, trying in their anguished blindness to leap and to attain the gleam and the comfort the only way these things could be done. And the big ones floated free, like all the slogans." (*BNYB*, 180)

Like Soyinka, Armah sees the common people in the dual image of victim and evildoer. But their evildoing is attenuated by their being vulnerable and lacking in social power. They are reproached for lacking the moral will to resist corruption, but it is also constantly pointed out that they are exposed unceasingly to the seductions of corruption. They observe those who adopt shortcuts to fame, wealth, and power, and the hardship which is the lot of the honest and the morally fastidious. Nothing is done to give respectability to morality. The few who hold on to their moral integrity, like the Man and his friend the Naked Man, become outsiders and are only saved from destruction by an indomitable pessimism and a tough-minded reliance on their individual integrity. They turn their backs on society and seek for strength within themselves, in the knowledge that everything else may collapse except the truth of individual conviction.

It is hard to agree that the answer to social corruption lies in withdrawal from active participation by good people. The Man does not actually withdraw, as the Naked Man does, but his resistance is too passive to provide an effective answer to social corruption. Soyinka's young activists and Achebe's Odili and Max present a more positive challenge to social corruption. Their response, like Dr. Stockman's in Ibsen's *An Enemy of the People*, is to fight back, not to turn their faces to the wall. And here is the difference, in the long run, between these writers. Achebe and Soyinka believe in vigorous social action to change the corrupt social order, while Armah thinks the situation is too far gone to be redeemed, at least in the near future. Achebe's young radicals believe in challenging the older, corrupt politicians for power, and Soyinka's "interpreters" attack and expose the hypocrisy and corruption of the ruling class. Armah, on the other hand, sees some hope in the distant future, but how this hope will be revived is not even remotely hinted at. "Someday in the long future," he writes, "a new life would maybe flower in the country, but when it came, it would not choose as its instruments the same people who had made a habit of killing new flowers." (*BNYB*, 188) The crucial point is that a "new life" can never come without preparation, a preparation which, in its most positive form, must involve the deliberate subversion of the old, corrupt life. Passivity and inaction are ways of postponing indefinitely this arrival of a desirable new order.

Interestingly, *The Beautyful Ones Are Not Yet Born* ends on a more positive note than the one on which it started. The Man, in helping the partyman Koomson to escape his pursuers on the day of the military coup d'état, partakes, literally and metaphorically, of the pervasive corruption. He subsequently has an invigorating swim and bath, undergoing a sort of purification, and is ready to continue the struggle, convinced that despite their corruption and human weaknesses, the people deserve to be saved.

NOTES

1. See Robert I. Rotberg and Ali Mazrui, eds., *Protest and Power in Black Africa* (Oxford, 1970), 1043.
2. "The Writer in a Modern African State" in *The Writer in Modern Africa*, ed. Per Wastberg (New York, 1969), 17.
3. Ibid., 14.
4. Ibid., 16.

5. Quoted by James M. Gibbs in "Wole Soyinka: Biography and Bibliography," *African Library Journal* 3, 1 (1972).

6. Ibid.

7. *The Political Dilemma of Popular Education: The African Case* (Stanford, California, 1969), 250.

8. Chinua Achebe, *A Man of the People* (London, 1966), 6. Subsequent references are cited as *MP* in the text.

9. Ayi Kwei Armah, *The Beautyful Ones Are Not Yet Born* (London, 1969), 6. Subsequent references to this work are cited as *BNYB* in the text.

10. Wole Soyinka, *The Interpreters* (London, 1965), 112. Subsequent references to this work are cited as *I* in the text.

11. Barbara B. Lloyd, "Education and Family Life in the Development of Class Identification among the Yoruba" in *The New Elites of Tropical Africa*, ed. P. C. Lloyd (Oxford, 1966), 164.

12. *Dark Eyes in Africa* (London, 1951), 16.

13. Frantz Fanon, *The Wretched of the Earth*, tr. Constance Farrington (Harmondsworth, 1967), 161–62.

14. Ibid.

CHAPTER 7

Victimization as a Theme

VICTIMIZATION is one of the main themes of African literature. African written works and oral tales and fables abound in examples of individuals—willing and unwilling, young as well as adult, male no less than female—who are occasionally sacrificed to the needs of society, to the pressures of tradition, or to the exigencies of religion. Others may be sacrificed to sustain the despotism of community, the all-consuming egotism of a dictator, or the absolutism of an idea.

Modern African writers no less than traditional artists have devoted considerable attention to this question of the victimization of the individual. In their role as the keepers of the conscience of the group and defenders of the values of individual freedom and human rights, they are not indifferent to a phenomenon that is neither hypothetical nor restricted to folklore. They are not indifferent to a situation that challenges their integrity and vision as humanists and the moral legislators of their people.

One point deserves to be made from the outset. The society, community, or group that sacrifices its members is already in a state that students of man and society would identify as unhealthy. A society, group, or community under pressure or tension is likely to sacrifice some of its members in its state of anxiety. It is therefore not difficult to see why victimization should assume such prominence in a continent that has endured such severe and sustained stresses and convulsions. African history over the last five hundred years has been one of a series of disasters, and therefore a history of innumerable victims.

Starting with the slave trade, the African peoples have probably produced more human victims than any other race of mankind in recent times. Imperialism and white racism on the continent have also generated human wastage. More recently still, the emergence of post-independence black dictatorships and bad governments has brought new styles and scales of human destruction that provide additional material for writers whose role it is constantly to explore and evaluate the state of social and psychological health.

African writing, from the very beginning, has been a literature of victims. From the texts left behind by eighteenth- and nineteenth-century Africans—texts consisting mainly of autobiographies and autobiographical fragments—it is easy to observe the pervasive insecurities among individuals who were

150

suddenly uprooted from their familiar surroundings and transported to the hostile, wider world of the Americas and the West Indies.[1]

It would, of course, be unrealistic to assume that traditional Africa, even if it had not undergone these upheavals, would have been completely free of victims. No human society, no matter how stable and well-organized, is without any victims whatsoever for the simple reason that no human society has so far attained a perfect state of stable equilibrium between itself and its numerous members. Traditional society never was, nor has it since become, the idyllic paradise of the romantic imagination. It has always had within it certain conditions that made the sacrifice of chosen victims inevitable. African realistic artists are not deceived into striking a purely idealistic stance when they appraise the position of the marked individuals within the traditional and modern societies on the continent.

African literary texts present the reader with two faces of victimization: collective victimization or the conversion of large segments of society into victims, and particularized victimization of single, isolated individuals. Collective victimization is sinister enough and embodies the terror that goes with any form of victimization, but because of its public and generalized nature, it operates less oppressively on the psyche than the more isolated and particularized cases of individual victims.

In one respect, however, collective and individual victimization cannot be neatly separated. Collective victimization tends to form a background to individual victimization and to reinforce it emotionally and psychologically. Where the group has already been victimized and has a consciousness conditioned by that experience, as in the case with the blacks in apartheid South Africa or the subjects of post-independent African dictators, victimization of separate individuals is taken for granted and regarded as an extension of group victimization. In fact, the individual tends to develop a victimization complex, which makes him almost expect to be victimized, as if it were in the natural order of things.

African writers deal with victimization on the two levels of group and individual consciousness. The theme is explored mainly in plays and novels because these are genres that offer full scope for the exploration of human experience in its extended dimension with the possibility of making a statement or clarification of a specific human condition or predicament. Each writer determines which form is more appropriate to his conception of this theme. There is no doubt, however, that a writer's conception of the meaning and nature of victimization goes a long way toward determining for him whether the drama or the novel form should be adopted. Where the scope of the action to be explored requires a detailed portrayal of the environment and atmosphere of victimization, the novel, which is an elaborative form, has generally proved advantageous. Where the treatment involves a symbolic or ritual approach, the drama has generally been favored. The novel offers the widest scope possible for examining of the conditions that give rise to the sacrifice of human victims, because it can trace motives and psychological factors that give significance and depth to action. Plays operate almost in the opposite direction, through a process of condensation and use of associative and symbolically worked-out movements and gestures. The three plays discussed here all deal with the victimization of individuals within traditional societies, while the two novels explore the predicament of the outstanding but doomed individual living in a transitional society or in the vitiated world of post-independence dictatorship.

SELECT PLAYS

I have selected three plays—Wole Soyinka's *Death and the King's Horseman* and *The Strong Breed*, and Tsegaye Gabre-Medhin's *Oda-Oak Oracle*—to see how their authors deal with the question of victimization. These works offer a fair sample of victimized characters and examples of situations and circumstances that make the sacrifice of human victims possible. They demonstrate that traditional societies existed in a metaphysical context that recognized the continuity between the past, the present, and the future, and, correspondingly, between the dead, the living, and those yet to be born. These societies widely accepted the need for occasional sacrifice to ease communication among the three stages of the continuum. On the other hand, outside the metaphysical context, human beings were often prepared to waive all human considerations and to sacrifice human victims to ensure their personal well-being.

Death and the King's Horseman, The Strong Breed, and *Oda-Oak Oracle* start from the traditionally accepted concept of sacrifice as a necessary ritual for cleansing society and oiling the wheels of transition that ensure the stability of the world. The writers examine the motives and attitudes involved and, at times, the suppressed pain, hopes, and fears that may be features of these sacrificial rituals. They deal directly, and at varying levels of artistic subtlety, with the sort of life that specializes "in finding scapegoats for anything that steered it from its dreary course."[2]

Each of the three plays is set in a communal society governed by custom, which, in turn, is sustained by an ancestral code of laws and conventions. The ancestors rule the world from the land of the dead, and because they also enforce the code by remote control, all manner of intermediaries and interpreters, including oracles, priests, diviners, and elders exist to determine their precise intentions, especially during difficult moments when real or hypothetical threats against the metaphysical order exist. The communal world is like an orb delicately poised on a tripod. One leg of the tripod represents the dead; the second leg represents the living; and the third leg represents those yet to be born. If any one of the legs suddenly gives way, the equilibrium is upset and the orb falls to pieces. It is the duty of the living to ensure that all three legs of the tripod are kept firmly fixed in their places in order to preserve the safety and stability of the world. The easiest way to upset this delicate balance is for the living to offend the ancestral laws and conventions. That would bring instant reprisals against the living, imperil the future of those yet to be born, and create an upheaval in the land of the dead.

Each play explores, explicitly, the metaphysical determinism of the communal world. In *Death and the King's Horseman*, the world trembles on the brink of the abyss when Elesin Oba, the king's horseman, fails to commit sacrificial suicide in accordance with the ancient custom that the king's horseman must accompany the king to the other world after the king's death. The metaphysical world-order is threatened in the *Oda-Oak Oracle* when Shanka, the strong son of the tribe who had a bride chosen for him by the oracle of Oda Oak, refuses "to know the warmth of his bride" because the same oracle has prophesied that the firstborn son of the marriage must be sacrificed to the ancestors. The attempt to forestall the "ordained" course of events leads not to one death but to the sacrifice of four people. *The Strong Breed* presents the perspective on the ritual significance of "the carrier" in traditional society, the recognition of the necessity for an individual to be "sacrificed" for the sake of society at large.

All three plays assume the ritual necessity of sacrifice of victims for the good of the communal society. In the details of presentation, however, the circumstances and inner rhythms of each plot differ considerably from those of the others; so do the motives and attitudes that underscore each drama. These differences are seen most clearly when the plays are considered separately.

Death and the King's Horseman

Soyinka explores the theme of victimization in *Death and the King's Horseman* from various perspectives. There is the metaphysical, communal perspective, which accepts without question the archaic custom that the horseman of the Alaafin must accompany the Alaafin at his death to the other world. Then there is the perspective on the individual caught in the web of a personal dilemma when it falls to his lot to become the sacrificial victim to serve what might appear to be other people's well-being. The outsider's perspective is also present when the action is viewed from a position of ignorance attended by skepticism.

In the author's note to the Eyre Methuen edition of the play, Soyinka inserts this interpretive guide—meant, no doubt, to lead the producer into the heart of the play and through the complexities of Yoruba metaphysics, which constitutes the intellectual underpinning of the action:

> The confrontation in the play is largely metaphysical, contained in the human
> vehicle which is Elesin and the universe of the Yoruba mind—the world of the

living, the dead and the unborn, and the numinous passage which links all transition. *Death and the King's Horseman* can be fully realized only through an evocation of music from the abyss of transition.[3]

The note is beneficial. The producer who adopts a purely secular and "materialist" view of the play will experience difficulty, very much in the manner of the Pilkings who, with the best of intentions and in an effort to do good, doubly confound the tragedy of those they set out to save. And not only producers but also critics who underestimate the metaphysical implications of the action will have great difficulty evaluating it. One has recently begun to hear epithets like "feudalistic" and "reactionary" being flung at Soyinka from the radical inkpots of some Nigerian critics. They are appalled that a writer of modern perceptions should use his gifts to sustain an archaic and outmoded worldview which sacrifices individuals to the "capriciousness" of a feudal-patriarchal social order.

It is not really necessary to attempt a detailed defense of Soyinka beyond saying that it is reasonable to absolve him from the more damnable imputations. Soyinka has done what any conscientious writer ought to do, which is to explore, with artistic fidelity, the historical event of 1946 when the Elesin Oba destroyed his own life to sustain the old tradition of his people after the intervention of the British authorities nearly caused a serious civil disorder. He has examined the underlying motives and delineated the intellectual and emotional impulses that conditioned the responses of those involved to wring out of the reconstructed drama the widest range of meaning and significance. If in doing this Soyinka has chosen to lean heavily toward a metaphysical interpretation of the action, it must be that a metaphysical interpretation is the one calculated to present it more truthfully and significantly than would a purely secular and physical interpretation, which might in the end trivialize the experience as well as misrepresent the true feelings of the dramatis personae.

The traditional perspective defines the mainline of the action. All the traditional characters—the Iyaloja, the Praise-Singer, Elesin Oba himself—and Olunde, Elesin's eldest son studying medicine in England, accept the custom of sacrificial suicide and the metaphysical view underlying it. They accept the cosmic unity of all existence as a first principle, which is that a metaphysical link exists between the dead, the living, and the unborn. When Elesin fails to fulfil his "destiny," partly because of his disinclination and partly because of his arrest by the District Officer, the Iyaloja accuses him of disrupting the ordered course of the communal world:

> He [Elesin] knows the peril to the race when our dead father, who goes as intermediary, waits and waits and knows he is betrayed. He knows when the narrow gate was opened and he knows it will not stay for laggards who drag their feet in dung and vomit, whose lips are reeking of the left-overs of lesser men. He knows he has condemned our king to wander in the void of evil with beings who are enemies of life. (*DKH*, 71)

The Praise-Singer is even more emphatic in condemning the Horseman: "You sat with folded arms while evil strangers tilted the world from its course and crashed it beyond the edge of emptiness . . . you left us floundering in a blind future. . . . Our world is tumbling in the void of strangers. . . ." (*DKH*, 75) Everyone, except the outsiders, recognizes the connection between the self-sacrifice of the horseman and the mystical welfare of the community, the preservation of the cosmic stability of the communal world. Olunde more than anyone else expresses the view that physical welfare is not unrelated to metaphysical peace. This comes out in the very long debate between him and Jane Pilkings in which the insider's and outsider's perspectives are sharply contrasted:

> Ever since I learnt of the King's death I've lived with my bereavement so long now that I cannot think of him [his father] alive. On that journey on the boat, I kept my mind on my duties as the one who must perform the rites over his body. I went through it all again and again in my mind as he himself has taught me. I didn't want to do anything wrong, something which might jeopardise the welfare of my people. (*DKH*, 57)

It is when this "welfare of the people" is put in jeopardy by his father's failure to perform the expected sacrifice that he himself takes over and pays with his own life.

Elesin recognizes the duty thrust upon him by tradition. It is a duty doubly reinforced by the demands of honor. He has enjoyed peculiar privileges as the king's companion and is quick to admit that these privileges are sometimes as great as those of the king himself: "Where there was plenty I gorged myself. My master's hands and mine have always Dipped together. . . . We shared the choicest of the season's Harvest of yams. . . . " (*DKH*, 14) And later still, as if to reemphasize the point, the Elesin stresses his obligation to fulfil a pact rooted in friendship as well as in honor:

> Life has an end. A life that will outlive
> Fame and friendship begs another name
> . . . . Life is honour
> It ends when honour ends. (*DKH*, 15)

Of him to whom much is given, much is expected. The personal indulgence allowed Elesin is in recognition of a role his destiny has carved out for him as a sacrificial victim. His life is made as comfortable as possible, as if a deliberate effort were needed to cover up the grimness of the destiny that awaits him at the very end. He is pampered by the people and is regarded as a special favorite of the gods. He is not only the king's companion but the king's confidant and trusted adviser. His fate may be grim, but everything is done to give it a human face. His last day's great splash, when he dances in splendor in the marketplace, shows indeed that the Elesin is "a monarch whose palace is built with tenderness and beauty." (*DKH*, 10) He is magnificently costumed by the women. He demands to enjoy a virgin bride as his last privilege. The Iyaloja, the arranger of this last tribute, testifies that Elesin is already in contact with the other world: "The voice I hear is already touched by the waiting fingers of our departed." (*DKH*, 21) His enjoyment is tinged with a shade of sadness.

The character of the man himself is attuned to receiving the communal tributes steeped in the unction of sensuality. He is described at the beginning of the play as "a man of enormous vitality, [who] speaks, dances and sings with that infectious enjoyment of life which accompanies all his actions." (*DKH*, 9) The critical issue of the play, therefore, becomes the question of Elesin's ability to shoulder his onerous burden, to fulfill his great destiny. As a sensualist with an enormous capacity for life and enjoyment, how would the Elesin confront a destiny whose fulfillment requires stringent self-discipline and social self-denial?

Both Iyaloja and the Praise-Singer recognize the risks involved in placing a godlike burden on a mere mortal. They are full of expectation, but the expression of this expectation is mixed with statements that suggest the possibility of disappointment and hints of doubt:

> **Iyaloja** The living must eat and drink. When the moment comes, don't turn the food to rodents' droppings in their mouth. Don't let them taste the ashes of the world when they step out at dawn to breathe the morning dew. (*DKH*, 42)

And the Praise-Singer, impersonating the dead king, tests Elesin's integrity:

> If you cannot come, I said, swear
> You'll tell my favourite horse, I shall
> Ride on through the gates alone.
>
> If you cannot come, Elesin, tell my dog,
> I cannot stay the keeper too long at the gate.
>
> If you get lost my dog will track
> The hidden path to me. (*DKH*, 42)

The anxieties of the market women, the Praise-Singer, and Iyaloja are justified in the end when Elesin grows reluctant to fulfil his obligation and commits what he himself calls "this blasphemy of thought," "the awful treachery of relief." (*DKH*, 68) But the nature of this blasphemy ought to be recognized. Elesin's sensuality is certainly a drag on his will, but he himself tells us that it would not have stopped his fulfillment of his obligation in the end. The decisive intervention of the District Officer alters everything. Not only is Elesin physically restrained from committing suicide but, and this is the blasphemy, he begins to feel a sense of relief that this intervention may have come as an act of the gods to free him from the obligation itself: "My will was squelched in the spittle of an alien race, and all because I had committed this blasphemy of thought—that there might be the hand of the gods in a stranger's intervention." (*DKH*, 69)

As he is soon to learn, however, the gods do not act so inconsistently and their will is not so easily set aside. The living, who in most cases interpret the will of the gods and act as their agents, see to it that fitting reprisals visit those who flagrantly attempt to set their will at nought. For Elesin is still driven to fulfill his sacrificial obligation by the combined pressures of his eldest son, the formidable Iyaloja, the Praise-Singer, whose song is now steeped in acid, and, by far the most persistent force of all, the voice of the brooding elders and people, speaking through the distant drums.

The major complication of the drama is supplied by the District Officer's intervention to stop Elesin's suicide. The intervention, even though well meant, is based on the outsider's perspective. This perspective is first introduced when Sergeant Amusa reports the unfolding drama in the following prosaic language: "one prominent chief, namely, the Elesin Oba, is to commit death tonight as a result of native custom." (*DKH*, 26)

It is clear that the outsiders are not capable of understanding or sharing the metaphysical world that demands the horseman's sacrifice at the funeral of the king. The polarization of perceptions is first handled as an intellectual argument between Olunde and Mrs. Pilkings, an argument that proves distressing and inconclusive. The limitation of Mrs. Pilkings's viewpoint is however shown in her conferring the status of heroic self-sacrifice on the action of the British captain who blows himself up with his ship in the harbor in order to prevent the death of people on shore, while regarding Elesin's impending self-sacrifice for the welfare of his community as barbaric and feudalistic. That the District Officer and his wife accept the captain's self-sacrifice as something noble and good while not conceding that even within a feudalistic context a man can sacrifice his life in the noble pursuit of the welfare of his people takes something away from the soundness of their view. This dramatic contrast indicates the author's rejection of the outsider's perspective and makes it easier to appreciate Elesin's tragedy.

Simon Pilkings's insight, built entirely on the secular conception of life, strengthens his determination to save the life of the horseman. He finds his confirming authority in a proverbial statement: "The elder grimly approaches heaven and you ask him to bear your greetings yonder; do you really think he makes the journey willingly?" (*DKH*, 64)

This insight cannot be dismissed out of hand because it is based upon a fact of human nature. No one is eager to die, even though all religions paint the blessings of heaven in attractive colors. From the first steps taken by Elesin Oba there grows a certain suspicion that the posture he has struck is not altogether genuine and is unlikely to carry him to the end of his onerous duty. There is something forced and frenzied in his sweeping movements that leave his drummers and praise-singer struggling to catch up with him. He is behaving like an elder who is approaching heaven at a running pace. We suspect he will not make the distance or, if he does, that he cannot arrive there in good grace. Elesin's references to the fear of death, coupled with such emphatic affirmations as "My soul is eager. I shall not turn aside—" (*DKH*, 14) this garrulity and rhetorical exuberance (the rhetoric is contra-dictory)—all create a certain uneasiness, as if the horseman were striving to fill up the time with anything but measured contemplation of the task which lies before him: that of dying with dignity, not living hectically. Even though he redeems himself at last, his path is rendered hazardous in the process, and much luster has gone from the act: "The passage is clogged with droppings from the king's stallion: he will arrive all stained in dung." (*DKH*, 76)

The horseman's dilemma, even when rooted in metaphysics, has its stem and branches in the open-air of secular objectivity. The reluctance to embrace death is deep in the human consciousness and manifests itself in spite of the seductions and promises of metaphysical rewards. The sacrificial victim is first and foremost a human being of flesh, blood, and bones before he is transmogrified into a metaphysical medium. His struggle to answer the needs of human nature may be blasphemous from the metaphysical viewpoint, but it cannot be altogether unworthy of the sympathy of all who are fully aware of the vulnerability of their human nature. Elesin Oba's tragedy is based on two factors: his realization of his responsibility to ensure the maintenance of the metaphysical stability of his people's world by the sacrifice of his own life, and his failure to live up to this responsibility because of his tenacious attachment to the pleasures of this life.

Oda-Oak Oracle

The efficacy of human sacrifice is also claimed by the valley people in the *Oda-Oak Oracle*. Here the sacrifice of the victims is to ensure the restoration of cosmic order that has been disrupted in the valley. In the words of First Elder, who is spokesman for the elders, only the sacrifice of the victims will restore the shattered world:

> Their deaths will prevent
> The wall of our tribe
> From breaking down.
>
> The gentle quiet
> That has been crushed
> From the land of the valley
> Will soon settle among us.
>
> The peace of the spirits
> That have escaped our mountains shall now
> Take over.[4]

The sacrifice of the protagonists is justified as a means of restoring metaphysical order and punishing the sin of defiance.

Shanka, however, is determined that, if the dead know no mercy, then he will never know his bride. His abstention is therefore an attempt to bring the prophecy to nought, which is itself a serious case of presumption—and impiety. His attitude is culpable from the traditional point of view. No true traditional character would publicly question the will of the dead ancestors as interpreted through the oracle and the elders. As Second Elder, who functions as Chorus says:

> The dead only demand
> In their ancient wisdom,
> Older than the memory of man.
> The living only obey
> Wondering. (*OO*, 5)

Shanka's second sin is his conscious attempt to use his friend Goaa to influence the oracle to change its mind:

> Go back to the Oda Oak, friend,
> And face the Oracle. (*OO*, 5)

Even after many months, when it is discovered that his bride has been made pregnant by somebody else, Shanka still questions the integrity of the elders:

> Why, Wise Elders,
> Must the dead feast
> On the sapping of life
> Of a babe,
> Who should have been materialized
> As part of my blood?(*OO*,33)

The reason why Shanka defies the "infallible" elders in this way is that he has been influenced by Goaa, his friend, "the inhibited by the strangers' ways," and can therefore appeal to a code of values outside those of the communal society. Even though this specific new influence is never mentioned explicitly, the oblique references would suggest that it is Christianity:

> You're more than a brother to me,
> Goaa, You imparted your knowledge
> Of the wisdom of the strangers
> To me. You did. You let me share the secret
> Of your happy obsession by the Word
> Which you said, is all loving.(*OO*,38)

Unfortunately, what might have become a concerted campaign against intolerable despotism disintegrates into an absurd revolt that is systematically suppressed by the implacable elders. Goaa proves to be neither a good man nor a moral man. He publicly denounces both Shanka and Ukutee, Shanka's neglected wife, who now bears Goaa's child. He tries to buy a separate peace from the elders. Shanka, now left unsupported, is totally alienated from tradition, although he is far from sure what sort of moral code he should use to oppose the absolutism of his persecutors:

> But yes
> For the cry of the new born!
> Yes, for the daughter of peace
> Yes, for the father and mother
> Who die to give it life.
> Yes, for the Word
> Who becomes All!(*OO*,51)

He suffers persistent oppression at the hands of the elders, and even though he is physically a strong and impressive man, the elders' tactics of attrition finally wear him out and his spirit is broken. He takes refuge in self-pitying lamentations:

> Strong, I am,
> Yet I am the weakest.
> The dead are my witness
> That many a dreary night
> I lamented like a
> woman.(*OO*,5)

It is as if the ancestors and the elders were determined to ruin him at all costs because every attempt to set himself right is interpreted as a criminal offense by the elders. The extraordinary self-control he shows by refusing to know his bride is interpreted as an affront, an attempt to see that the oracle of the ancestors will not be fulfilled. His sin of presumption is said to cause heart-burn and teeth-gnashing among the spirits and natural upheavals in the valley. He is accused of betraying the tribe. In the trial the elders conduct, he is condemned to fight a duel with Goaa, but his survival of that ordeal is not thought punishment enough. He is doomed to extinction.

Goaa, the inhibited, is accused of sowing perversity in the society as a result of his having been influenced by the ways of the strangers. One does not see much evidence of his subversion except through Shanka's claim that he has indoctrinated him into the mystique of the Word. The Oda-Man's verdict is very severe for Goaa's offenses. His crimes are identified as, first, letting his head turn into a cavern "where the ghosts of strangers lingered,"(*OO*, 52) and second, allowing his "inhibited soul" to instill fertility into the chosen bride of the spirits. He is condemned to vagrancy in death and life. There is a hint of suspicion that the elders are more worried about

the foreign influences in the mind of Goaa than about his tampering with
the bride of the spirits:

> But true, Goaa,
> Because of your inhibition
> Of the strange ones
> You defied the wisdom
> Of our by-gone fathers,
> And aroused their curse
> Upon all. . . .(*OO*,26)

Ukutee is just as severely punished as the others even though she rightly
pleads extenuation. She is a victim of neglect; when her lawful husband refuses
to know her warmth she succumbs to temptation. But her pleas are set aside
and heavy sentence is pronounced upon her:

> And you, woman,
> Comforter
> Of every man's sweat,
> The creature in you
> Shall not come forth.
> Ever.(*OO*,30)

And so the court of severity dispenses Draconian justice. The three victims
are predictably sacrificed, as well as a fourth non-active-participant in the
triangular tragedy, the newly born child.

But it seems the author has the last word in the matter. Toward the end
of the play, when the menacing mob is about to bear down on both the
Elders and the culprits, Shanka poses the following significant question:

> Who rages for sacrifice?
> Our dead?
> Or our living?(*OO*,53)

To which First Elder supplies the answer:

> We need a sacrifice
> To cool the fire
> Of the raging mob.

And Third Elder agrees:

> Let them have Shanka
> With this child of shame,
> Before they have us.(*OO*,53)

Shanka and the child are fed to the fury of the raging mob, but he has at
least obtained some illumination that had eluded his tortured soul until then.
Sacrifice is demanded by the living for the sake of the living. The sole ben-

eficiaries are the living, who have bought their peace at the cost of those sacrificed. And, as if to emphasize the human factor in the untangling of the metaphysical web, the oracle predicts that Ukutee's unborn child shall be a boy:

> You shall deliver
> A new son, woman,
> Strong and fierce
> Like a young leopard, yes
> He shall grow
> To become man of the tribe.(*OO*,45)

When the child is born, it turns out to be a girl, who is ultimately to be fed to the fury of an angry mob. The author does not indicate whether the dead ones are playing tricks on their oracle, or the oracular vision has been dimmed by the human factor.

The Strong Breed

In *The Strong Breed*, Soyinka presents two perspectives on the ritual significance of the carrier in communal societies. The recognition of the necessity for an individual to be "sacrificed" for the sake of the society at large is common to two societies suggested in this play, but there is a basic difference in general attitudes and procedures. Whereas in the first, there is a lot of evil associated with the ritual, in the other, the carrier's role is somewhat heroic and nearly sacred.

The meaning of the carrier is first suggested by the mysterious girl under Eman's window: "Do you mean my carrier? I am unwell You know. My mother says it will take away my sickness with the old year."[5] The carrier is conceived as a metaphysical medium whose role it is to purge society (at specific seasons) of its evil through a symbolic physical act. This is further confirmed by the same girl later in the play, in her words to Ifada, who has been playing with her "carrier": "But just because you are helping me, don't think it is going to cure you. I am the one who will get well at midnight, do you understand? It is my carrier and it is for me alone."(*CP*,120)

But attitudes to the carrier differ radically between Jaguna's village and Eman's village. In Jaguna's village, where a good part of the action is set, the carrier is seen as an outcast, and the people make use of him opportunistically. They victimize him for their own well-being and treat him abominably. In Eman's village, on the other hand, the carrier is not only a respectable member of society, but also a bearer of a special responsibility for which society is indebted to him. The lot of the carrier in Jaguna's village is outlined by Jaguna himself in this exposition at Eman's house: "A carrier should end up in the bush, not in a house. Anyone who doesn't guard his door when the carrier goes by has himself to blame."(*CP*,128) His next in command, Oroge, goes a little further:

> This is not a simple matter at all. It is not a simple task for anybody. No one in his senses would do such a job. Why do you think we give refuge to idiots like him [meaning Ifada]? We don't know where he came from.(*CP*,128)

Sunma, the alienated eldest daughter of Jaguna, gives frantic expression to the evil involved in the selfish, opportunistic attitudes of the people of her village. She repudiates them and renounces her ceremonial role as Jaguna's eldest daughter. She warns Eman against the villagers: "You are wasting your life on people who really want you out of their way. . . . I know they are evil and I am not. From the oldest to the smallest child, they are nourished in evil and unwholesomeness."(*CP*,120–21) It is possible to see her anxiety as the selfish concern of a girl for her man's safety, but the more dignified context in which the role of the carrier is established in Eman's native village and the subsequent development of the action vindicate her position. In Eman's village, as revealed in the flashbacks, the role of the carrier is a special one, peculiar to a special family. And here it is devoid of the ignominy and contempt that characterize it in the other village. The Old Man, Eman's father, reminds him of the sacredness of the role: "Ours is a strong breed, my son. It is only a strong breed that can take this boat to the river year after year and wax stronger on it."(*CP*,133) A special deterministic force seems, however, to be acting on the chosen family that makes it inevitable for its members to be found out in foreign places and given the burden of their destiny. The old man informs Eman of this inevitability and the futility of his attempt to leave his village in order to escape the carrier's destiny: "Your own blood will betray you, son, because you cannot hold it back."(*CP*,134) And his blood does betray him in Jaguna's village, because even though Eman is living there as a fugitive in search of psychological peace, he intervenes to save Ifada, the village idiot selected for the role of carrier. He takes over the burden instead and is hunted down and hanged upon a tree. In the end, his father's prophecy, that his blood would betray him and that he would waste his strength among those unworthy of his redemptive calling comes true. However, the bestiality and viciousness of the people at the festival render the exercise futile. Oroge and Jaguna finally admit that it has been a night of curses and that, despite everything, there remains so much contamination in the air. At the critical moment when the carrier should have been burdened with curses, the villagers only "looked up at the man and words died in their throats."(*CP*,140)

It remains a question whether Soyinka intended in this play to examine two conflicting approaches concerning the role of the carrier, recommending the one and rejecting the other, or whether he simply wanted to point out the futility of such sacrificial attitudes to life.

All these plays highlight the predicament of the doomed individual in the traditional, communal society. A haunting sense of loneliness and feeling of abandonment are shared by all the protagonists. Their physical terror is only matched by the spiritual terror that seizes them from the very first moments of their victimization. The exclusion from the mystical communion of those who have decided to sacrifice them presents its own psychological problem to the victims; for, in every case of victimization, there is total separation of the victim from the rest of humanity and abandonment to a fate that must be confronted alone. The sacrificial situation represents a peculiar dialectic in which the victim ceases to be humanly autonomous. He becomes an instrument, an agent, and a means toward achieving an end, which is the well-being of those who sacrifice him.

Implicit in this relationship is a confrontation of interests, with those of the sacrificial victim subjugated to those of the beneficiaries, who gain from the sacrifice. The nature of this gain, or sacrificial efficacy, is explored in the three plays. On one level, it is interpreted metaphysically as the restoration of the cosmic order to a previously disturbed world. On another level, this gain is interpreted in terms of mass psychology, a certain craving of mobs for excitement through the humiliation of carefully chosen victims. Rulers of communities, aware of this tendency in the collectivity, periodically stage such shows to draw attention away from themselves. They sacrifice scapegoats to keep the crowds happy.

J. Bronowski, in *The Face of Violence*, observes in the chapter "Death as a Spectacle" that "every spectacle has an element of this; Mr. Punch and the circus clown, and the hero of Greek tragedy and the dying gladiator alike give to those who watch their defeat a stab of shameful pleasure in the collapse of human dignity."[6] And Frantz Fanon seems to endorse the same view in *Black Skin, White Masks*: "In every society, in every collectivity exists . . . a channel, an outlet through which the forces accumulated in the form of aggression can be released."[7]

In other words, the sacrificial drama, elaborated often by rituals, incantations, and music and, sometimes by scenes of violence and bloody orgies, provides collective catharsis and purges communal societies of more destructive internal upheavals. The annual expulsion of the carrier or the occasional sacrifice of a human victim insendates society from grosser forms of violence and destabilizing disorders.

SELECT NOVELS

Gabriel Okara's *The Voice* and Ngugi wa Thiongo's *The River Between* treat the theme of victimization with great concentration. Numerous other African novels deal with the theme in a more or less diffused manner. They are not lacking in victims, because the newly established post-independence regimes are still stumbling along, lacking assurance and consistency, and are therefore more likely than not to hunt down individuals or groups and to offer them up as scapegoats to divert attention from their own failure to meet the challenges of independence. The apartheid regime of South Africa continues to sacrifice Africans, singly and as a group, in order to ensure the continuity of that totally inhuman, exploitative, and discredited system. Different novels deal with different aspects of the deliberate sacrifice of an individual or a group in order to prolong the existence of a tyrannical, unjust, or perverse and exploitative social order. *The Voice* and *The River Between* are single-mindedly devoted to this theme.

Perhaps what makes these two novels so attractive is their choice of self-conscious, messianic victims. Okolo and Waiyaki are active victims. They carry a special burden; they are engaged in a specific mission for the redemption of society. They are committed men who espouse a noble cause and pay with their lives to bring salvation to their people. Other victims are either too passive altogether or too lacking in vision and clarity of view about the task to be performed to be interesting, even as victims. Compared with Okolo and Waiyaki, Loyaan (*Sweet and Sour Milk*) is too ensconced in his suffering, subjective soul; Willieboy (*A Walk in the Night*) is too passive in his victim's predicament; and Modin (*Why Are We So Blest?*), too vague in his vision of life. It would be difficult to see to what extent regenerative possibilities exist in their sacrifice. Okolo and Waiyaki are sacrificed, but their campaigns have a certain earnestness about them that ensure that their impact will survive after the victims have been sacrificed. The handling of the theme by Ngugi and Okara is competent, revealing numerous insights and refreshing technical innovations that greatly enrich the novel form.

The Voice

The plot of *The Voice* is very slight. The hero, Okolo (which in Ijaw means "the voice"), after having studied and lived abroad, returns home to the village of Amatu. He is appalled by the moral decay he finds everywhere and, more particularly, by a persuasive and all-pervasive materialism that has corrupted the souls of the people both within the village and in the neighboring town, Sologa of the Big One, and destroyed the people's moral vision of life. Okolo feels called upon to draw attention to his people's moral predicament by going round and asking them if they have got *It*, thereby stimulating moral revival in their lives. He assumes for himself the mantle of reformer, prophet, and messiah, but like all such moral revolutionaries, he antagonizes the corrupt establishment and is, quite predictably, crushed just when his message is beginning to take root.

There is hardly any doubt as to the tradition to which Okara's tale belongs. The moral campaign the hero mounts right from the beginning, the morally dominated atmosphere, and the inside details of the plot point irrevocably not only to an obvious analogy but to a close patterning on the Passion story of the Gospels. In his excellent study *The Novelist and the Passion Story*, F. W. Dillistone writes about such novels:

> The . . . possibility open to the novelist is to write about his contemporary
> world openly and frankly but with the essential pattern of the Passion narrative

forming the inner framework of his own story. It is, of course, impossible for him to do this unless he believes that the successive stages in the recorded life of Jesus do correspond to the general sequence of events which may be traced in the career of every heroic figure who carries out a mission of redemption for his fellow men. Such a mission may be performed by an individual seeking consciously to follow in the steps of the Christ and to fashion his life after the pattern displayed in the Gospels. But not necessarily so. In dedicating himself to the service of his fellows he may almost unconsciously find himself caught up into a sequence of temporary acceptance, growing opposition, rejection, suffering, dereliction, vindication, strangely similar to that which marked the career of Jesus of Nazareth himself.[8]

Though *The Voice* is not as closely patterned on Christ's life as, say, Kazantzakis's *Christ Recrucified*, there is enough of the Passion story in it to justify attention being drawn to the fact. Okolo carries on his moral campaign from a position of moral superiority—he possesses *It* while the people whom he sets out to convert do not possess *It*. He is single-mindedly devoted to his mission in spite of the obvious personal risks involved. His complete commitment to his messianic mission actually contrasts with the different kind of commitment evident in the artist who "puts his shadow into creating faces out of wood"[9]—a kind of creative virtue which, though commendable in itself, is too subjectively centered to have a wide, cleansing impact on the moral environment.

Okolo, like Christ, is the man who cares whereas everyone else is content to let things slide. In a world where everyone else is a comedian (to use Graham Greene's famous distinction), he is the only tragedian. He has an awareness of the extent of moral ruin that has overtaken his society, and he is prepared to risk life and security to assault the forces of darkness. One of Okolo's main targets of attack, like Christ's, is the establishment, which is not only corrupt in itself but corrupts the rest of the people. Chief Izongo and the Elders of Amatu may be correlated with the Scribes and Pharisees; the white colonialist, in charge of the Big One's security service that imprisons Okolo in Sologa, is analogous to Pontius Pilate. We even have the equivalent of Nichodemus in the Elder Tebeowei who comes to Okolo at night, not to learn more about his message, of course, but to persuade him of the futility of his efforts. Okolo's collaborators and converts, the outcast Tuere and the cripple Ukule, could be likened to Christ's humble disciples. Most of the evils denounced by Christ are the same evils deplored by Okolo in the village of Amatu and the town Sologa of the Big One—the leadership of which corrupts the ordinary people by its concupiscence and self-love as well as a general moral laxity distinguished by too much love for material security and too little concern with social morality.

All the main stages in the Passion story are present in Okolo's life— notice that the actual drama of Okolo's moral campaign is very short-lived. As with the story of Christ, the most formative period of the hero's life remains inexplicably shrouded in obscurity. Also, like Christ, Okolo goes through the stages identified by Dillistone—temporary acceptance (because people are beginning to listen to his moral promptings, the autocrats have to move quickly against him), suffering (Okolo has a good deal of this both in the village and in the town), dereliction (the very limit is marked by Okolo's death by drowning, tied with the unfortunate Tuere in a rudderless canoe that drifts from one bank of the river to the other like "debris carried by the current" until drawn into a whirlpool), and vindication: there is more than an ordinary hint that Okolo's mission will triumph over the forces of human tyranny. Ukule the cripple assures Okolo before he is led away that "your spoken words will not die."(*V*,127) But even before this time, a convert to Okolo's viewpoint has said emphatically:

> "Nobody withstands the power of the spoken word. Okolo has spoken. I will speak when the time is correct and others will follow and our spoken words will gather power like the power of a hurricane and Izongo will sway and fall like sugar cane."(*V*,110)

The story leaves no doubt that the cause for which Okolo dies will, in the end, triumph, just as the cause for which the Christ was crucified has since triumphed.

This patterning on the Passion story is interesting, but even more impressive are the means whereby Okara creates for us an overwhelming vision of evil and corruption, the vision of a wholly corrupt environment within which everyday activities are distorted into a dreamlike nightmare comparable only to life in a lunatic asylum. Here is an extract from the incident of Okolo's first arrest:

> Okolo seeing the messengers, recognized them and questioned them. But the men, in spite of their grim faces, opened not their mouths. The remaining crowd hushed. The silence passed silence. The three messengers faced Okolo, opening not their mouths. A man from the back of the crowd pushed his way to the messengers. The four of them put their heads together while with their eyes they looked at Okolo. They put their heads together for a while and walked towards Okolo, as if stalking an animal. And Okolo stood looking. They moved nearer. Okolo stood. They moved nearer and, suddenly, pounced on Okolo. Okolo and the men fell to the ground. Hands clawed at him, a thousand hands, the hands of the world. Okolo twisted free. He ran. Running feet followed. He ran. A million pursuing feet thundered after him. He ran past his house without knowing and ran into another. A woman giving suck to her baby screamed. Out Okolo sprang and ran. The running feet came nearer, the caring nothing feet of the world. Okolo turned a corner and nearly ran into a boy and girl standing with hands holding each other. They did not look at him. He turned a corner. A dog barked at him. Okolo ran. He was now at the ending of the town. Only one hut was left and beyond it the mystery of the forest. Okolo ran and as he ran past, a voice held him. "Come in," it said, "Come in quickly."(*V*,15–16)

In Okolo went, instinctively, and in the gloom stood panting. And here is a description of Okolo's first night in Sologa of the Big One:

> Through the black black night Okolo walked, stumbled, walked. His inside was a room with chairs, cushions, papers scattered all over the floor by thieves. Okolo walked, stumbled, walked. His eyes shut and opened, shut and opened, expecting to see a light in each opening, but none he saw in the black black night.
>
> At last the black black night like the back of a cooking pot entered his inside and grabbing his thoughts, threw them out into the blacker than black night. And Okolo walked, stumbled, walked with an inside empty of thoughts except the black black night.
>
> When Okolo came to know himself, he was lying on a floor, on a cold floor lying. He opened his eyes to see but nothing he saw, nothing he saw. For the darkness was evil darkness and the outside night was black black night. Okolo lay still in the darkness enclosed by darkness, and he his thoughts picked his inside. Then his picked thoughts his eyes opened but his vision only met a rock-like darkness. The picked thoughts then drew his legs but his legs did not come. They were as heavy as a canoe full of sand. His thoughts in his inside began to fly in his inside darkness like frightened birds hither, thither, home-less. Then the flying thoughts drew his hands but the hands did not belong to him, it seemed. So Okolo on the cold cold floor lay with his body as soft as an over-pounded foofoo. So Okolo lay with his eyes open wide in the rock-like darkness staring, staring.
>
> Okolo for years and years lay on the cold cold floor at the rock-like darkness staring. Then suddenly he saw a light. He drew his hands and his hands came. He stood up with his eyes on the light and walked towards the light. As he moved towards the light, the light also moved back. He moved faster and the light also moved faster. Okolo ran and the light also ran. Okolo ran, the light ran. Okolo ran and hit a wall with his head. Okolo looked and the light was no more. He then stretched his hands forth and touched the wall. His fingers felt dents and holes. Okolo walked sideways like a crab with his fingers on the wall, feeling dents and holes, dents and holes in the rock-like darkness until his feet struck an object. As Okolo stopped and felt the object his body became cold. His heart-beat echoed in the rock-like darkness and his head expanded. Still, he felt along the object until his fingers went into two holes. As his fin-gers went into the holes he quickly withdrew them and ran. He ran and fell, ran and fell over other objects. He ran and knocked against the wall and fell. Still he ran, then suddenly stopped. He saw a light in front of him. He moved gently crouching forward like a hunter stalking game. Then when he nearly reached the light, he rushed forward.(*V*,84–86)

These two passages have been selected because they illustrate the quality, range, and variety of Okara's art. In fact, what is most striking about them is the careful, deliberate manner in which Okara works the different rhetorical devices into a sustained and singularly successful medium to convey the peculiar experience we find in *The Voice*. Okara's art would reward study because he is easily the most "artificial" of all West African writers. We use the word *artificial* in connection with Okara's style in the word's old and modern connotations of "having constructive skill" or art and as the opposite to "natural."

The most outstanding feature of Okara's art is his reiterative rhetoric, his repetition of single words, phrases, sentences, images, or symbols to produce diverse emphatic effects. Notice, for example, the mood suggested in the first passage by the repetition of "Okolo stood" and "They moved nearer." It is as if Okolo were fixed on the spot under a hypnotic spell while his sinister adversaries make their sharp, furtive moves, full of menace and danger to the hero. The image already suggested in "as if stalking an animal" is fully justified by what happens. In the very next lines the sinister, nightmarish quality of the episode is reinforced by vividly described physical activities. The assailants "pounce" on Okolo and a struggle ensues.

Nightmare is the only word that adequately describes the physical sensation of "a thousand hands" and "the hands of the world" that claw at Okolo as he "twisted," "struggled," and "kicked" at his four adversaries. To Okolo, the hands of four men in that brief and silent struggle produce the sensation of "a thousand hands"—the reader feels this sensation, just as he feels the sensation of being pursued by a million "thundering" feet in the dark silent night. Because the drama is so vivid, so concrete the reader feels that he is Okolo, sees things through Okolo's haunted eyes, experiences the thrill of horror that Okolo experiences when the four silent men suddenly pounce on him, and when the whole crowd begins to pursue him in the dark.

The reiteration of the action in short dramatic sentences like "Okolo ran," reinforced by clearly hyperbolic expressions like "a million pursuing feet" give rise to a terrifying concrete physical sensation that is felt in the very marrow. Notice also Okara's method of giving concreteness to the action by the repetition of the proper name rather than the personal pronoun—"Okolo stood," "Okolo twisted," "Out Okolo sprang," "Okolo turned a corner," "Okolo ran."

The use of reiteration to give physical concreteness to a situation is even more developed in the second passage. Here, the reiteration of "black" imbues the darkness of the night with a near-tactile quality in expressions like "black black night," "black night like the back of a cooking pot," "the blacker than black night." The sinister nature of the darkness is very much heightened by its being raised to a physical sensation. In fact, the symbol of "darkness" is so pervasive, not only in this passage but also in the rest of the narrative, that the atmosphere of the story could be said to be completely dominated by it. Light appears intermittently and merely helps to emphasize the darkness, not to dispel it.

The reiterative image of darkness in this passage is particularly effective, especially as it is further reinforced by Okara's invocation of the horrific in terms of the human senses—eyes trying to pierce an impenetrable darkness, hands and feet that refuse to move in one moment and then shoot out in a singly automatic movement in the next, the groping of the fingers into dents and holes, the crablike movement, the head knocking on the wall, the body becoming cold, the heartbeat echoing, the head expanding, the running and falling—all these physical actions and sensations, which are given great vividness, assume a dreamlike, nightmarish quality because they take place in the dark.

Now this evocation of horror and nightmare would have been a point of weakness in Okara's art, mere sensation-mongering, if it had been indulged in for its own sake. But it is not. It provides a superb background to the serious moral issues with which Okara is dealing in the novel. This is not a normal world but one that has been terribly distorted by evil and corruption. The very prospect of living in it assumes an aspect of physical danger and spiritual terror, especially for the only man who is courageous enough to challenge its standards of morality, its rotten values, as well as the invidious forces that dominate it.

Of course, the story is a parable with the universal theme of man's indomitable struggle against the evils of spiritual oppression and social corruption, as the blurb says, but we can only derive the maximum of its rich moral significance by apprehending it on the levels of both particularity and generality, and on the literal and symbolical levels, because each level tends to reinforce the other. To realize his theme of "good versus evil," Okara has had to build up the physical aspect of his environment, a horrific and nightmarish environment, within which we feel, through physical sensations, the oppressive presence of evil, as well as the heroic suffering and torment of a soul implicit in the hero who campaigns against it. Thus the theme has both universal significance as well as a contemporary application: the novel's setting is both the world and an African country in which dictators have set up police states and destroyed their people's liberties. Okara's reiterative rhetoric makes real the physical implications of the moral problem and quite effectively represents the moral situation through physical action and physical sensations. But there is more to it than that.

Okara brings his poetical gifts to bear on his choice of images and symbols. He uses metaphors, similes, and other figures of speech to give concreteness and body to the heavily oppressive moral environment he builds up. By such devices even the most abstract notions are reduced to physical realities. Okara is, in this sense, more than any other West African novelist, a materialist, because he attempts to reduce actions, feelings, and sensations to material or physical realities. This tendency in Okara's technique can be regarded as a process of "reification"; the process of giving the quality of "thingness" to mental and abstract constructs. Okara, for example, describes Okolo's confusion of mind in the dark room by likening it to "a room with chairs, cushions, papers scattered all over the floor by thieves"; Okolo's "thoughts in his inside began to fly in his inside darkness like frightened birds hither, thither, homeless." There is an example of the use of synecdoche to give concreteness to the squalid moral outlook in the town of Sologa: "So Okolo walked in Sologa of the Big One passing frustrated eyes, ground-looking eyes, harlot's eyes, despairing eyes, nothing-caring eyes, dust-filled eyes, aping eyes. . . ."(*V*,90) Only by evolving a consistent style with its own inner logic can Okara make "eyes" do duty for him in this bold unconventional manner.

The process of reification in *The Voice* is greatly enhanced by the rhythm of Okara's prose, the rhythm of words spun under the immediate pressure of what is being done, felt, or suffered. When accompanied by Okara's reiterative rhetoric, this can enhance dramatic immediacy as well as fix impressions in a concrete and vivid way. The tremendous power of the second passage is the result of Okara's ability to capture the rhythm of action and of physical sensation through common everyday words that thus acquire sensuous and sinister overtones—words like "dents," "holes," "the thing." What gives ordinary, innocent words like these their quality of creeping terror is the context in which they occur, and the way they are woven into the hero's movement in the dark. When the hero's fingers, for instance, enter into the "two holes" and he immediately withdraws them, we feel without really knowing why that we are in a room where there are human skeletons. We are chilled and experience horror and revulsion along with the hero. Perhaps the term that best describes Okara's ability to produce physical sensations and attendant emotions by manipulating words, actions, and the rhythm of language is T. S. Eliot's famous phrase, "objective correlative."[10] The accumulation of physical sensations and emotions fixes our moral reaction to the issues the writer has so clearly stripped bare before us.

The main impulse in *The Voice* seems to derive from the oral tradition, especially the folktale. Okara's rhetoric, more especially his deliberate repetitions, his metaphoric and hyperbolic elaborations, and his colloquial rhythms, belong essentially to that tradition. The ghoulish and the nightmarish, which are so well developed in *The Voice*, are the regular features of the folktale. Okara's interest in the Ijaw oral tradition goes much further than any other novelist's, for Okara, of all the writers, attempts to reproduce not only literal meanings from the vernacular (as is evident in expressions like "Okolo had no chest," "he had no shadow," "all his inside," "with all his shadow"), but also actual syntactical forms in sentences: "Who are you people be?" "If you are coming in people be, then come in." Even the process of reification already noted may have been derived by Okara from the vernacular, since it is quite well-developed in West African languages.

It has been suggested that Okara wrote the story in "ordinary English" and then as an experiment translated it into "this medium." This may well be so, but it is equally true that Okara's experiment with language and imagery in *The Voice* was clearly foreshadowed in his poetry. We find in *The Mystic DRUM*, for instance, expressions like "in my inside," "with their shadows," "the eye of the sky," and this sustained image: "and smoke issued from her nose and her lips parted in her smile turned cavity belching darkness,"[11] which may have prepared the way for the dominant symbol of darkness in *The Voice*. Another poem, "Adhiambo," suggests the theme of *The Voice*. The opening lines read:

> "I hear many voices
> Like it's said a madman hears;
> I hear trees talking
> Like it's said a medicine man hears.
> Maybe I'm a madman,
> I'm a medicine man.
> Maybe I'm mad,
> For the voices are luring me,
> Urging me from the midnight
> Noon and the silence of my desk
> To walk on wave crests across a sea." [12]

The hero of *The Voice* is also a visionary and is said by the people to be a madman. What is being hinted at here is that *The Voice* is, perhaps, the sublimation in prose fiction of Okara's poetical visions of his mission, through literary creativeness, to reform and purify society. The poet-reformer will bring out of his creative imagination the full image of the appalling corruption of society, so that all those who see this image will be shocked into a mood of moral revival. Thus, the real key to why Okolo is a Christlike rather than a Promethean hero may actually lie in the fact that Okara conceived him essentially as a poet-reformer and not as a political revolutionary, as a man who appeals to the soul and the finer faculties and emotions of people rather than one who stirs their emotions into revolutionary violence. Okara gives us in a very vivid way a terrifying picture of society completely corrupted by totalitarianism and extreme materialism, but his moral positive remains vague, veiled in elusive poetic suggestion. The *It* is the quality of moral excellence the autocrats have emasculated in their subjects: "For him it has no name. Names bring divisions and divisions strife. So let it be without a name: let it be nameless."(*V*,112)

The novel is sometimes criticized for taking a too rigid moral stance. But this criticism is hardly fair. As a parabolic tale whose effect depends on a certain rigidity of moral positions, the novel may be excused for adopting a one-sided moral outlook to bear out the theme of the tale.

The River Between

In *The River Between*, the protagonist is another messianic bringer of salvation to his people. Under the pressure of European settler imperialism, which alienates the land from the people, the rift between the Christian converts and the Gikuyu Council of Elders deepens into a chasm of distrust and antipathies. In the prevailing climate of zealotry, fanaticism, and funda-mentalism, the people are hopelessly divided. Assuming the mantle of redeemer and teacher, Waiyaki attempts through modern education, love, and tolerance to bridge the rift and reconcile the people. However, at the critical moment, he forgets that the real cause of the pain in the hearts of the people is their loss of their independence and right to their land. His efforts to unite the people fail, and he is rejected by Christians and traditionalists alike. He is brought to trial, convicted by the people's assembly, and handed over to the Council of Elders to face execution for breaking his oath of loyalty to the people.

Two perspectives are presented in this narrative: the traditional and the Christian perspectives. Each is essential to the action. The Gikuyu community is a traditional community, but Christianity has since been introduced there and has become part of its total reality. The writer's perception of the action in this novel, therefore, necessarily takes account of this reality in advancing the themes and sharpening the focus of action. The perspectives explain the dilemma of the protagonist, whose education and consciousness have been conditioned by both tradition and Christianity.

In presenting the traditional perspective, myths and legends are deeply drawn upon to provide a support for the framework of action. The world is viewed through the myth of its origin and the legends of its continuity; its foundation is set firmly and rooted in the land which, to the agrarian Gikuyu, is the most important factor of life:

> Murungu brought the man and woman here and . . . showed them the whole vastness, the land. He gave the country to them and their children and the children of the children, *tene na tene*, world without end. . . . From here, Murungu took them and put them under Mukuruwe wa Gathaog'a. There our father and mother had nine daughters who bore more children. The children spread all over the country. Some came to the ridges to keep and guard the ancient rites.[13]

People are strengthened in their lives and actions by their myths. The Gikuyu's attachment to the land is total. Land is a force drawing them to their deepest aspirations, to their origins and roots; it is hallowed by its being harnessed to their fundamental myth. When, therefore, later in the narrative it becomes clear that Waiyaki has missed the point that his people's relationship to the land is a special one, and a very emotional one, it becomes equally clear that he has missed one of the life-sustaining truths concerning the Gikuyu and is bound on a course of defeat.

Next only in importance to the myth of origin and creation is the myth of a prophecy, an ancient belief that in some unspecified future some strangers would come to Gikuyuland and would break the people and their way of life apart: "There shall come a people with clothes like butterflies. . . ." But the prophecy also predicted that a savior would arise from among the people who would rescue the people from their invaders. The existence of prophecy assumes the appearance of prophets and interpreters, or seers or sages, who reiterate the old idea or explain it to the masses to give it perpetuitive validity. Waiyaki's credential as leader is based on his being of the line of these seers and prophets. His father, Chege, reminds him of his special destiny, which is rooted in tradition:

> Now, listen my son. Listen carefully, for this is the ancient prophecy. . . . I could not do more. When the white man came and fixed himself in Siriana, I warned all the people. But they laughed at me. Maybe I was hasty. Perhaps I was not the one. Mugo often said you could not cut the butterflies with a panga. You could not spear them until you learnt and knew their ways and movement. Then you could trap, you could fight back. Before he died, he whispered to his son the prophecy, the ancient prophecy: "Salvation shall come from the hills. From the blood that flows in me, I say from the same tree, a son shall rise. And his duty shall be to lead and save the people!"(RB,24)

The coming of the missionaries and the white settlers in their wake is regarded by Chege as the fulfillment of the first part of the prophecy—the arrival in Kikuyuland of "a people with clothes like butterflies." The fulfillment of the second part Chege places on the shoulders of Waiyaki, his son, who is the last of the line of the much revered Mugo wa Kabiro. Considerable space is devoted in *The River Between* to establishing the credentials of Waiyaki as a redeemer; he comes from the right place and is the proper scion.

The induction of Waiyaki into traditional life is accomplished through the rites of passage and incorporation, with the circumcision rites as climax. These rites, in addition to providing great avenues for communion through musical celebrations and dancing, offer a severe test of courage and endurance. But, even more importantly, they provide the foretaste of the sacrifice the individual may be called upon to make at any future stage in the furtherance of the people's destiny. In a number of unobtrusive authorial remarks, we are informed that the shedding of the individual's blood during the process of circumcision is a sacrificial act, prefiguring, perhaps, the demands the land will require of initiates in promoting the collective heritage, and signifying the offering of the circumcised victims to the service of the tribe and its interests, and the preservation of its code. On Waiyaki's circumcision the author comments: "Blood trickled freely on the ground, sinking into the soil. Henceforth a religious bond linked Waiyaki to the earth, as if his blood was an offering."(RB,52–53) And much later we read: "To her left was open ground where the candidates for circumcision went to shed their blood. Muthoni too had come here on the morning of her sacrifice."(RB,132)

It is necessary to draw attention to this matter of circumcision, sacrifice, and the preservation of the tribe because it helps us to appreciate the importance of the circumcision rites in the polarization of the relationship between Christians, who abominate these rites and exclude those from their membership who go through them, and traditionalists, who reject anyone who might decide not to undergo the rites. Circumcision for the traditionalists is a pact of blood in furtherance of the social, economic, and cultural life of the tribe; and, since the intention of the Christians is to transcend this life, there is no better strategy than for them to strike at the heart of the traditional life by destroying circumcision rites.

Ngugi presents tradition as having a validity that ensures its continuity; within it are contained the vitality and power that secure its survival and perpetuity. Thus, with the extension of the settlers' power into the hills and ridges and the people suffering "the bite of injustice," and with the campaign by Christians against tradition becoming serious, people constitute a revivalist Kiama "to preserve the purity of our tribal customs and our way of life."(*RB*,95) When serious events require the mobilization of the emotional solidarity of the people, the people's assembly is a great force and tribunal that resolves great issues of social survival. The true strength of the traditional system is demonstrated in times of emergency when the mobilization of its psychological forces has taken place. At such moments, the operators of the system who recognize the trigger-points of its peculiar energy press those points and release their concealed vitality.

Oath taking is one of the means adopted by traditionalists to galvanize the emotional vitality of tradition, a means of unifying the response of the people and linking their contemporary conditions to the past and future destiny of the race. Circumcision rites integrate individuals into the traditional system, but an oath binds the same individuals emotionally and psychologically to the society's aspirations in a pact of life and death. The collective oath is the people's highest covenant, their call to their members to keep faith with the things that give cohesion to their lives and provide continuity of action and aspirations to past, present, and future generations.

Waiyaki's attitude to the oath, as also his inability to realize the significance of land to the Gikuyu, shows him as very ill-informed in the ways of the tribe and poorly equipped to survive within it. When his friend and colleague Kinuthia warns him that oaths are being administered in his name, he does not see at once how that shows that his work as the teacher of his people is being assimilated into the collective consciousness of the tribe, and when he lets the people down by appearing to go over to their enemies by aspiring to marry Nyambura, Joshua's daughter who is uncircumcised, he is somewhat bewildered at the virulence of the same people's rejection and anger. The people who idolize him for bringing education to their children now bellow, "The Oath! The Oath!" at him, with anguish and bitterness in their voices. But Kinuthia's warning had clearly prefigured both responses:

> Be careful, Waiyaki. You know the people look up to you. You are the symbol of the tribe, born again with all its purity. They adore you. They worship you. You do not know about the new oath in your name. In the name of the Teacher and the purity of the tribe. And remember Kabonyi hates, hates you. He would kill you if he could. And he is the one who is doing all this. Why? The Kiama has power. Power. And your name is in it, giving it greater power. Your name will be your ruin.(*RB*,127–28)

Waiyaki is in the end not careful enough, for to be careful in the circumstances is to adhere to the principles of action, as well as to satisfy the codes, mores, and conventions of the traditional system. It would mean sacrificing Waiyaki's personal aspirations, including his love for the Christian Nyambura. It would mean allowing the extremists in the Kiama to bear down on the Christians and probably create great devastation and unhappiness. Waiyaki's regret that he ever resigned from the Kiama, which left the field open to Kabonyi and the diehards, shows how little he understood of the traditional system before the truth came to him, too late, on the eve of his tragic defeat.

It is speculated, and with substantial justification, that Waiyaki's inadequate integration in the traditonal system is a result of his upbringing early in life in Livingstone's Siriana mission school. It is suggested that as a result of his Siriana background, he underwent incipient alienation from tradition that never leaves him to the end. It blurs his sensitivity to the demands of tradition.

Ngugi's perspective on Christianity is not as fully elaborated as the traditional perspective. This is not at all surprising. The vast majority of the Gikuyu are traditionalists, compared with the few who have only recently been converted to Christianity. The framework of the action is, therefore, largely the traditional system. Christianity plays around the fringes of the traditional system and disturbs its inner harmony and stability, but it cannot replace it altogether and so cannot claim the same attention as the former.

The Christianity presented in this novel is redemptive and is explored through Joshua and his partisans. Every one of these adherents accepts the redemptive importance of the Christ as the main ideological prop. Every one is also determined to achieve deliverance not only from personal sins but also from contamination through the ways of the tribe, which are considered sinful. Joshua's is a religion of faith mixed with self-righteousness; it is a fighting religion whose interest lies in supplanting of the ways of the tribe. It is therefore an overzealous religion bound on a collision course between its members, "the people of Joshua," and its enemies, "the people of the tribe." But the redemptive strand in its ideology remains a great inspiration to the less volatile of its adherents.

Waiyaki absorbs its messianic impulse during his education in the Siriana mission. Ironically enough, his admission into that school is engineered by Chege, his traditionalist father, as part of what he envisages as the necessary preparation of Waiyaki for his messianic role: "Arise. Heed the prophecy. Go to the mission place. Learn all the wisdom and all the secrets of the white man. But do not follow his vices. Be true to your people and the ancient rites."(RB,24)

Like Ezeulu in Achebe's *Arrow of God*, this move to steal the enemy's thunder is doomed to defeat for it is not easy to acquire the white man's skills and knowledge without assimilating some of the white man's attitudes and values.

Consequences arise from Waiyaki's exposure at the Siriana mission school. Firstly, the Siriana connection provides Waiyaki with a model upon which to build his messianic vision: "The element of love and sacrifice agreed with his own temperament. The suffering Christ in the Garden of Gethsemane and His agony on the tree had always moved him."(*RB*,114) He recognizes the merits as well as the weaknesses of Christianity and is prepared to build a bridge between it and traditional religion—and between its adherents and those of the traditional religion:

> Waiyaki knew that not all the ways of the white man were bad. Even his religion was not essentially bad. Some good, truth shone through it. But the religion, the truth, needed washing, clearing away all the dirt, leaving only the eternal. And that eternal that was the truth had to be reconciled to the traditions of the people.(*RB*,162)

This quest for the reconciliation of extremes remains the most positive aspect of Waiyaki's messianic career. Where Joshua and his adherents pursue their single-minded path of puritanism and fundamentalism, Waiyaki, no less than Joshua's two daughters, Muthoni and Nyambura, pursues a course of integrating the traditional and the Christian worlds. And Ngugi seems to suggest, at this stage at any rate, that this reconciliation is necessary to avert a terrible tragedy built upon intolerance. It is significant that all three people who share the vision of reconciliation are sacrificed. It is also significant that all three find sustaining comfort in the life and sacrifice of the Christ.

The convergence of the traditional and Christian impulses in the defining of Waiyaki's mission of redemption is possible because Ngugi devotes considerable effort to describing them and how they shape the messianic temperament of the protagonist. It is clear, however, that even though greater comprehensiveness is achieved in exploring the traditional background of the action, the decisive messianic inspiration seems to have come from the brief formative Christian influence of the Siriana mission school. It is, in the final analysis, with Christ that Waiyaki identifies himself and not with Mugo wa Kabiro and the Gikuyu seers in his attempt to "lead the tribe to light."(*RB*,125)

Waiyaki builds his strategy for redeeming the people upon modern education and pursues it singlemindedly. Much is done to show evidence of his success in building schools and infecting his people with his enthusiasm for education. But, alas, he forgets to build into the content of this education, and to preach at the appropriate moment, the lesson of tolerance and love. From this point of view, success in the educational experiment turns into defeat when the very people, who idolize the Teacher, in the end reject the Redeemer. The failure of the educational vision finally compromises the task of redemption.

One aspect of *The River Between* deserves to be spotlighted. It is Ngugi's successful use of setting to focus the mainlines of narrative development. The ridges and hills, sacred trees, and the Honia River are given concrete existence in the narrative by their being related to the internal details of the story. But, even more significantly, the physical features define the rhythms of action and aid plot development. Thus, when the ridges and hills are in a relative state of stability, which corresponds to the state of relative peace among the people, the features are likened to "sleeping lions." The graphic analogy is convincing. And when the life of the region is disturbed, the sleeping lions are said to be awakened. The metaphoric extension is worthy of note, but there is also another sense in which a literal condition should be inferred. The spread of education across the hills and ridges, the conflict between the converts and the Christians and the alienating of the Gikuyu land right up to the ridges and the hills by the settlers, these appear to disturb the atmosphere physically and to increase the tempo of the crisis that plunges the people into tragedy. The landscape is peaceful and almost without people when the hills and ridges are described as "sleeping lions." But a certain restlessness and constant human movement results when the lions are awake. The effectiveness of this novel is a result of Ngugi's successful integration of setting, character, and selected myths and legends which are fused into a well-condensed statement on the theme of victimization.

Next to the uniqueness of setting is the uniqueness of Ngugi's use of language in *The River Between*. Commentators have noted with justification the simple, colloquial rhythm of the novel's language. Others have accurately called this use biblical. The fact is that the virtue of a language used simply but to a profoundly great effect cannot be lost on the reader. Here, for example, are two passages taken from the great debate at the people's assembly when the protagonist, Waiyaki, and the antagonist, Kabonyi, first bare their swords publicly and set the stage for that which, in the end, will consume the hero:

> He [Kabonyi] reminded them of the poverty of the land. The dry months had left the people with nothing to eat. And the expected harvest would not yield much. He touched on the land taken by the white man. He talked of the new taxes being imposed on the people by the government post now in their midst. And instead of Waiyaki leading people against these more immediate ills, he was talking of more buildings. Were people going to be burdened with more buildings? With more teachers? And was the white man's education really necessary? Surely there was another way out. It was better to drive away the white man from the hills altogether. Were the people afraid? Were there no warriors left in the tribe? He, Kabonyi, would lead them. That was why he had formed the new Kiama. He would rid the country of the influence of the white man. He would restore the purity of the tribe and its wisdom.(*RB*,109)

> Then he Waiyaki opened his mouth and began to speak. And his voice was like the voice of his father—no—it was like the voice of the great Gikuyu of old. Here again was the saviour, the one whose words touched the souls of the people. People listened and their hearts moved with the vibration of his voice. And he, like a shepherd speaking to his flock, avoided any words that might be insulting. In any case, how could he repudiate Kabonyi's argument? Waiyaki

told them that he was their son. They all were his parents. He did not want to lead. The elders were there to guide and lead the youth. And youth had to listen. It had to be led in the paths of wisdom. He, Waiyaki, would listen. All he wanted was to serve the ridges, to serve the hills. They could not stand aloof. They could never now remain isolated. Unless the people heeded his words and plans, the ridges would lose their former dignity and would be left a distance behind by the country beyond. . . .(*RB*,110)

We observe that the two speakers use their words simply. They are the words of everyday speech. But we are also aware that the matters at issue are deadly serious. They touch upon the things which affect the collective well-being, things like poverty, drought, imperialism and its expulsion, the problem of leadership, and the question of age and experience in the determination of a leader. The words are simple but the questions touch the very fundamentals of the community's life and survival. We can, even within this limited context, discern certain essential differences in the characters of the two speakers. One speaks almost demagogically, to score points and win arguments; the other speaks in a way that "touched the souls of people." One speaks rhetorically, using numerous questions that suggest their answers to the audience; the other speaks plainly and with candor. One man is a politician; the other, a redeemer.

This use of the language of everyday speech in very clearly and precisely structured movements around serious and fundamental issues of life and death is Ngugi's fictional asset. It is what helps most to create the sacrificial atmosphere of this novel. Everything is kept understated through the low profile of the language. There are no big speeches, full of high-blown, emotion-saturated phrases. Adjectival and adverbial elaborations, which add intensity, are kept to the minimum. The appeal is to common sense and, through common sense, to the common good and the common destiny of a people unified by their traditions, myths, and mystical environment. The lack of linguistic excitement is not a result of the absence of linguistic vitality but the conception of language as a means of making contact with the rational and deeper levels of people's responses. At the end of this spoken encounter, the justness of the position of the Teacher is established and collectively endorsed. The demagogue is temporarily defeated, though he lives to fight and win another day.

What sort of people are victimized? They are often individuals who evince certain qualities of independence and openly or implicitly threaten the custodians of tradition and the maintainers of the status quo. The elders, the priests, the oracular class, and all those who constitute the ruling class of the communal society have a stake in keeping the system pure from the virus of subversive questioning. People who manifest independence sooner or later find themselves accused of some demonstrable crime against the gods and are, in the nature of things, sacrificed as victims, so that the communal social order can go on undisturbed.

The victimization of Shanka, the strongest son of the tribe, and Goaa, who indoctrinates him, and Ukutee, who allows her personal passions to vindicate her individuality, has its roots in their having been "inhibited" (a more modern word would be "alienated") from tradition by their contact with the new subversive ideas based on the mystique of "the Word." The victimization of Okolo, the visionary quester after moral excellence, becomes inevitable when he attacks the corrupt values of post-independence African dictators. And that of Waiyaki results from his assuming a redemptive leadership role in opposition to the ambitions and intrigues of powerful elders.

These authors' handling of the theme of victimization varies considerably from play to play and from novel to novel, but they share one dominant attitude in common. That attitude is ambivalence. They see the sacrifice of victims as logical to the communal system and to certain types of human situations, but their sympathies lie always with the victims and the victims' struggles to defend the flicker they carry within themselves, which is indeed the light of their own lives.

NOTES

1. See E. N. Obiechina, "Africa in the Soul of Dispersed Children: West African Literature from the Era of the Slave Trade," *Nsukka Studies in African Literature* 4 (January 1986): 101–60. This essay deals with the memoirs, reminiscences and autobiographical fragments of Ayuba Suleiman of Bondu, Salih Bilali, Abu Bakr al-Siddiq, Ali Eisami, Samuel Crowther, and James Wright, in *Africa Remembered: Narratives by West Africans from the Era of the Slave Trade*, ed. Philip D. Curtin (Madison, 1967); "Autobiography of Omar Ibn Said, Slave in North Carolina, 1831," *American Historical Review* 30 (1984):789–95; *Letters of the Late Ignatius Sancho, An African* (London, 1783); Ottobah Cugoano, *Thoughts and Sentiments on the Evil and Wicked Traffic of Slavery and Commerce of the Human Species* (London, 1787); Phillis Wheatley, *Poems on Various Subjects, Religious and Moral* (London and Boston, 1773); James Albert Ukawsaw-Gronniosaw, *A Narrative of the Remarkable particulars in the Life of James Albert Ukawsaw-Gronniosaw: An African Prince, Written by Himself* (Bath, 1774); Olaudah Equiano, *The Interesting Narrative of the Life of Olaudah Equiano or Gustavus Vassa, the African, Written by Himself* (London, 1789); Venture Smith, *A Narrative of the Life of Venture, A Native of Africa, but Resident above sixty years in the United States of America, related by Himself* (New London, 1835).

2. Alex La Guma, *A Walk in the Night* (London, 1968), 48.

3. Wole Soyinka, *Death and the King's Horseman* (London, 1975), 5–6. Subsequent references to this work are cited as *DKH* in the text.

4. Tsegaye Gabre-Medhin, *Oda-Oak Oracle* (London, 1965), 41. Subsequent references to this work are cited as *OO* in the text.

5. Wole Soyinka, *The Strong Breed* in *Collected Plays I & II* (London, 1974), 118. Subsequent references to this work are cited as *CP* in the text.

6. J. Bronowski, *The Face of Violence* (Cleveland, 1967), 15–16.

7. Frantz Fanon, *Black Skin, White Masks*, tr. Charles Lam Markmann (New York, 1967), 145.

8. F. W. Dillistone, *The Novelist and the Passion Story* (London, 1960), 19–20.

9. Gabriel Okara, *The Voice* (London, 1964), 84. Subsequent references to this work are cited as *V* in the text.

10. T. S. Eliot, *Selected Prose*, ed. John Hayward (London, 1932, 1969), 107–8.

11. Gerald Moore and Ulli Beier, eds., *Modern Poetry from Africa* (Harmondsworth, England, 1963), 123–24.

12. Ibid., 124–25.

13. Ngugi wa Thiong'o, *The River Between* (London, 1965), 21. Subsequent references to this work are cited as *RB* in the text.

CHAPTER 8

Nsukka: Literature
in an African Environment

POSSESSION OF LITERATURE, written or oral, modern or traditional, is one of the distinguishing characteristics of Homo sapiens. There are no people anywhere in the world who, in the course of their evolving an integrated social life in their encounter with their environment, have failed to develop structurally organized rhetorical modes for giving expression to their emotional impulses and for verbalizing, in rhythmic sequences, their deepest human aspirations. There are no people who have not been able to dramatize, in symbolic and aesthetic terms, the major ritual, religious, and secular events of their collectively shared experiences. Possession of literature strongly supports the sense of individual identity as well as reinforces the attachment of individuals to the community. It supplies the emotional matrix that cements the reciprocal interaction of the individual with community and community with the individual.

This could hardly be otherwise; for, in its widest functional context, literature guarantees for a community a certain stabilization of its structures of action. It helps the community to clarify its basic ideas of morality, its sense of what constitutes the beautiful, the sublime, and the comical in human affairs. It offers individuals in society their best scope for expressing their feelings of joy and sorrow, their triumphs and defeats, their heightened appreciation of their vital forces no less than the depths of tragic pathos into which they occasionally fall in their full realization of their vulnerability as human beings. All this is of significance in the discussion of literary experience in the Nsukka country in the eastern part of Nigeria.

The people of Nsukka participate, in full measure, in the creative awareness which literature brings, whether by way of its defining for them the limits of the achievements of the human imagination or of revealing to them, forcefully and dramatically, the nature of life itself, its numerous and intractable dilemmas, its paradoxes, and the ambivalences that surround man from his birth to his death.

The environment of Nsukka provides a great impulse toward literary creativity: its breathtaking scenic beauty, its round green hills that roll away from the observer's view until they embrace the distant skyline, revealing in this embrace exquisitely formed breasts of the earth-mother goddess; its enchanting sunsets splashed over with known and unknown colors—from the deep, rusty yellow that forms a halo round the hills to the multiply tinged red and orange mix that hangs down like a magic tapestry between the hills; surmounting the riot of colors is the majestic sun itself, huge, round, like a ball of fire. Divinity and mystery are compounded here to create a thing of grandeur and primeval fear.

Geography and history play their part also in making Nsukka a unique creative center. And herein exists a real paradox. Nsukka is in the northern fringe of Igboland and yet, in terms of its cultural commitments and artistic loyalties, it seems more central than the so-called Igbo heartland.[1] Cultural practices that have since decayed or been superseded in the heartland still continue to survive in a vigorous state within the Nsukka environment. Songs and dances that formed part of the lost repertoire of Igbo artistic tradition survive here. Above all, the cyclical festivals, with their attendant rituals and communal drama, which have long been undermined by an aggressive, proselytising Christianity in most of Igboland, have survived here and remain a vibrant phenomenon of the environment. The integrated humanism of traditional Igboland has been better preserved here than anywhere else. The pastoral simplicity that characterized that tradition in the past has been less eroded in this environment than elsewhere, where a high-swinging and seductive materialism has already subverted the peasant virtues of traditional life.

The physical setting of Nsukka offers a plausible explanation. Characterized by chains of rounded hills that helm in fertile plains that look like food bowls, the ecological formations strongly enhance the preservation of cultural identity. Each bowl provides arable farmlands; while brows of hills provide easily defended and stockaded settlements. Each community in this environment is therefore very much aware of its peculiar solidarities and identity.

Two contrastive outlooks have developed as a result: namely, an attitude of neighborliness as well as robust independence. These outlooks in combination prove highly conducive to cultural development and artistic (including literary) creativity. Numerous cultural expressions, whether in the form of songs, music, dance, literature, drama, narrative, painting, plastic arts, or costumery, are attracted to the Nsukka "bowls" and are trapped and preserved there long after they have elsewhere receded into limbo. In that respect, Nsukka offers the best chance for cultural/artistic retrieval to anyone who intends to document the dying cultural and artistic traditions of Igboland.

Historically, also, the border situation of Nsukka and the frequent incursions there by warlike, horse-riding neighbors to the north and west, gave rise to a tenacious and lively cultural nationalism which the people of Nsukka used to oppose their invaders and to assert their independence and autonomy. Cultural and artistic expressions have, for this reason, remained vigorous in this region of Igboland.

The third factor of creativity in the Nsukka environment arose out of an ordinary accident. The siting of Nigeria's second university within the Nsukka region is one of those lucky events that seem to transform the history and destiny of peoples. When the founders of the institution took a fancy to Nsukka, its cultural and artistic uniqueness was probably the furthest thing from their minds. What was probably more obvious at the time must have been the beautiful scenery of the region or the general coolness of its climate, which sharply contrasts with the climate of other parts of eastern Nigeria. No sooner, however, was the university established than the creative, new works pouring out of Nsukka began to arrest the attention of commentators on African literature. They began to identify what was vaguely referred to as the "Nsukka School of Poetry," while to other observers, the center of literary creativity in Nigeria was shifting from Ibadan to Nsukka.

What is incontestable, however, is that there has been an upsurge of literary creativity at the University of Nigeria, Nsukka, as a result of a combination of auspicious coincidences, including the convergence there of a number of highly talented and creative minds soon after the opening of the institution, the deliberate promotion of creativity within the English academic program, and the stimulating nature of the Nsukka environment itself, with its inspiring scenery and the vigorous cultural and artistic activities still going on in the region and quickening the imagination with the touch of their magic. It is not too much to assert that the establishment of the University of Nigeria at Nsukka brought into being a new dimension of creativity that registered most emphatically in the abundance and fine quality of creative literature that emerged from that region. The reciprocal relationship of the university and its environment will be explored further in due course; but for the moment, it is enough to state that the blending of traditional cultural and artistic creativity with modern creativity has given rise to one of the most exciting developments in the literary and artistic history of Nigeria.

THE TRADITIONAL SETTING

Various forms of oral literature have existed in Nsukka from time immemorial and have survived more or less authentically to the present time. The most ubiquitous of these forms are the folktale and animal fable, which constitute a domestic medium through which the basic realities of the environment, including the moral values of the community, are transmitted to the young. Whether in form of fireside narratives at mother's hearth or as village-arena entertainment, the simple tale, often livened up with ditties, has remained an important portion of the cultural repertoire of Nsukka. It is especially available to the young before they attain adolescence and helps to shape their emotional responses and to prepare them for adult responsibilities.

The exploits of tortoise the trickster, of lamb the prudent, of wolf the bully, and tiger the tyrant are still generously disseminated. The gods and spirits of earth, sky, hills, and rivers still assume a place of relevance in the unraveling of numerous tales. The evils of ingratitude, treachery, jealousy, and oppression are still castigated in moral tales, just as many phenomena and natural realities find their explanation in etiological tales. Why are sky and earth equal in their sizes? Why does the mosquito sing into the ear? Why did disease and death come into the world? How did human beings develop the depression in their backs? Why does the lizard always nod its head? Why does the tortoise shell look as if put together from fragments? These and many more observable "facts" find expression in the fireside tales. Local trees, animals, and birds find roles in numerous tales. Orphan, hunter, obdurate child, wicked foster-mother, vicious servant or slave, all these and more are the stock characters of fireside and village-square tales.

Certain present-day developments within Nsukka are beginning to threaten the folktale tradition. Modern, classroom education and the fact that young school-goers are given work to do at home cut into the time they would have used in the past to tell folktales. These days, children are as likely to be found clutching their homework textbooks in the evenings as telling stories by the fire. A fair number of children also live away from home with their relations and nonrelatives, and are thus cut off from direct participation in folktale sessions.

The oral narrative tradition still survives, but not as vigorously as before the arrival of the modern era of "those who walk backwards" (which is how Nsukka people described strangers who came by lorries in those days, in which they constantly sat with their backs facing the front and were, therefore, metaphorically said to "walk" backwards).

The same fate that has overtaken the folktale and animal fables has also diminished interest in riddles, tongue-twisters, and other forms of oral literary entertainment that flourished in the Nsukka environment. One positive prospect, however, remains to redeem the situation. These tales are increasingly being written down and will still be available, even if only in watered-down form, to the children, in the context of modern education. The loss of the oral tradition is being made good by the spread of a written tradition. Far from being played out therefore the narrative tradition would seem to be undergoing a slow transformation that will include new forms and a widening scope of narration. In addition to the tales and fables, the schools are introducing more complex and comprehensive narratives, of which the novel is the best example. There is developing, then, a profit-and-loss situation in which the gains might, in the long run, offset the losses. There is even the possibility, more desirable than the supplanting of an oral narrative tradition by a written one, that both traditions may continue to exist side by side, with one tradition reinforcing and enriching the other.

Next in extent and importance, after folktales, animal fables, and riddles, the Nsukka region boasts a highly developed tradition of minstrelsy. Its open, savannah country encourages open-air life and group activities. The people love to form crowds under any kind of stimulus: the birth of a child, a wedding, the return of a kinsman from foreign sojourn, success of the year's harvest, a successful hunting expedition, the taking of a title. The individual Nsukka man is highly gregarious. He loves festivals and public gatherings. He loves rituals and has an imagination and sensibilities deeply enriched by this abiding love. He relishes huge spectacles and processions. He is a fanatic about the exhibition of masquerade fiestas. Most cyclical festivals and ritual fiestas have perished elsewhere in Igboland except for a few isolated spots, but not so in the Nsukka region. Here, fiestas are plentiful and pulsate with life and excitement. Every village, every clan, exhibits its own fiestas and cycle of ritual observances. There is hardly any time in the Nsukka region when something or other is not being celebrated. A man can spend his life in this place moving from one fiesta to another, savoring one excitement after another.

Reincarnating the very soul of revelry and festive excitement is the minstrel. The Nsukka minstrel who sings with his tongue of honey, the man who has drunk from the purest springs of an ancestral tradition, is the link between the people and their deepest emotional attachments. The minstrel organizes the people's emotional responses; he touches the chords that regulate their collective heartbeat; he takes his audience back in high poetical flights through the enormous labyrinths of their ancestral journeyings into the dark womb of time.

What is it that goes into the making of an Nsukka minstrel? I do not think an answer can readily be found to this seemingly mundane question. Scholars have not, after several scores of years and agonizing questioning and research, made a dent in the igneous hardness of the Homeric Question. Why should the Nsukka case be different? The minstrel is the inspired performer, the speaker with the voice of a spirit, the medium through which the purest imaginative waters flow to wet the parched hearts and souls of men. That much seems clear.

Even though we cannot unravel in detail the intimate processes that go into the fashioning of a communal poet, we do know, or can at least reconstruct, the physiosocial and psychotherapeutic basis of the ritual festivals. The festival is a form of transformation, a purification of the soul of society in order to render it continually utile. All the people open up like buds to the morning sun. Heady wine flows like water through the veins of the most sober-minded men and women; food is available to anyone who cares for it. Promiscuous eating and drinking drive the people into one another's arms. The community becomes one little-differentiated mass of heaving humanity. Differences of status and station dissolve, social hierarchies and categories sink to the bottom of a sea of conviviality. Today, the beggar will dine with kings, the basic democratic nature of man is asserted again, and the spirit of communal egalitarianism is on the wing. Sobriety and self-consciousness disappear, and a new chaos that absorbs everything in its formlessness is born; life and death embrace each other in the melting pot of all contrarities;

life and death become a continuum and not a dichotomy; the masked spirits symbolize the bridging of life and death, an end that prefigures a beginning and a sterility immanent with fertility. Out of the fusion of extremes the purest poetry is born.

The minstrel, saturated with wine and food, incarnating the spirit of chaos and formless excesses, is the medium through which the best cadenced lyrics are released, the most heightened linguistic effects are produced, and the most powerful images are carved. All the grossness is purged through the verbal magic of this possessed performer. Order is restored, society is purified, and feelings are refined. There follows a sort of calm that comes with heavy rain after a dust storm. Peace reigns, and that unique perception of the nobility of man, which is at the base of all humane religiosity, emerges. The society is reinvigorated and the strings that bind its people together are strengthened. Values of moral excellence that seemed suspended in the brief interlude of ritual exuberance are reasserted with tripled vigor. Death, which had been symbolically submerged in the totality and unity of being and experience, reappears now, with its attendant awe mixed with pathos, as an identifiable and individuated phenomenon.

The fact of death, especially death as a vital unit of human experience, provides another major impulse toward literary creativity within the Nsukka environment. Everyone accepts the inevitability of death, but instead of subjectifying the phenomenon and being preoccupied with particular, individual deaths, the matter is objectified, distanced, and poeticized. Dirges, which are the peculiar poetry of the objectified fact of death, are among the best-known poetic genres in the Nsukka region. The death of a kinsman or woman, of a husband or wife, of a personal friend or respected age-mate, becomes the occasion for the production of poetry of great lyricism and euphonic beauty.

Some need exists to have the dirges recorded to make them available for prosodic analysis, though the problem of finding how this can be done without overt intrusion of gadgetry into solemn contexts of ritual and mortuary observances remains a major obstacle. Nothing is calculated to vulgarize ritual solemnity so much as the appearance on the scene of the "weapons" of mass communication. And yet, a proper study of the dirges requires that texts should first of all be collected, compiled, and archived for literary analysts and probably musicologists as well, to work on.

For the present, a purely impressionistic view of the dirges reveals that they embody certain discernible characteristics. The virtues and excellent personal qualities of the dead person are itemized and sung or chanted in fitting monodic cadences in which the voice quivers between a sob and an assertion. In these praises, images and symbols are drawn from the physical environment, from the hills and valleys, plants and animals, the moon, the sun and the stars, the weather and the seasons. The common occupations of farming, hunting, trappings and palm-wine tapping form the foci of the praises, and poetic effects are increased by the use of figures of language, including similes and metaphors, personification, and euphemism. Sound effects are produced by assonance, alliteration, onomatopoeia, and judicious repetitions. Through the use of these devices, dominant sentiments, and moods are established by the dirges.

By far the most significant achievements of the creative imagination within the Nsukka environment are the great dramas that take place at various fixed periods in the different parts of the Nsukka region. These dramas represent the most integrated artistic experience in the traditional life of the Nsukka people. They center on the cult of the ancestral spirits and arise from these mysteries even though their total impact spreads far beyond the scope of the cult of ancestral mysteries. But that this cult provides the centralizing principle of the drama is not in doubt. The cult of ancestral spirits is so strong in this part of Igboland that each of its three regions is distinguished by the dominant ancestral spirit for that part of Nsukka. The three groups of Nsukka people are known as Igbo-Omabe (where the Omabe masquerade is dominant), Igbo-Odo (where Odo is dominant) and Igbo-Mmanwu (where conventional masquerades dominate the scene). Igbo-Omabe is the largest group and inhabits the largest area of the present Nsukka province. It embraces almost the whole area of the present Nsukka local government division, Igbo-Eze local government area, and parts of Isi-Uzo local government area, parts of Igbo-Etiti, and parts of the town of Nkpologu in Uzo-Uwani local government area. The Igbo-Odo group, somewhat less widespread than Igbo-Omabe, is to be found in several towns of Igbo-Etiti local government area, including Umunko, Umunna, Ikolo, Onyoho, Ochima, Aku, Ukehe, Uzueme, and Akpugo. There are also the towns of Eha-Amufu, Ikem, and Leke in Isi-Uzo Division. The third group, the Igbo-Mmanwu people, also occupy an area much smaller than the Igbo-Omabe group. It is predominantly situated in Uzo-Uwani area and the whole western Igbo-Etiti, without Nkpologu and Nrobu which belong to Igbo-Omabe area. Other regions of Igbo-mmanwu are Ogbori, Ayamelum, and Umulokpa.

These dramas take place once in two years in most of the region, once in four years in some others, and annually in a few places. Each drama is a grand enactment of the most important of the people's waking realities, as well as the dominant archetypal ideas that inform and control their collective unconscious. Each drama is a reenactment of the cycle of life and death, of the agricultural cycle of planting and reaping and planting again. The dramas present the rhythm and continuity of life, the ebb and flow of the human stream. From agricultural experience, we know that planting is followed by germination, growth, maturation, and harvesting; from man's experience, that there is birth, growth, and death, and a perpetuation through the cult of the ancestors. Through these dramas, ancestral spirits return periodically, reunite with the living, shed their munificence among the living, and then depart to reappear during the next cycle of ritual celebration. The greatest gift the ancestors bring to the living is fertility: children for the childless, and agricultural abundance to reward the labors of all.

The setting of the drama is the entire pastoral life of the village—the whole terrain made up of the hills, valleys and plains, the households and their approaches, the shrines and religious groves, the village squares and marketplaces, the village paths that lead to the streams, farms, and markets, the streams themselves, and cult houses.

Participation is diffused throughout the population and takes in the adult males who have been initiated into the cult of the ancestral spirits. But children and women also play a role at some stages of the action. In some respects, whole clans are engaged in the various rhythms and movements of the action. Household units also participate at some stage. The communion of the living and the dead includes all the people. The destiny of the community is celebrated; promises are made in the interest of the whole community; the interests of all the people are pledged for protection.

The procession that takes place at the end assumes an aspect of a theater-on-the-round in which the ancestral spirits process according to their clans and pass through all the contiguous village squares. The departure is also organized as a series of gradations in which the principle of clan seniority comes much into play, in the places of assemblage and order of procession. The pageant coalesces in the full assemblage of spirits, when they form a huge panoply, a grand spectacle full of colour and grandeur. Song and poetry, music and dancing, religion and ritual, myth and mysticism, all converge in this open-air theater which draws in all the people and unites their destiny, sublimates their aspirations in an action formalized and structured mainly by rituals, and emotionally united by basic myths.

The impression that these dramas are baggy, poorly structured pageants, dominated almost exclusively by spectacles is a false one. Each drama has clearly defined units all of which combine to create a totally conceived action. It is true that much of the action is ritualized and that the movements are sustained by central myths, but the organization of parts in order to create a wholly conceived action is the very hallmark of all drama. These general remarks can be fairly well illustrated from a close look at the Omabe festival drama, which is a dominant form in a very large section of the Nsukka environment.

The Omabe drama is arranged in a two-year cycle. After every celebration, two years will pass before the appearance of another celebration. Each dramatic period lasts for six months, which should immediately alert those aware of the conventions of the unity of action, time, and place as an aspect of modern literate drama, that the Omabe drama (as well as the Odo drama) is a different genre from the modern, conventionalized stage drama that takes place in three hours or less. The method of organizing the units of this drama is crucial to our determination of whether or not the festival drama is drama at all or a mere ritual spectacle and pageant.

There are five main components of the action of the Omabe festival drama: (1) Preparation, (2) Return, Welcoming, and Procession (3) Communion, (4) Dedication, (5) Departure and Blessing. Each of these units of action deserves to be looked at in more detail.

Preparation

It takes six months to prepare for the festival drama and another six months to complete it, from the return of the spirits to their departure. The emotional incubation and the full flourishing of the rituals and the spectacles encompass the year.

The sense of expectation takes time to build up. Once the custodians of the ritual calendar put their official seal on the period of the great drama, all necessary preparation is put into motion and a great sense of expectancy electrifies the atmosphere. Necessary materials of the drama begin to be assembled. Costumes and masks are made. Cult houses called "okiti" or "ulo-mmo" are erected if old ones have fallen into disrepair. These houses remain the retirement chambers when the Omabe have actually arrived. Roads are cleared for the occasion. The public square of each clan is made ready, cleared of debris and all untidiness, and a sitting pavilion is built. Each family clears its compound, smoothens and beautifies the walls of individual houses with decorative designs. The gods must find the people ready when they arrive.

As the date for the festival draws closer, the general preparation and anticipation reach fever pitch. People begin to exchange visits and to become more generous with their drinks, food, and kolanuts. Ballads and minstrels rove around entertaining small audiences with songs, poetry, and music. Here, for example, is part of a recording made of one of the roving minstrels announcing the expected arrival of the spirits and setting the scene for the poetic effusion that characterizes the entire Omabe festival:

THE PERFORMANCE

Nka bu olu Ugwu Nnamani; Onye Umuoda, Lejja. One awu egara maka Omabe na alata echi bu Orie.

Ugwu Nnamani   (*with a metal gong as an accompanying instrument*)
     O—Ogidie
     O—Ogidi ori Ukwueze Nwa Akpu
     Nwa agbara izere.
     Ike na chi kpara ero nwa ori Ukwueze Nwakpu
     Ah nne nwa nne nne O—

     O—Ogidi Nwakpu Nwaba
     Keletusu O—, Keletusu O—

Amako Igbo nne m
Onye Igbo mma.
Ah nne nwa nne nne amako igbo (nne m)
Onye igbo mma
Ho—Ho—Ho—o—
Ho—Ho-Hoo

Keletusu Nwa Opata
Amako igbo nne m onye igbo mara
Nwatakiri Oyi Ogerenyi.
Ebelebe nina O
Ugwuja Ebelebe Nina Odobo
Ike jiri okeoku n'abo go ukwu nya
Imenyi ji n'ani ago ukwu ha
Nwa nna Ogbo m O
Ah nna ogbo m Ugwo O
Ah nna ogbo m ooo
Ugwuja Ugwu udu le Chigbo

Nwa Arua Nwa Ebonyi
Ah Nwasogwa Edem n'Eke
Deje nwa Ofere Ogbo (*saluting a new comer*).
Nwa Orinyima Enyi na Edem n'Eke.
Nwa nne kworo nwa nne nya—O
Nke Ogu aenigi ya—O

Damianu nwa Opata—O
Umu nne umu nne chiri ekwa—O
Onigi adara anyi okwu—O
Umu Orefi-O-Umu Orefi Ukwuapi
Anyi ezugide k'anyi shi aga-O
A umu uwelu—O
Nwa Ugwoke Eze ibea O (*saluting another person just
  arriving*)
Madu Nwaeze Nwaogoro Nwa Ogbuebo Nwasogwa (*another
  newcomer*)
Egbe ji m Ugo ji m-O
Ike m nna zugworo Orie bia zu Nkwo
Nwaeze Nwaogoro Nwa Ogbu Nwasogwa (*accomp.*)
Udele Igwe Nwagbo—O
Anaku Nwagbo—O
Igwe chi ebo Nwagbo—O)
Ogburu Ogori Nwagbo—O) (*twice accomp.*)
Omabe Ugwuanyi Eze-O
O—maba Ekwu Eme
Nwada nna nwa nne Ogori
Ojiri Otubo Omaga Nwasogwa Nwa Igwurube (accomp.)
Nwasogwa Eze Nwa Ogoro
Nwa Ogbebo Nwasogwa—O

Frederick	Ekwu Eme (*being response by the person just called*)

Ugwu Nnamani	Nwa Ogbuebo Nwa Ogoro
Frederick	Eh! (*The person called above answers again*).
Ugwu Nnamani	Frederick Njogo O (*accomp.*)
Frederick	Eh!
Ugwu Nnamani	Ekad' Ogo Nwaeze Inugwonu nkem—O Nwaeze Nwa Ogbonna (*calling another person; also accomp.*) O Umu nna m O, Umu Uwelu (*calling the whole people*) Nne Nne Eze Nwa Okori—O (*another person*) Nwa Asogwa Echara—O (*the latest person's father*) Onye ukwu egbe ala egbe Ozoko minyi ebugu eputu Mi idide ekwumugu ajarija n'ohu (*accomp.*)
	Baibulu Nwa Ogbu Nwaeze, Ezeugwu (*accomp.*) Baibulu Nwa Ogbu Nwaeze, Ezeugwu (*accomp.*) Nwa Alumona Nwa Omaga Nwa Alumona Nwa Omaga Ogwu kporo onye vu uzo Onye kpe azu jide onwe nwa te-O (*accomp.*) O Ogbu Nwaede Ogbu Nwaede, O Ogbu Nwaede Ishiwu Nnadi Eze—O O Chiya Nnadi Ugwu! O Umu nna m—O O umu uwelu—O Oke Jacob Njogo (*accomp.*)
Jacob	Eh!
Ugwu Nnamani	Oke Jacob Njogo
Jacob	Ujo Adigi
Ugwu Nnamani	Unu siri m kwu-de Umu nna m—o?
Group	Kwu—a, kwu-a, kwu-a-a-a-a.
Ugwu Nnamani	Oliji Ogele Eze Nwa Omaga Nwasogwa Nwa Idenyi Ugwu Ugwuanyi Eze-e Ugwu Ekwu eme, Nwa Olibeja Ojiri Otubo nne m Omaga nwa Ada nna Nwa Adanna nwa nne Ogori Ugwuoke Eze Nwa Omaga Ugwuoke Eze Nwa Omaga Ugwu Igwurube Nwasogwa (*accomp.*) Oh—ho—, OO—, oho! oh-hoo, Obe! Obe Oyi m Ogbonnah Nwa Ukwueze Aba Izu gabu n'onu agu (*accomp.*) Umu Uwelu—O, Umu Uwelu—O Umu Uwelu—O!

This poetry, even where it exhibits the main characteristics of orality, has peculiarities all its own. With other forms of oral poetry, it shares the familiar features of brevity and ellipticity of syntax, parenthetical intrusions, end-stoppage, parallelism, sonority, including the use of names that in their accumulation evoke a sense of grandeur in their so-called heroic rumble. Alliterative and assonant devices also abound, especially in the rounding off of some units of the verse. This poetry is essentially beamed, as poetry was originally meant to be, to the ear. Its aural inspiration is indicated by the full tonal stress and inflection given to every syllable in each line and by the various forms of repetition that serve several needs, including the need for emphasis, elaboration, and the "easing" of the memory before the next movement of the mind.

THE PERFORMANCE *(translation)*

This is the voice of Ugwu Nnamani of Umuoda Lejja. He is chanting about Omabe that will make its reentry, tomorrow being Orie.

Ugwu Nnamani   O—Ogidi—e
Ogidi Ori Ukwueze Nwakpu
It's only the great one who holds conversation with his
  personal god
Nwa Ori Ukwueze Nwakpu, who as a child was headed by
  your parents
Ogidi Nwakpu Nwaba, dearly held mother
Cletus—O, Cletus—O
You who hail from a people famed for producing
  masquerades
Lover of your motherland, you
Dearly beloved son of his motherland
You hail from a people famed for producing masquerades
Ho—Ho—Ho—o o
Ho—Ho—Ho—o

Cletus Nwa Opata
Beloved son of his motherland who is known by people
  beyond
A child who is accepted in the company of elders
Ebelebe Nina O
Ugwuja Ebelebe[2] Nina Odobo
Great one who at a go offered two cocks to his god
When others offer one cock at a time to their gods,

Kindred of my father
Kindred of my father, Ugwu—O
Kindred of my father
Ugwuja Ugwu Udu nu Chigbo

Son of Arua Nwa Ebonyi
Nwasogwa of Edem that observes the Eke market day
I salute you son of Ofere Ogbo

Son of him who plants so much yams that the
Elephant finds impossible to consume
You from Edem that observes Eke market

When a brother carries his brother at his back
There is no more question of quarrels
Damian Nwa Opata—O
When brothers take up musical instruments
They always beat to the same rhythm
Children of Oriefi, Children of Oriefi Ukwuapi
We are now gathering as we move together
Kinsmen of Uwelu
Nwa Ugwoke Eze, have you come?
Madu Nwaeze Nwa Ogoro, son of Ogbebo Nwasogwa
Kite that holds me, Ugo that holds me,
The valiant one with whom
I first go to Orje[3] before going to Nkwo[4]
Nwaeze Nwa Ogoro, son of Ogbu Nwasogwa
Udele Igwe Nwagbo—O
Anaku Nwagbo—O
Sky that has two children, Nwagbo,
Sky that has two children, Nwagbo
Ogburu: Ogori Nwagbo
Omabe that does whatever it says
Nwada nna, the brother of Ogori
Ojiri Otubo Omoga, son of Nwasogwa begot by Igwurube
Nwasogwa Eze, son of Ogoro
Son of Ogbebo Nwasogwa
Son of Ogbebo Nwa Ogoro

Frederick Njogo　—O
He who does things in a big way
Are you listening to me?

Ugwu Nnamani　Ekad' Ogo Nwaeze
Do you hear my voice?
Nwaeze son of Ogbonna
My kinsmen, kinsmen of Uwelu
Dearly beloved Nwa Okori
Son of Asogwa Echara
Fleet-footed one always accompanied by gun-shots[5]
He who struggles for water does not fear soiling himself
    with mud
And the earthworm grows no hairs on its buttocks

Bible Nwa Ogbu Nweze, Ezeugwu,
Bible Nwa Ogbu Nweze, Ezeugwu
Son of Alumona Nwa Omaga
Son of Alumona Nwa Omaga
When a thorn pricks the person at the forefront
He who walks behind should tread more carefully
Ogbu Nwaede, Ogbu Nwaede, Ogbu Nwaede,

	Ishiwu Nnadi Eze
	Ochiya Nnadi Ugwu
	O my kinsmen
	My kinsmen of Uwelu
	Valiant Jacob Njogo
Jacob	Eh!
Ugwu Nnamani	Valiant Jacob Njogo
Jacob	Have no fear.
Ugwu Nnamani	My kinsmen, should I continue talking?
Group	Yes, speak on, speak on.

You who eat yams cultivated near the Ogele[6]
Son of Nwasogwa begot by Idenyi
Ugwu Ugwuanyi Eze
Ugwu that does whatever it says
Son of Olibeja
Nwa Adana, brother of Ogori
Ugwoke Eze Nwa Omaga
Ugwoke Eze Nwa Omaga
Ugwu Igwurube Nwasoga
Oh—ho—OO—oho—ho—Obe!

My friend Obe Ogbonnah
Son of Ukwueze Aba
The meeting place is now at Onu-Agu[7]
Kinsmen of Uwelu, kinsmen of Uwelu
Kinsmen of Uwelu.

But the evocation is centered mainly on genealogy. Everyone around is placed in the network of family relationships by having his paternity established and publicly recognized. Certain distinctive qualities of the characters being sung about are thrown in to set off some point about the uniqueness of the persons concerned. Omabe, the real pretext for the poeticization, is referred to now and again, but the genealogical motif is dominant: A is the son of B who, in turn, begets C. All this is relevant because the festival itself revolves around the theme of kinship and communal solidarity. The spirits of the dead will visit the living, bringing with them numerous gifts and blessings. The festival serves to underline the strong links uniting the living, the dead, and those that are yet to be born. The poeticization of kinship is a method of creating anticipation and of defining the direction of the action of the larger drama when it develops. The eve-of-festival revelries and minstrel music foreshadow the emotive direction of the action and some of the controlling motifs which would, in the fullness of time, become the organizational focus of the entire festival drama.

Return, Welcoming, and Procession

The Omabe are expected to rise from the river. They make their appearance first from dry valleys if there is no stream in the neighborhood. The Omabe appear in procession, splendidly costumed. The lower, exposed parts of the body glisten in the sun the way the skin would if suddenly released from the stream. The procession heads for the cult houses, where the Omabe and elders undergo the first communion. Then the procession heads for the major landmarks of the immediate environment, including the hills. The most splendid sight is the Omabe in their full formation descending from the hills, with the sun gleaming on their flashing costumes and their glistening lower parts. There is no better expression to describe the beauty of the scene than "poetry in motion."

There are three main types of Omabe. First are the ones with huge, carved heads called ishi-mma. The head can be as much as four feet long. Such Omabe are regarded as the incarnation of the founding spirits of the clan units in which they appear. After the Ishi-mma follows the Ugwoke Omabe, variously known as "Ujam," "Ugele," "Igele," and "Ugwoke Oku." This is the most beautiful and richly costumed of the Omabe masquerades. The maskless head is surmounted with eagle-feathers. These are probably the most costly Omabe to fit out. The third type is the "Ugwa" or "Ori-Okpa." These are menial spirits that carry out errand duty and police functions at the festivals; they appear earlier than the superior Omabe and attempt to prepare the way for the emergence of the other Omabe.

Communion

This stage centers on communal feeding in the village square during which the people renew their sense of common belonging by sharing a meal together. The Omabe retire to their cult house and there again commune with the elders. Choicest food, drinks and meat are stowed away for the Omabe and the elders. The communion continues in the homes of individuals as the Omabe begin their rounds of visits to every household, in order to impart their blessings on the households. Choicest food, meat, and palmwine are brought before the Omabe.

Dedication

As Omabe begin their final rounds and preparation for departure, people bring their troubles before the spirits and pledge to make some sacrifice if in the interval the Omabe will intercede to rid them of the troubles. Such problems as childlessness, failing agriculture, constant illness, are brought to the Omabe, with the promise that if succor comes, the Omabe will be greeted with the specified gift at their next return.

Departure and Blessing

Finally, the Omabe retreat in grand processions in which clan superiority comes into play. All the Omabe of one clan may depart in one procession, making sure that proper order or seniority of the component units of clans is adhered to. As the Omabe depart, they bless the people and their society and promise to bring them ample rewards, in the form of blessings and banishing evil.

Throughout the festival, much poetry is created by the men who follow the Omabe around. They eulogize the spirits in language noted for its imagery and figures of speech. The Omabe music itself is provided by a grand orchestra of ten xylophones of different pitches, vibrations, and tonality, strongly supported by wooden drums known as ekwe-Omabe. The music is so rich in variety and suggestiveness that the phrase "ancestral polyphony," heard more frequently these days in ethnomusical symposia, may well have its basis in fact in this festival. The Omabe music, strongly led by the leading xylophonist, coupled with the panegyrical effusions of the followers of the Omabe spirits, gives emotional direction to various stages of the drama and defines the total emotional response that is created during the festival. The poetry is taken up largely with the praises of Omabe, the beautiful, the magnificent, the munificent, the reviver and regenerator of life, and bringer of diverse gifts precious to man. But the full emotional impact is achieved by the communion and unification of all parts of life's experience, the exuberance and reconciliation of all nature, to be followed inevitably by the tragic fact of separation as represented by the departure of the benign spirits—a poignant reminder of the impermanence of things.

THE MODERN SETTING

When we consider the place and formal significance of literature in the modern age, we cannot but confront the question of the "town-gown" situation as it affects literature in its broad and narrow definitions. We are faced with such questions as: Does the university as a sensitive center feel the existence of a rich literature in the local tradition? How is this sensitivity expressed? Is there any kind of cross-fertilization between the literary developments in the two sectors of literary experience? Is there a continuing dialogue, and how is this dialogue articulated? What kind of presence does Nsukka have in the literary artefacts that are fashioned in the University of Nigeria? Has the environment itself advanced or impeded the development of literature in the university? Other questions might be raised, but these provide a convenient starting point.

The answers to these questions, individually and collectively, must necessarily be many and, perhaps, diverse. One fact, however, is beyond doubt: it is that the Department of English of the University of Nigeria is fully aware of an oral literary tradition in the Nsukka region. Even though this awareness has not been made use of adequately in terms of the promise of available material, some start has been made which, in the long run, may become a source of growth and development far above its original inspiration.

The expression of this awareness can be seen on two levels. The first, one might refer to as a public, symbolic, and gestural level. The epithets should not be interpreted to imply an absence of seriousness or sincerity but to recognize that the existence of a rich literary culture in the local environment is given mere surface expression in the Department of English. For example, when *The Muse*, a magazine of the English Association, appeared in 1963, the perceptive and imaginative young people who founded the journal sensibly saw their Nigerian muse as Watermaid or Dancer. The figure, as subsequently analyzed, combines the elusive beauty and mystery of the various water spirits with the otherworldly beauty and delicacy of such a female spirit as *Agboghommo*, with all the connotations of the classical muses. It also embodies the idea of *Ala* (the Earth Goddess) represented in the Mbari tradition as the patroness of art. This felicitous symbol has since been immortalized in the cover sketch of *The Muse* made by Obiora Udechukwu.

In 1972, when a departmental poetry journal was founded to reinforce *The Muse*, the discovery of an appropriate name did not present too great a problem. From the culturally exciting environment, a name seemed to leap out. What other name, suffused already with the felicities and suggestions of rooted poetic tradition, than *Omabe!* And just as a reminder, each issue of the journal carries the following explanation: "*Omabe* is the name of the cult music and poetry from the shrines of Nsukka."

This level of awareness would be merely opportunistic if it represented the limit of the university's identification with the creative literary tradition in the Nsukka environment. But this is not so. There is the second level of deeper identification and more critical and responsible interaction. The university, after all, must function as a creative center no less than as an intellectual clearing house. It should act as a sensitive needle, recording all that is vital, significant, and profound in human experience, as well as examining, with equal sensitivity, the very components of each relevant object with the purpose of categorizing, differentiating, and sifting its essence. This is surely a level of creative and scholarly commitment far superior to symbolic naming or an intuitive recognition of the significance of certain surface realities.

The Department of English in the University of Nigeria, happily, recognizes and lives up to this second and higher level of responsibility. It is not just that, in broad relief, a study of the oral literatures of Africa has been seriously initiated in the literature program of this university, but that the oral literature of Nsukka presents important specimens for testing theories and hypotheses formed under general consideration.

To take just one illustration, scholars within the department, especially those with a strong interest in drama, are beginning to examine the Omabe and Odo communal dramas and relate them to dramatic traditions inside and outside the African continent. So far, two schools of thought seem to have crystallized around what one could reasonably call evolutionary and relativistic theories. The evolutionist theory is well represented in an article by Professor M. J. C. Echeruo called "The Dramatic Limits of Igbo Rituals."[8] Professor Echeruo uses the Odo festival to illustrate his thesis. His central proposition is that this festival, like the Greek Dionysian and Apollonian festivals, contains dramatic elements capable of future development into full-bodied drama. Ritual and myth, in his view, would first of all be shorn of their coagulating sacredness and rendered sufficiently to be used in a secular drama built on the destiny of differentiated, individual characters.

The relativistic view flatly contradicts the evolutionary one and insists that the ritual festivals in Africa represent full and authenticated drama that should be recognized as such; that they are communal dramas which differ from secular, individuated modern drama with its precise separation of stage from auditorium, actors from audience, and fictitious time from the duration of the action on the stage.

The Department of English has holders of both views on its staff, which means that for a long time to come the argument will remain active. It is necessary to establish an area of general agreement and isolate the main issue of controversy. I believe it is generally accepted that the Odo and Omabe festivals of Nsukka broadly resemble the Greek Dionysiac and Appollonian festivals. The combination of a number of features—revelry, wine-imbibing, music, dance, poetry, ecstasy, and mystery—makes the comparison inevitable and even justifiable. The analogy itself, with particular reference to the fertility, death, and resurrection of nature, is reasonable. The main point of divergence of view, however, is the insistence by the holders of the evolutionary position that modern drama in Africa needs to follow the identical linear development of the classical Greek drama from the Dionysian and Apollonian festivals. This insistence is somewhat dubious since Greek cultural and historical development differed extensively from the African cultural and historical experience. The evolutionists' problem, it seems, is their lack of helpful anthropological insight.

The story is told of an American tourist who, having heard that the Watusi of Central Africa are a race of giants, when he saw a pigmy grandfather with white hair and beard, exclaimed to a traveling companion, "By Golly, Andred, what a handsome Baby Watusi!"

One might object that the American was not very observant, otherwise he would not have failed to see that the pigmy was not at all a baby but a full-grown adult, indeed, a grandfather. The fact is that a pigmy is a pigmy, a Watusi a Watusi. They are both Africans, but each of them has an autonomy peculiarly his own. The Omabe and Odo communal dramas, in like manner, are different from modern, individualistic, and literacy-mediated dramas, but they are drama all the same. It is quite possible that the evolutionists have been misled by too great a reliance on writing and the facilities it provides and by too little confidence in an oral tradition. They can eulogize the Greek dramatic genius and its contribution to the Greek awakening because the works of Aeschylus, Sophocles, Aristophanes, and others exist in written form and can be readily studied and analyzed and staged. The same thing cannot be said of the Greek communal drama that had existed for several centuries in an oral, performing context. There is no script from which such drama can be reenacted or analyzed. From this distance, Greek communal and festival drama cannot but present an aspect of a fragmentary phenomenon yielding, at best, mere resource material for the fashioning of the fuller, better-documented Greek drama of the fifth century B.C.

Taking a fragmentary view of Greek ritual drama is, therefore, understandable; not so is holding the same view of Igbo communal and festival drama. It is even less defensible to regard the Greek situation as paradigmatic of every dramatic development. If that were so, the drama history of even Far Eastern Asia would have taken the same line of development. We know, of course, that this is not so. There is no incontrovertible reason why the Greek example must be repeated everywhere else. Nor is there any compelling necessity to describe drama entirely in terms of the proscenium stage and its conventions. Why must drama be seen from the point of view of a distinct stage and auditorium, of actors and the audience? Is there any particular reason, except that of meeting the specifically practical pressures of the present age, why an enactment should last only two or three hours instead of six months? Is the sense of organic unity that we assume in the modern theater and its conventions not possible on an extended scale among a people whose sensibilities are trained to absorb more diffused ritual and symbolic significances of action? Is a broad communal canvas not more suitable for painting more inclusive social and emotional action than the mere mouse-tongue platform called the modern stage?

I raise these rhetorical questions because it seems to me useful that the debate between the relativists and the evolutionists should be encouraged to continue. It is a means of clarifying the particular and general issues of cultural and artistic continuity in contemporary Africa. The evolutionists have, up to the present time at any rate, lost the arguments to the relativists; but their vigorous advancement of an identifiable and combative viewpoint has often acted as a goad to the relativists and driven them out of the seductive highways of intellectual complacency into the narrow, winding paths of painstaking scholarship.

It has earlier on been stated that the University of Nigeria has seen, from its inception in the sixties, a flourishing of creative activities, especially in the field of poetry. Some suggestions have been made as to what were the major causes of this literary renaissance. These causes can now be examined in greater detail.

Looking at the Department of English curriculum of the 1960s, one is struck by a number of features that seem to have been dropped altogether or modified radically since the end of the Nigerian war. One is struck, for example, by the inclusion of three courses on creative writing in the program. These have disappeared since 1970. The reason is historical. The Americans, who supervised the development of the University of Nigeria in its first ten years, believe that creative writing can be taught, and so they made provision for it in the curriculum. The predominantly British-trained and oriented dons who took over the department in 1970 do not seem to share this belief.

It is not my intention to go into the debate of these two opposite views on the matter, but it seems fair to say that the effort to teach the writing of poetry, especially, produced a crop of young men who have since distinguished themselves by their finely textured verse. Peter Thomas, the don who handled the course, was himself a highly enthusiastic and inspiring teacher who carried the creative interest outside the classroom. With his equally enthusiastic students, he encouraged a small informal group within which discussions on the nature of poetry and the creative process were hammered out. Almost as if to reinforce the creative stimulation, the late Christopher Okigbo, poet, prophet, and prodigal, the child prodigy of Nigerian poetry, was working as an assistant librarian at the university and became part of the creative coterie that was, in a matter of a few years, to make far-reaching contributions to African literature. In addition to Okigbo himself, names of such good poets as Pol Ndu (whose collections include *Golgotha*, *Golgotha Re-visited*, and *Amerika*), Okogbule Nwanodi (author of *Icheke and Other Poems*), and Romanus Egudu (whose poems have been heavily anthologized) stand out in the varied landscape of Nigerian creative contributions.

Other younger writers have since emerged and constitute the second generation of Nsukka poets. Their writing has been sensibly anthologized by one of their number, Chukwuma Azuonye as the second *Nsukka Harvest*. This harvest, appearing soon after the civil war in which most of the contributors participated, contains harrowing, individual experiences of the traumas of the struggle. But, in common with the first harvest, there is constant introspection and exploration of the creative process and the relationship of the artist to his community and his community's manifold destiny. There is also in many of the individual poems a vibrant invocation of the beauty of the environment and its artistic qualities. The subjective, inspirational and atmospheric emphases of the poems lend them a certain mood and texture that are readily associated with the poetry of the European Romantic movement. In fact, Echeruo is right when he refers to the poets of the second *Nsukka Harvest* as "a gathering of Romantics."

A DRAWING TOGETHER OF STRANDS
THE LEGACY OF OKIGBO

I think the picture of the creative development in the Nsukka environment would not be complete without specific reference to what one could call "the legacy of Christopher Okigbo." Here, the major creative strands in the traditional and modern sectors meet and fuse into something unique, beautiful, and historically significant.

Christopher Okigbo spent 1961 and part of 1962 at the University of

Nigeria, Nsukka, as assistant university librarian. Brief as this period was, it marked a major watershed in the development of creative literature within Nsukka itself and, perhaps, in Nigeria as a whole. Professor Sunday Anozie has given a fairly comprehensive view of those very exciting times in his book on Okigbo, *Christopher Okigbo: Creative Rhetoric.*[9] According to Dr. Anozie:

> There was no big literary event in the old Federation of Nigeria, or in Africa for that matter, in which Okigbo did not play a leading role. Nor are there many poets in Nigeria today who have not first of all passed through his 'forge,' so to speak, or received his blessing and encouragement. In fact to the young generation of poets, such as Okogbule Wonodi and Polycarp Ndu, both of whom have been published, Okigbo was as Pound was to Eliot. It is in the works of these poets that Okigbo's greatest influence will be sought later.[10]

The truth is that Okigbo influenced not one but two generations of poets, both of which made Nsukka their habitat, the generation of Wonodi and Ndu, and the civil-war and post-civil war generation of Obiorah Udechukwu, the late Kevin Echeruo, Chukwuma Azuonye, Onuora Enekwe, Akomaye Oko, among others. The question that necessarily arises is: where does the Nsukka environment come into all this? What does Okigbo's very brief sojourn at Nsukka have to do with Okigbo himself and his poetry and the two generations of Nsukka poets?

The answer seems obvious to me and should be to anyone who has looked closely at the matter. Okigbo inspired the Nsukka poets in the same way that he himself had been inspired by the Nsukka environment. To Okigbo, the richness and immense plenitude of cultural and artistic wealth of the Nsukka environment marked out that environment as the soul land and creative heartland of the Igbo race. Nsukka, for him, was the source-spring of creative inspiration. I have looked at his poems before and after his two eventful years in Nsukka. His pre-Nsukka poems, the *Four Canzones* written while he was schoolmastering at Fiditi Grammar School are, without doubt, underdeveloped, full of wild, unassimilated borrowings, and verbal prolixity, and dressed in sentences that drag rather than flow. The images protrude uneasily and seem to await the master's hand to vitalize them. Okigbo himself, the best critic of his own poetry, saw the inadequacies of these poems when he wrote later, in "Lament of the Flutes":

> Tidewash . . . Memories
> fold-over-fold free-furrow
> mingling old tunes with new[11]

and admonished the poet to:

> Sing to the rustic flute:
> Sing a new note. . . .

The Nsukka environment provided him with a congenial setting, abundant natural inspiration, and an unparalleled variety of artistic and cultural models out of which his creative soul could distil new notes and new songs.

Dr. Anozie sees the abundance of traditional images in Okigbo's poetry as strongly influenced by the romantic and pastoral verse of the Roman poet Vergil and the Greek Theocritus of Syracuse, both of whose poetry fall in large measure within the pastoral tradition. That is probably so, especially in the *Canzones*, since Okigbo, a graduate of classics, must have had more than a passing contact with classical pastoral poetry. The greater reality, however, is that the Nsukka environment with its abundance of natural scenery, a flourishing tradition of ritual drama, and exciting artistic exhibitions of song, dance, and music, offers a more immediate creative impulse to the poet whose senses are open to receiving direct impressions. Some of Okigbo's poems that embody the evidence of his maturity were written here or started here. They include *Heavensgate*, *Limits*, and the first part of *Silences*. In these poems, the Igbo musical instruments (ubo, ekwe, ogene, oja), which abound in the Nsukka environment, are celebrated. Some of these poems are even written for specific instruments. The impact of the traditions of minstrelsy and masquerade music are felt. So also are the ubiquitous hills, which strongly define the Nsukka terrain and determine the ecology and occupational patterns of the region. In such lines as

> So would I to the hills again
> so would I
> to where springs the fountain
> there to draw from

the presence of the hills is no longer just a physical landmark but a creative signpost.

Christopher Okigbo's poetic career was informed by one central passion, the attempt by the artist as a quest-protagonist to make contact with the spiritual and creative inspiration of his race, in particular, and of humanity in its all-embracing totality, in general. That quest, even when it assumes an aspect of physical terror and a threat to personal life, will not be abandoned. It requires no other justification but itself and is, in the long run, its own truest validation. Behind such a view lies what can be identified as a heroic view of man and his destiny, with heroism seen as man's capacity to defend his deepest inspiration with the most precious thing that he has, his own life. Sophists and cynics have strained interminably to devalue heroism of this kind as mere folly and Ali Mazrui has even gone further to put Okigbo on trial in a novel entitled *The Trial of Christopher Okigbo*, because, in Mazrui's consideration, Okigbo abandoned the relatively superior calling of a poet for the relatively inferior profession of a soldier. Obviously, the sort of vision that motivated Okigbo to defend the Nsukka zone of the Nigerian war and lose his life in the process is far beyond the grasp of earth-bound intellectuals like Mazrui. But to the second generation of Nsukka poets who grew up, even vicariously, under the shadow of Okigbo, he was a hero, a saint and martyr who inspired some of their best poetic efforts. I quote here a few

examples from Obiora Udechukwu, a highly gifted poet and scholar of fine
and applied arts:

(1) Drumless Monody

> Tonight the masquerade walks
> The dual-pathway of the anthole,
> But there are no drums for the descent,
> There are no flutes for his return
> And we, dumb as our drums,
> Dumb as our flutes,
> Can only moan, silent. . . .[12]

(2) Sacrifice for Rebirth

> That a minstrel
> dry of throat
> may not cease to sing
> and we, keyless at the Gate,
> may yet listen to his flute
>   send to Idoto
>   tongue-tied at dusk
>   not looking back
> a black ant and a white hen
> for in a palm grove
> somewhere beyond the hills
> the blood of her sunbird
> merged for ever with sand
> at the confluence of seven seas
> the sunbird and his lioness
> at the confluence of seven deserts
> a new bird takes shape[13]

(3) Salute

> You . . .
>   lone voice that subdued the echoes
> You . . .
>   shrub that pierced the forest
>   and knocked the poplars with his jaw
> You . . .
>   who changed your lunar flute
> for a spear
> that future generations
> might not bite sand. . . .[14]

This kind of poetry is a product of the Nsukka environment. Echoes of
Okigbo's lines are embedded in the poems, and the physical and cultural
realities of Nsukka are also competently assimilated. Odo poetry, as anyone
who has read R. N. Egudu and D. I. Nwoga's *Igbo Poetical Heritage*[15] will

attest, provides the inspiration for the third poem. In these, as in most of Okigbo's poetry, the impact of minstrel music and song is very strong.

The legacy of Christopher Okigbo continues to make itself felt and to be perceived as a major creative force in the Nsukka environment. Okigbo has immeasurably enriched the literary legacy of the Nsukka environment after being himself most vitally formed by that environment. Perhaps it is correct to say that it takes the interaction of two factors, a very sensitive and creative individual and a very stimulating environment, to produce the great creative epochs in the history of any people. A study of the major literary developments within the Nsukka environment lends support to this fact of cultural history. The Nsukka environment seems destined to become the cultural and creative center of this part of Nigeria. Its immense potential is only just beginning to be recognized.

NOTES

1. Background information on Nsukka is available in numerous studies, including A. E. Afigbo, "Nsukka Before 1916: The Making of a Frontier Igbo Society" in *Ropes of Sand: Studies in Igbo History and Culture* (London, 1981), 69–115; C. K. Meek, *An Ethnological Report on the Peoples of the Nsukka Division, Onitsha Province* (Lagos, 1931); C. A. Abangwu, *Nsukka Handbook* (Enugu, 1960); Parbati Sircer, ed., *Nsukka Division: A Geographical Appraisal, Nigerian Gopgraphical Association Proceedings*, 1965; G. E. K. Ofomata, ed., *Nsukka Environment* (Enugu, 1978); Austin J. Shelton, *The Igbo-Igala Borderland: Religion and Social Control in Indigenous African Colonialism* (Albany, 1971).

2. *Ebelebe*—a rare tree of great medicinal efficacy and metaphysical significance.

3. *Orie*—The market day on which the Omabe makes its appearance.

4. *Nkwo*—a major marketplace patronized by all the Lejja people. Two days after the reentry of the Omabe, it is Nkwo market day. On this day, all Omabe masquerades from all the villages in Lejja assemble and perform at this market for the people.

5. Gunshots—During the performance of the Omabe masquerade, its closest kinsmen fire volleys in the air to celebrate the successful emergence of the spirit.

6. *Ogele*—A very large well dug by the people at the public square where the Omabe house is located. Water collects in this well and is used to irrigate the area and keep it fertile.

7. *Onu-agu*—where the young men go to herald the Omabe before it makes its public appearance.

8. Michael J. C. Echeruo, "The Dramatic Limits of Igbo Ritual," *Research in African Literatures* 4, 1 (1973): 21–31.

9. This is the first book-length study of the poetry and background of this most enigmatic of African poets.

10. S. O. Anozie, *Christopher Okigbo: Creative Rhetoric* (London, 1972), 17.

11. Christopher Okigbo, *Labryinths with Path of Thunder* (London, 1972).

12. Obiora Udechukwu, "Drumless Monody" in *Nsukka Harvest*, ed. Chukwuma Azuonye (Nsukka, 1972). This and other poems by Udechukwu have now appeared in a collection titled *What the Madman Said* (Bayreuth, West Germany, 1990), 14.

13. Udechukwu, *What the Madman Said*, 17–18.

14. Ibid., 16–17.

15. R. N. Egudu and D. I. Nwoga, eds., *Poetic Heritage: Igbo Traditional Verse* (Enugu, 1971).

CHAPTER 9

Christopher Okigbo
Poet of Destiny

Hear the voice of the Bard!
Who Present, Past, & Future sees;
Whose ears have heard
The Holy Word
That walk'd among the ancient trees,

Calling the lapsed Soul,
And weeping in the evening dew;
That might controll
The starry pole,
And fallen, fallen light renew![1]

IT SEEMS APPROPRIATE to open this discussion with "The Bard," a poem by the British poet, William Blake. Blake was a poet of the romantic movement who, in the true tradition of romanticism, made large claims for poetry and appropriated sublime attributes for the poet, the bard, "who Present, Past & Future sees!"[2] The poet, in the romantic conception, is no ordinary mortal but a divinely inspired artist, a possessed performer through whom hidden truths of the spirit are revealed and through whose influence mankind undergoes regeneration and spiritual rebirth. The poet, in the romantic tradition, functions severally as priest, prophet, and legislator for mankind, as a man speaking to other men with a voice of moral authority strengthened by heightened sensibility. He is a man imbued with an understanding and suffering soul, a kind of a god. Wordsworth echoes a similar view when he wrote in "Resolution and Independence," "By our own spirits are we deified."[3]

The idea of the poet as an inspired performer, a composite prophet or seer, priest, and madman, is much older than the romantic movement itself and is quite familiar in different cultures of the world. It has remained strong in European literary history and was well explored by Plato in some of his dialogues, especially in *Phaedrus* and *Ion*. The romantic movement represented one of the highest watermarks of this concept, in more recent times.

Christopher Okigbo conceived of his poetic career in these serious and responsible terms. For him poetry is no mere aesthetic pastime, no simple celebration of verbal ingenuity, no indulgence of intellectual gymnastics. It is a sacred vocation espoused by persons who feel specially called and set apart from all other persons to carry the grave responsibility of speaking for their people about those matters of weight and moment of which a benign Providence has granted them the inspiration to speak with the authority of priests, prophets, and moral legislators.

In a sense, if one takes the totality of Okigbo's self-image and the matter and measure of his poetic output, one would be justified in regarding him as one of the last of the romantic poets, and, in our African context, as the greatest African romantic poet.[4] One could, with equal justification, regard him as Africa's greatest poet of destiny because, in the final analysis, what distinguishes the great poets of romanticism from those of other movements and orientations is their belief, to a point of obsessive inevitability, that they carry a certain destiny that binds them inextricably to the fate of those for whom they speak, who may be their specific peoples or humankind in general.

The enticing paradox surrounding poets of destiny is their embodying at once distinctly individual drives and identities and the most essentially communal attributes: they are, in one breath, intensely themselves, as well as being of the people whose aspirations they articulate in their poetry; they are at one and the same time poets' poets, no less than what the French call "les bardes de communauté," almost in the archaic sense in which the poet sings his song for the edification of his community under his community's powerful impulses.

That Christopher Okigbo saw himself as a poet of destiny, and his creative mission as closely linked to the fate of his community, is without any doubt. The evidence is writ large in *Labyrinths*, a collection of his poems selected, reorganized, and edited by himself, with an unmistakable air of finality in the awesome statement that "the versions here . . . are final."[5] In his introduction" to *Labyrinths*, after providing a brief commentary on his poem sequences, Okigbo sums up his poetical intentions in what appears to be a very carefully prepared manifesto:

> A poet-protagonist is assumed throughout; a personage, however, much larger than Orpheus; one with a load of destiny on his head, rather like Gilgamesh, like Aeneas, like the hero of Melville's *Moby Dick*, like the Fisher King of Eliot's *Waste Land;* a personage for whom the progression through 'Heavensgate,' through 'Limits' through 'Distances' is like telling the beads of a rosary; except that the beads are neither stone nor agate but globules of anguish strung together on memory.
>
> Every work of this kind is necessarily a cry of anguish—of the root extending its branches of coral, of corals extending their roots into each living hour; the swell of the silent sea, the great heaving dream at its highest, the thunder of splitting pods—the tears scatter, take root, the cotyledons broken, burgeon into laughter of leaf; or else rot into vital hidden roles in the nitrogen cycle. The present dream clamoured to be born a cadenced cry: silence to appease the fever of flight beyond the iron gate.[6]

The introduction of which the above passage is a part presents certain procedural problems to the critic. The poet himself has told us what his poetry is about: "a poet-protagonist is assumed throughout; a personage. . . with a load of destiny on his head." We have here an actor who is also a commentator on his own actions, a writer of his own footnotes. The situation does seem bewildering, if not outright anomalous, to the "professional" critic. That little difficulty deserves to be got out of the way if we are to see our way clear to appreciating Okigbo's poetry in the context of his self-appointed role as "a poet of destiny."

Luckily, we do not have to accept with docility everything a creative writer says of himself, his intentions, and his work. In fact, there are many reasons why we should not trust writers when they turn commentators on their own work, and why we should be on our guard and attend to a writer's self-analysis with more than mild skepticism. In the first place, the process of creativity itself is so complicated and defiant of precise formulations and analyses that even the brightest of writers might yet encounter "areas of dark impenetrability" in the attempt to guide his audience with his own light into the sanctuary.

Another and, perhaps, more compelling reason than the first would seem to arise from the creative and the critical processes tending to draw from different faculties and abilities that are rarely combined in the same persons. One might, of course, be confronted with outstanding exceptions, such as Longinus, Horace, Sidney, Dryden, Johnson, Arnold, Eliot, Sartre, Tolstoy, Henry James, and, in our own day and place virtually every prominent writer— Soyinka, Achebe, Ngugi wa Thiong'o, Clark, Awoonor, and so on. They combine the vocation of creative writer with the profession of literary scholarship. But one must be quick to counter that these examples seem only superficially separated from the generality that validates the truth of the observation. If any of these writers is put on a scale and weighed, the balance would tilt inevitably toward the creative writer or the literary scholar. Even where a fair balance is established, it is soon obvious that readers go to the writer at different times for one or another of his offerings, either for his creative work, or his critical opinions, rarely for both.

There are at least three distinguishable types of author-critics or author-commentators. There are those whose critical views are broad enough to transcend their work and creative intentions, and others whose critical views encompass only their own work. The writers in the first group present no great difficulty to the "professional" critic. They may, as a matter of fact, be successful critics in their own right. The problem is with the author-commentators who take their readers by the hand and conduct them through their work. Apart from the attempt itself being somewhat gratuitous, it also smacks too much of an a posteriori apologia and a validation of consciously chosen stances and creative procedures. When this situation arises, the professional critic is inconveniently required to discuss not only the creative work itself but also its author's commentary, which accompanies it.

The third category of author—commentators with whom the critic has to deal—differs from the two categories mentioned above in the particular sense that the writers' comments and manner of presenting them constitute an extension of the statements contained in their creative texts. These writers are, more often than not, seriously committed to certain ideas that then become their creative inspiration. Such writers feel compelled to expose and extend those ideas outside the "creative" contexts proper. In other words, the critic is not just dealing with commitment to artistic validity, strictly speaking, but, more significantly, is touching upon areas of deeper commitments and responses for which art offers only one medium of exploration. The essay form, whether couched in conventional prose or less conventionally in poetic prose, offers yet another level of reaching a statement that should not be lost sight of.

Writers in this third category tend to see themselves as committed to more seriously objectified concerns than the self-validating artists. They espouse the idea that they carry a special destiny and that their visions are animated by concerns which, even though arising subjectively from within themselves and their intimate knowledge of themselves, lead them through this knowledge toward wider, more socially validating concern with the world around them, a situation in which their subjectivity is objectified by this widening of interest to accommodate the condition of things outside the limited self. Such writers invariably ripen through their creativity and visions into prophets and spokesmen of their people and, sometimes, of humanity at large. The Old Testament world and ancient mythologies and religions have a fair number of these poet-prophets. Names like Ezekiel, Jeremiah, Nehemiah, and Habbakuk in the Old Testament readily come to mind. The New Testament has Paul of Tarsus and that uncanny author of the Apocalypse, John the Divine.

It is obvious from the evidence in his introduction to *Labyrinths* that Okigbo saw himself as a poet-prophet and his poetical career as that of a bearer of special destiny and spokesman of the time and the people. In other words, he belongs to the third category of writers, whose artistic integrity comprehends their individualities and creativeness, as well as their special commitments and functions as articulators of the aspirations, hopes, and fears of their people and times. This assumption is so fundamental and serious that it should be critically tested before we can reasonably give it credence or proceed from it to explore the wider implications of Okigbo's claim to being a "poet of destiny."

The first task that immediately comes to view is to examine the credentials of the poet-prophet, in much the same way as the Jews of old used to examine critically the personal credentials of their prophets. In a world swarming with noisy, self-appointed spokesmen of the people, a world full of charlatans and confidence tricksters (they also exist among "artists"), the least that can be expected of the aspiring spokesman of the people and humanity is a sign that his inspiration inclines him to high seriousness, to understanding of the inner springs of himself as prophet-aspirant, a sensitive understanding of the nature of man, of human problems and predicaments, and a wholesome assimilation of the self and its interest to the broad, inclusive destiny of a people and the world of people. We must demand of our poet-prophet clarity of view and personal integrity as reliable guides to our better understanding of the forces that tyrannize us. In other words, we must seek to be reassured that the poet *is* of us, that he possesses adequate intellectual scope and breadth of sympathy to understand our problems, that he has the personal integrity to tell us the truth as he sees it, and that he is sufficiently assimilated to our destiny to share our sufferings and agonies, our joys and hopes, our dreams and reveries. We must insist that he should adequately internalize these things in order to become the sensitive needle that probes and locates our emotional traumas, our anxieties, elations, and fears, no less than our hopes and aspirations. We cannot trust him otherwise.

One point requires clarification to avoid the type of error to which a number of critics of Okigbo's poetry are prone. When I say that the poet of destiny should be "of us," I do not imply that he should be like everyone of us, individually or collectively. To become that, he would first of all have to abdicate his poetical vocation, since most of us are not only non-poets but devastatingly prosaic in our individual lives and in our perceptions of life. There is developing currently a certain prescriptive-cum-proscriptive literary opinion, pushed aggressively, and not very wisely, by African literary scholars based mainly in the United States of America, who insist that the African poet, to be genuinely African, must write like everyone of us. In a recent article, the most outspoken of these critics accused all those poets who do not meet this demand (chief of whom is Okigbo) of suffering from Hopkins's Disease.[7]

I find this prescription quite unreasonable. We are not all poets and we value our poets because they are poets. We would not care too much for them if they were no poets at all or if their poetry merely reflected our own far-from-poetical levels of expression. We would probably not expect them to assume the role of spokesmen or to articulate our aspirations with sensitivity, intelligence, and integrity; for, even though a fair number of people may lay claim to intelligence and integrity, what they very often lack are poetic sensitivity and the capacity for imaginative reordering of experience for optimum effect.

It ought to be recognized, however, that an aspect of the poet-prophet's identification with the people for whom he functions as spokesman must be aesthetic as well as historical. In his essay "Tradition and the Individual Talent," T. S. Eliot makes the significant statement that "every nation, every race, has not only its own creative, but its own critical turn of mind,"[8] and, referring specifically to the peculiar relationship of the poet's individual creativity to the general pool of his people's tradition, he writes:

> If we approach a poet without . . . prejudice we shall often find that not only the best, but the most individual parts of his work may be those in which the dead poets, his ancestors, assert their immortality most vigorously.
> . . . Yet if the only form of tradition, of handing down, consisted in follow-

ing the ways of the immediate generation before us in a blind or timid adherence to its successes, 'tradition' should positively be discouraged. We have seen many such, simple currents soon lost in the sand; and novelty is better than repetition. Tradition is a matter of much wider significance. It cannot be inherited, and if you want it you must obtain it by great labour. It involves in the first place, the historical sense, which we may call nearly indispensable to anyone who would continue to be a poet beyond his twenty-fifth year; and the historical sense involves a perception, not only of the pastness, but of its presence; the historical sense compels a man to write not merely with his generation in his bones, but with a feeling that the whole literature of Europe from Homer and within it the whole of the literature of his own country has a simultaneous existence and composes a simultaneous order. This historical sense, which is a sense of the timeless and of the temporal together, is what makes a writer traditional. And it is at the same time what makes a writer most acutely conscious of his place in time, of his own contemporaneity.[9]

It is convenient to lean on T. S. Eliot here because his very lucid view helps to settle one of the most vexing questions concerning Okigbo's poetry, namely, its individuality and the poet's insistence on the role, essentially historical and communal, of prophet, priest, and spokesman—in other words, as a poet of destiny. The poet of destiny fits most patently Eliot's description above, because, like Eliot himself, P. B. Shelley, and W. B. Yeats, among others, the poet of destiny is constantly aware of temporality and timelessness as major determinants defining the totality of his creative commitments; he is aware of traditional continuities as well as the vibrancy of each passing moment of experience. Both factors contribute ultimately to the full impression of the self, its roles, and the relative significance of things. Okigbo says of himself and his perception of his role as poet of destiny:

> When I knew that I couldn't be anything else than a poet—I can't say whether the call came from evil spirits or good spirits. But I know that the turning point came in 1958, when I found myself wanting to know myself better, and I had to turn around and look at myself from inside—I mean myself, just myself not the background. But you know that everything has added up to building up the self—and when I talk of looking inward to myself, I mean turning inward to examine myself. This of course takes account of ancestors.
>
> . . . I am believed to be a re-incarnation of my maternal grandfather, who used to be the priest of the shrine called Ajani, where Idoto, the river goddess, is worshipped. The goddess is the earth-mother, and also the mother of the whole family. My grandfather was the priest of this shrine, and when I was born I was believed to be his incarnation, that is, I should carry on his duties. And although someone else had to perform his functions, this other person was only, as it were, a regent. And in 1958, when I started taking poetry very seriously, it was as though I had felt a sudden call to begin performing my full functions as the priest of Idoto. This is how it happened.[10]

If we believe Okigbo's statement, and there is no good reason why we should not believe him, then we should agree that the major ingredients existed from the very beginning of his poetical career—defining him, by his self-appraisal and appointment, as a poet of destiny. The ingredients are, if we should reduce them further into their relevant constituents, the poet's perception of his unique role as spokesman, priest, and prophet, his perception of the destiny of man or of the specific community within which he places this role, and his perception of the creative process itself through which he communicates his visions. These constituents must be taken one by one and examined with attention so that we can determine whether indeed they exist as essential ingredients of Okigbo's poetry and poetic posture and, therefore, whether the poet has succeeded or failed to carry through his self-appointed role as a poet of destiny.

A poet of destiny must have a definite identity. Even though his destiny tends ultimately to merge with the destiny of his community, he cannot afford to be anonymous or to be seen merely as a blurred presence against the powerful backdrop of themes, techniques, and intentions. The significance we attach to the poetry must necessarily take in our perception of the personality of the poet himself. His integrity must be of an overt kind, since explicitness is essential for a proper rapport between the poet and the people. Homer was not mistaken when he announced to the Greeks for whom he composed or collected *The Iliad* and *The Odyssey* that if anyone should ask them about the maker of the poems, they should say it was "the blind man who sings in the Chios." The strong communal nature of the epic poem does not exclude the presence of an organizing spirit who must be seen as a living presence investing the poems with aura and distinctiveness of authentic human warmth. In like manner, the poet of destiny must have a certain concreteness of identity to help his audience to identify with the matter of his poetry, especially insofar as his credibility and the impact of his poetry depend on the distinctness of his voice, the clarity of his visions, and the integrity of his sentiments.

In the poetry of Okigbo, the personality of the poet is distinctive and visible. We are aware of the poet-protagonist, not only as a speaking voice but also as a physical human presence embodying a feeling and suffering soul. The poet speaks, it is true, through a mask or persona, as a convenient convention, appearing now as a prodigal son returning in penitence to a neglected patrimony, now as a sunbird, a weaverbird, an oracle, or as a town-crier, as befits each particularized occasion and its dominant mood. But the evocative nature of the poetry keeps alive and very much in the fore the distinctive personality and identity of the poet to the very end when, under the severe pressure of events, he dispenses with the mask and appears as his true self with: "I, Okigbo, town-crier, together with my iron bell."[11] A little later, the following lines occur in "Elegy for Slit-Drum":

The mythmaker accompanies us (the Egret had come and gone)/Okigbo accompanies us the oracle enkindles us/the Hornbill is there again (*the Hornbill has had a bath*) Okigbo accompanies us the rattles enlighten us —(69)

Inevitably, the establishment of identity begins with initiation rites. Through initiations, the individual is inducted into distinctly defined roles and is given the psychological and emotional resources to meet the demands of those roles. We are made aware through these processes of the human but privileged presence of the poet, of his sensitivity, imaginativeness, and alertness in the probing of the exterior and interior existences and realities both of man and of the world that surrounds him.

In "Heavensgate," the first sequence of poems in *Labyrinths*, the protagonist is delineated from childhood through adolescence to adulthood, his personality explored through quests that develop the consciousness and lead to an understanding of the self, of the world that impinges on it, and the destiny that entangles the self with the world. We see the poet-protagonist initiated into the triple mysteries that prepare him for the unique role of a poet of destiny: he is initiated into the ancestral role of priest, then into the alienating membership of the Christian religion, and finally into the cult of poetry. Each initiation reveals in more than bare outline the personality of the initiate and the determinant attitudes and moods that are reinforced by the particular experience.

As might be expected, the organization of these experiences does not follow this order strictly. The opening unit, called "The Passage," presents the protagonist as a supplicant at the village stream, Idoto, sacred to the earth-mother goddess. He brings with him an attitude of total humility and surrender, becoming to a returning prodigal son. The idea is that the protagonist, having already been initiated into the Christian faith to the neglect of his obligations to Idoto, the tutelary deity of the community, can only return to the traditional obligations in a mood of repentance and humility:

> *Before you, mother Idoto,*
> *   naked I stand;*
> *before your watery presence,*
> *   a prodigal*
> *leaning on an oilbean*
> *   lost in your legend*
>
> *Under your power wait I*
> *   on barefoot,*
> *watchman for the watchword*
> *   at Heavensgate;*
> *out of the depths my cry*
> *   give ear and hearken—*
>
> (3)

The sense of the poet's inadequacy and humility is written all over this sequence. He stands "naked" before the deity and is a returning prodigal son, as lost as a young bird whose mother has been caught on a spray. His inexperience is conveyed through the analogy with a newly arrived chicken which, the Igbo proverb says, always stands on one leg. The attitude of humility and self-effacement is also typical of Igbo traditional priests face to face with the awesome presence of their deities. But, just as commitment to traditional religion and way of life has a certain imperative, so initiation into the Christian religion and, more particularly, into the Roman Catholic sect of it, is a reality that cannot be wished away. There is a character, a scar or mark of this initiation which remains ineffaceable and as a major conditioner of the poetic consciousness, especially through the centrality of the cross and its association with the redemption of humanity. The crucifix is a powerful image that arrests the sensitive imagination and bends it toward a revolutionary intent. A poet of destiny cannot ignore the significance of the cross, since the self-sacrifice of the Christ never fails to stir the soul out of its torpidity to grasp and preserve the emotional anchor that comes from the contemplation of its powerful image. The permanence of the impact of the cross on the initiate is stated most concretely in the opening verse of "Initiations:"

> Scar of the crucifix
> over the breast,
> by red blade inflicted
> by red-hot blade,
> on right breast witnesseth.
>
> (6)

The poet of destiny, because the rhythm of his own inner existence embodies some messianic inspiration, finds in the lesson of the cross one of his deepest impulses to action, an impulse driving him towards heroic self-sacrifice. Okigbo describes this impulse metaphorically when he says of the poem: "The various sections of the poem . . . present this celebrant at various stations of his cross". (xi)

The Christian faith itself, in its barren orthodoxy, especially in its abstract morality ("life without sin"), is the least satisfactory as an influence because to preach "life without sin" is, in the poet's view, to preach "life without life"

> . . . which accepted
> way leads downward
> down orthocenter
> avoiding decisions.
>
> (xi)

It can only lead to moral passivity. But the cross is different. It symbolizes the ultimate triumph of the spirit over human weaknesses; it represents the more durable aspects of the initiation into Christianity:

> —United in vision
> of present and future,
> the pure line, whose innocence
> denies inhibitions.[11]
>
> (x)

The logic is, of course, that experience is essential to cultivate goodness. To act is to experience, and to experience is to be alive and responsive. Even if in action one makes mistakes, it is still better to learn from such mistakes than to stay passive, "avoiding decisions." The cross is a symbol of action, of redemptive action, and therefore central to the initiation of a sensitive person into heroic virtue. Empty husks of dogma and Christian orthodoxy breed all manner of hypocrites and moral deviants whom the poet identifies through geometrical shapes and patterns:

> Square yields the moron
> fanatics and priests and popes,
> organizing secretaries and
> party managers—
> the rhombus—brothers and deacons,
> liberal politicians,
> selfish selfseekers—all who are good
> doing nothing at all;
> the quadrangle, the rest, me and you.[12]
>
> (7)

The poet presents details of this initiation that indicate how deeply embedded in his consciousness the experience has been. He remembers Kepkanly, who brought him into the church, and also those whimsical, semidemented minstrels and village wags, Jadum and Upandru, who complement the picture of those early exciting days. What, one may ask, is the use of bringing up events long submerged in the memory of more recent, more significant happenings? What have the random songs and disjointed speeches of demented villagers got to do with a poet as up-to-date and modern as Okigbo?

The reason is clear. Initiations are stages through which the intellectual, psychic, and emotional development of an individual are brought about. Each stage is stored up in the memory and contributes, when activated, to defining and highlighting ultimately the totality of the individual's experiences and actions. Earlier in this discussion, the point was made that the poet of destiny should be "of the people," that his experiences, in the nature of things, should approximate those of the people, although in some particulars he would be expected to transcend those experiences. By drawing from the memory bank such common currency as the sayings and actions of generally known characters like Kepkanly (and his unfortunate connection with Harragin), Jadum the half-demented minstrel and his songs "after the lights," and Upandru with his corny maxims, the poet is exhibiting an aspect of this identification with the community, especially with its folk outlook that leads to the recognition of the importance of individuals, be they ever so demented, grotesque, or waggish. Such references have the effect of locating the poet close to the center of his people' folk imagination that takes in everyone and everything that stimulates its responses. In these special interactions, arising from initiation rites, in which the individual is bound more closely to the group and the group more closely to the individual, no experience is too trivial, no action too inconsequential; each experience, action, speech, and gesture helps to provide the emotional scaffolding that sustains the communal world from which the artist draws to enrich his sensibilities and the texture of his work.

In "Watermaid," the third section of "Heavensgate," which deals with initiation into poetry, the experience is largely personal. But the representation of the muse as a watermaid has acquired in recent times fairly wide acceptance, especially within the group among whom Okigbo matured his poetic visions. Hitherto, and over a wide area of West Africa, the belief that the watermaid is reputed to bring wealth and other favors to her favorites is very well known. What Okigbo and the poets of his connection have done is to appropriate the existing belief to the service of poetry. The encounter with the watermaid is therefore a private experience with wider evolving implications.

This initiation is full of anguish because the muse cannot be possessed; the questing protagonist can only obtain occasional glimpses of this source of inspiration and cannot therefore sustain long periods of poetical output. The brevity and brittleness of poetic inspiration drives the poet to a state of near despair:

> So brief her presence—
> match-flare in wind's breath—
> so brief with mirrors around me.
>
> (11)

The muse is described as "maid of the salt-emptiness sophisticreamy." And yet, the experience itself is magnificent and inspires some of the most splendid poetic evocations of the collection. The beach scene is detailed with fine and sensitive discrimination and the Watermaid is described in all her brilliance and other-worldly splendour:

> Bright
> with the armpit-dazzle of a lioness
> . . . .
> wearing white light about her,
> and the waves escort her,
> my lioness,
> crowned with moonlight.
>
> (11)

But the brevity of this experience of poetic inspiration, this encounter with the muse, leaves a hollow feeling of isolation in the poet.

Part of the lesson of this initiation is that isolation is the burden all special and inspired people—priests, poets, prophets, and even philosophers—have to bear. The very intangible nature of their concerns brings them face to face with the despair and loneliness of their situation away from the din and bustle of the world of ordinary people. Initiation into the cult of poetry is, in this respect, a retreat into loneliness and isolation, into areas where the best reward may be a fleeting or fragmentary vision which, if not captured opportunely, is soon lost again—like "gold crop/sinking ungathered." But momentary inspirations become the decisive factors in the making of a poetic career, for, in a process of creativity, it is that flashpoint of intensive experience that gives rise to the most successful poetry. As the poet aptly puts it, what matters is being able to capture that moment of heightened sensitivity and intuitive grasp of the core image inspired by the muse:

> Stretch, stretch, O antennae to clutch at this hour,
> fulfilling each moment in a broken monody.

(13)

Thus, the third initiation is the most problematic but, at the same time, the most relevant in determining the nature of the poetic personality. The feeling of abandonment and isolation, of becoming "an island," sharpens the poet's intuition, enabling him to "clutch" at the flashes of inspiration that come like "match-flare in wind's breath," even while providing the essence of poetic direction.

Initiation is often accompanied by ceremonies of purification and ritual sacrifices. The initiate must throw off the old self and put on a new self, refined and rendered sacred by the appropriate ritual cleansing. The fourth movement of "Heavensgate," "Lustra," concerns this ritual cleansing that reinforces the protagonist's preparation for the poetic vocation. In this development, the conjunction of the previous experiences becomes evident, for here nature becomes the medium through which the three kinds of initiation previously undergone are united. The hills become the focus for the reconciliation of traditional religion and Christianity and provide a core motif and whetstone to the evolving poetic genius of the initiate. Or, to put the matter differently, the poet's initiation into nature, with its corresponding mystical suggestions, resolves the apparent contradictions between the traditional religious impulses and the messianic impulse in the development of the poetic sensibility of the initiate. Sacrifice, which is at the center of both religions, becomes a unifying factor in the poet's experience, and his deepest inspiration.

The logical organization of the verse here requires a comment because it illustrates the best example of a skillful manipulation of material referred to by Okigbo earlier on as "logistics." "Logistics" is a word many commentators on Okigbo have tended to uproot from its context and misconstrue as "acrobatics," or "gymnastics," which they, in turn, interpret as verbal trickery. But "logistics" simply suggests a careful and deliberate deployment of existing material to optimum advantage. There is nothing in this to suggest a forcing of such material into inappropriate positions by mere cleverness or legerdemain.

The first three units of verse prepare the scene for the sacrifice and anticipate the salutary effects of that sacrifice by opening the eyes of the poet to the underlying unity of nature, religions, and poetic inspirations:

> So would I to the hills again
> So would I
> to where springs the fountain
> there to draw from
>
> And to hill top clamber
> body and soul
> whitewashed in the moondew
> there to see from
>
> So would I from my eye the mist
> so would I
> thro' moonmist to hilltop
> there for the cleansing
>
> Here is a new laid egg
> here a white hen at midterm.
>
> (14)

The process of purification, of cleansing, is accomplished by a free and easy exposure to nature, followed by its impact on the poetic consciousness. "Body and soul" must be exposed together; the poetic imagination "draws" from the natural inspiration; the poetic "eye" is cleared to see the hidden likenesses between things apparently dissimilar, to see mystery lurking behind exposed realities. With the poetic imagination thus sharpened, the vital associations are formed to further emphasize the links. Thus, dew-covered flowers suggest "weeping" by nature in remembrance of the death of the Christ, "for him who was silenced." This is further reinforced by the three memorable lines:

> *Messiah will come again*
> *After the argument in heaven*
> *Messiah will come again—*
>
> (15)

The association of ideas is the hallmark of successful poetic organization. For, here, the initiations and purifications are not an end in themselves but a means to the preparation for the ultimate sacrifice to which all sensitive beings are in the end driven by the very logic of their purity. The intimations are fully established and are centered on the traditional religion. The palm grove is the physical representation of this commitment, while the "long-drums and cannons," which ordinarily symbolize death, here signify the awakening of the somnolent spirit. The poet's return is complete after he has partaken of this revitalization of the spirit through nature and sacrifice.

Two events seem deducible from this highly concentrated versification. First, the spirit of the ancestral dead, as represented during traditional drama festivals like those of the Odo and the Omabe of the Nsukka region, "is in ascent," summoned by the "long-drums and cannons." So also the spiritual consciousness of the poet-initiate is awakened by the newly found integration through appreciation of nature and ritual sacrifice. The overall effect is a certain assurance that the prodigal has indeed come home and can now partake of the richness and glory of the ancestral heritage.

The concluding lines of "Lustra" celebrate this newfound strength and confidence:

> I have visited;
> on palm beam imprinted
> my pentagon—
>
> I have visited, the prodigal . . .
>
> In palm grove,
> long-drums and cannons;
> the spirit in the ascent.

Perhaps it is useful to pause at this stage and look at the oft-repeated but erroneous view of some critics of Okigbo that initiation for him means a flight from Christ to Idoto, a rejection of Christianity in favor of traditional religion.[12] That view seems an oversimplification of a patently complex question. There is no flight, but an affirmation; a discrimination, but not a rejection, since total rejection of Christianity would become a repudiation of one of the most active ingredients of Okigbo's poetic inspiration. What are rejected are the empty husks of theoretical Christianity, the dogmas, which all manner of charlatans push and behind which they perpetrate atrocities against their neighbors and humankind. The critics ought to be more careful by following the signposts so well established by the poet. Okigbo does not talk about "Initiation" in "Heavensgate"; he talks of "Initiations." The preference for the plural word in place of the singular is deliberate and therefore significant in our discussion of his intentions. It is clear that as a poet of destiny, Okigbo cannot afford to shut out of his consciousness experiences that vitalize his imagination and prepare him more adequately to fulfill his chosen task.

In "Newcomer," which concludes "Heavensgate," Okigbo gives poignancy to his acceptance of the Christ motif as an important strand in the fabric of his poetic inspiration:

> Time for worship—
> softly sing the bells of exile,
> the angelus,
> softly sings my guardian angel
>
> Mask over my face—
>
> my own mask, not ancestral—I sign:
> remembrance of Calvary,
> and of age of innocence—.

(17)

It is true that he recognizes the Christian connection as a kind of exile, but it is also a part of the functional reality of his total experience. It provides him with one of his many masks which, as he is careful to state, is a personal rather than an ancestral one. In this, as in other similar statements, the poet's integrity is disarming. He does not conceal anything behind a facade of sophistry. He acknowledges sources which individually and collectively account for the richness of his poetry. In this regard, it is useful to note that a major source of his inspiration is the poet's exposure to the world culture through his formal, Western education and, consequently, his grounding in the classics, and, through a variegated reading, in the literatures and mythologies of diverse peoples, countries, and ages. Much of this accumulated knowledge is assimilated in the poetry, in one form or another. Okigbo acknowledges these sources in his introduction to *Labyrinths* in a welter that includes Hopkins's "The Wreck of the Deutschland," Debussy's "Nocturne," Melville's *Moby Dick*, Eliot's "The Waste Land," the work of Malcolm Cowley, Raja Ratman, Stéphane Mallarmé, Rabindranath Tagore, García Lorca, and Peter Thomas.

The same point was made by Okigbo in an interview given to *Transition Magazine* when he said: "I think that I've been influenced by various literatures, right from classical times to the present day in English, Latin, Greek and a little French, a little Spanish."[13] What this means is that the poet's initiations must necessarily take account of his formal education and induction into the literatures and cultures of diverse peoples, places, and times that serve to sharpen his intellectual and emotional responses and to prepare him for the special role as a poet of destiny.

This point is important. Knowledge is necessary for the enrichment of experience, and that enrichment is vital to the sharpening of the imagination and promotion of creativity, because a mind suffused with knowledge is more readily drawn upon in situations requiring firm authoritative statements on the human predicament or aspects of that predicament than one circumscribed and confined within a narrow intellectual groove. Matthew Arnold, one of the originators of modern literary criticism, was right to observe that a successful writer must be a knowledgeable and widely educated man. That condition is even more imperative for the poet who perceives his role as spokesman for his time and people since the framework of his poetic exposition comprehends not just the destiny of himself as an individual but the collective destiny of his community, his race, and mankind in general. Indeed, the matter and manner of prophecy in poetry demand this godlike assurance arising from a certain rootedness in the concrete world of solid and miscellaneous learning. It should be understood, of course, that learning by itself, no matter how profound, cannot satisfy poetic expectations unless it passes through the transforming sieve of the poet's imagination and reissues as a new and refined artefact worthy of aesthetic appreciation.

The uniqueness of Okigbo's poetry and the man's poetic career derive from his successful assimilation of numerous formative influences into an organically unified verse. His poetry answers the strenuous demands of both art and social message and is able to contain great depths and layers of meaning within the most consistently lyrical or poetic framework in the African creative scene. While being the most self-consciously personal of African poets, Okigbo is, at the same time, the most profoundly public in the sweep and spread of his social, political, and cultural commitments.[14]

If we regard Okigbo's sequence of poems in "Heavensgate" as the poet's intellectual, psychological, and cultural preparation for the self-appointed task of oracle and prophet, we would be right to assume also that the sequences known as "Limits" afford the poet an opportunity to test the level of his achievements in terms of his self-assessment and his handling of public and momentous themes. The first four sequences, captioned "Siren Limits," the poet devotes to both a celebration of his newly won inspiration and the successful initiation into the mysteries of life and the bardic cult. But here again the poet's integrity asserts itself in a mixture of excited self-assertion and the recognition of the limitations of vision and performance. The opening glee is soon tempered with the knowledge that fullness of creative stature is still a long way off. That is why the first sequence, which opens with

> Suddenly becoming talkative like weaverbird
> Summoned at offside of dream remembered

and ending with

> Queen of the damp half-light,
> I have had my cleansing,
> Emigrant with air-borne nose,
> The he-goat-on-heat

is followed by the second sequence that opens soberly with

> For he was a shrub among the poplars
> Needing more roots
> More sap to grow to sunlight
> Thirsting for sunlight,
>
> A low growth among the forest—.
>
> (23–24)

This is no case of self-denigration. The poet expresses a reality born of the awareness that poetic maturity is not attained by sudden flight, that the muse is niggardly in dispensing of her bounties, and that there still remain numerous obstacles separating the initiate from full growth. There are, metaphorically, "Banks of reed/Mountains of Broken bottles" (25) to surmount before attaining maturity and developing an authoritative voice of prophecy. For the present, the poet must be contented to remain an acolyte and must not strain for a recognition that has not been adequately prepared for:

> Then we must sing, tongue-tied
> Without name or audience,
> Making harmony among the branches.
>
> (25)

The images here are blurred—mist, twilight between sleep and waking, damp half-light, shadow, dream, and anaesthetic suspension of active consciousness. But the important fact is that the task of poetic composition must go on; the dream must be told, in spite of its evanescent quality; the exploration of the poetic process and the labor to cultivate an appropriate voice cannot be abandoned. In fact, the poet has soon to put his achievements to the test, by venturing, even if only tentatively, into themes of public concerns, in the second half of "Limits," called "Fragments Out of the Deluge."

In these "Fragments," the apparent lack of secure confidence is visible and pushes the poet into using an elaborate framework based on Eastern mythology. Mesopotamian and Egyptian images sound impressive but do nothing to enhance the development of a personal voice and vision, and hardly help the reader, in spite of the explanatory footnotes by the author, to obtain more than a precarious and flighty sense of the poet's meaning. Those who accuse Okigbo of deliberate mystification and obscurity bordering on pedantry might find the opening part of this sequence supportive of their accusation. But the rest of "Fragments," which deals with the assault on native authenticities and the despoiling of African traditions, is handled with greater assurance and fine discrimination. The symbols and images are appropriate, the cadences easy, the meanings pithy, and the arguments firm and hard to fault.

In a sense, "Fragments out of the Deluge" ought structurally and thematically to belong with "Silences" and to lead on to "Path of Thunder." They constitute, in varying forms and degrees of intensity, the areas of poetic and prophetic statements. The other sequences—"The Passage," "Initiations," "Watermaid," "Lustra," and "Newcomer" that make up "Heavensgate," "Siren Limits," and "Distances"—demonstrate the various stages of the poet's preparation for the prophetic, bardic role, including his initiations, self-explorations, and testings of the possibilities of poetic statements. A little shuffling of the arrangement of the poems from the way they are organized by Okigbo to the affinities outlined above would do greater justice to his full design and intentions, since establishment of the self-identity of the poet and exploration of the poetic process serve the higher interest of fulfilling the task of prophecy.

It may be argued, of course, and with considerable validity, that the moods, attitudes, and tones of the different sequences, as presented in *Labyrinths with Path of Thunder*, constitute more accurate bases for the division of the parts than thematic affinities; in which case, it might be prudent to follow the poet-editor's arrangements of the sections of the organic poem. The slight difficulty that arises from the choice between the approaches in this discussion is, fortunately, not insurmountable, once it is noted that the author's appraisal of his intentions and designs cannot be accepted as the last word. As stated earlier in this discussion, the artist is not always the best judge of his own creations.

It could be observed, for example, that the posture of innocence and naïveté assumed by the poet up to "Limits" is not altogether justified in view of the skill and excellent control of statement and poetic form achieved in the second part of "Fragments." There is no doubt that Okigbo's maturity of view and control of his medium had reached in this section a high point only marginally surpassed by the later sequences. The gift of prophecy is already assured; the training in divination is complete, and the public spokesman has already emerged. The preparation for the role of poet of destiny is almost complete. What is left is the very delicate probing of the inner man abstracted from the obstacles of flesh and bones, which he carries out in "Distances."

By the time Okigbo came to write "Distances," the incipient disorders of the body politic of the independent state of Nigeria had become a roaring inferno and had begun to evince all the symptoms of a totally uncontrolled and perhaps incontrollable state of social disintegation referred to by sociologists as a state of anomie. We have here a society heaving backward toward chaos.

The role of the creative artist infused with a sense of destiny is quite clear at a time such as this. He would direct his creative energies in an opposite direction from a world propelled toward its chaotic beginnings; it is his duty to attempt to create order out of chaos, and a cosmos out of refractory materials driven by human weaknesses and nature's law backward to their primeval sources. The creative process, in other words, becomes a struggle against the encroaching chaos and attendant disasters. To create is to impose order where active agents hurtle toward a lack of order and in obedience to Hobbesian imperatives. The artist, pulling away from the dominant force of a world in disarray and attempting to steady it and steer it away from its course of disintegration, encounters many-faceted terrors and dangers. The task is made doubly dangerous because it involves taking a positive stand against the primitive impulses and passions that govern man, especially the passion to destroy, to stop the process of creation, to restore chaos, and to perpetuate it. The creative artist is thus up against principalities and powers, against the immense and ingenious machine designed by man for the emasculation of the truly beautiful, the pure, the sublime, and the productive.

For the poet of destiny, the choices in this sort of emergency are even more limited. He has to oppose himself actively through his medium to the agents of chaos and the destroyers of a people's dreams for true liberation. He has to espouse antithetical values to those of a society wheeling toward chaos, with full awareness of the risks and dangers involved which, ultimately, must include the reality of death and physical dissolution. To prepare himself therefore, to meet the challenge of chaos, the poet of destiny must steel himself against that eventuality toward which the logic of his avowed commitments will inevitably carry him.

In "Distances," Okigbo allows himself to experience the reality of death, as a means of bracing himself for the dangerous struggle against the forces of chaos. He recognizes that it is only in the full realization of the consequences of death and dissolution can he, as a quest-protagonist, undergo the final ritual preparation without which the task cannot be followed to its logical conclusion. It is only when the poet of destiny has gone through his initiation into the mysteries of death that he is ready to undertake the final and most dangerous task of his vocation without the inhibitive fear that comes from absence of knowledge.

Okigbo explores the reality of death as a sort of homecoming, as the experience takes him back to the very beginning of things. He experiences moments of rare vivid insight and glimpses of the horrors that await the poet-protagonist in his attempt to reverse the world from its rush toward chaos:

> anguish and solitude . . .
> smothered my scattered
> cry, the dancers
>
> lost among their own
> snares; the faces
> the hands held captive;
> the interspaces
> reddening with blood;
>
> and behind them all,
> in smock of white cotton,
> Death herself,
> the chief celebrant
> In a cloud of incense
> paring her fingernails . . .
>
> At her feet rolled their heads like cut fruits;
> about her fell
> their severed members, numerous as locusts.
> Like split wood left to dry, the dismembered
> joints of the ministrants piled high
>
> She bathed her knees in the blood of attendants;
> her smock in entrails of ministrants. . . .
>
> (55)

Okigbo calls "Distances" a poem of homecoming in its spiritual and psychic aspect, a process of sensual anaesthesia and of total liberation from all physical and emotional tension. It is important to observe that this liberation from what a writer has called the tyranny of form and matter is inevitable to give the poet-protagonist the final exposure that qualifies him for the role of prophet and poet of destiny. Until now, exposure and preparation for this role has been sustained in concrete terms, in images and symbols of initiation that chain the mind to the sensitive body. The prodigal at heavensgate is a physical being: naked, standing barefoot, leaning on a sacred oilbean tree. Nature images abound here, and when the ground shifts to initiation into

Christianity, the concreteness of the cross is pervasive and even moral states are not abstracted but are given concrete, geometrical patterns. In the "Water-maid" sequences, the sea and the beach and all kinds of marine scenery are presented; so also are the sky and the stars. In "Lustra" and "Newcomer," the hills, the palm groves, flowers, and long-drums and cannons provide appropriate setting for the ritual preparation for the long quest. "Siren Limits," in which the quest itself is already under way, presents the protagonist's self-appraisals largely in concrete images and symbolic terms: he is "a shrub among the poplars," "a low growth among the forest," "little stream to the lake." In "Distances," however, everything is dreamlike, evanescent, intangible— "from flesh to phantom." This is the most difficult level of experience to capture and the most essential to complete the cycle of preparation for the apocalyptic role for which the poet has been building up his resources and initiatives.

Nor should we be surprised that the exploration of this level of poetic consciousness should be reserved for the last stage in the evolution of the actions and the terrible events that challenge the very limits of the poet's resourcefulness and affirmations. The vision imprisoned in solid matter may appear adequate at the beginning when the stakes are relatively low, but with the escalation of the crisis to the threat of total collapse of the state and the dream behind it, new issues come to view, and new questions necessarily arise that radicalize our expectations of the poet of public commitment. We ask: does this spokesman know enough? Is his experience adequate to qualify him as spokesman? Has he felt the terror of the intangible, of the inchoate and fluid state of being from which the process of creation began? Can he speak authoritatively of those deep mysteries that surround humanity, es-pecially in those harsh moments when we are helplessly pushed back toward the sources? Can the poet bear the terror of dissolution and death, or will he lose heart at the first sight of the massive, heaving movement toward the chaos of the beginning? Can he endure the painful immensity of isolation and abandonment, and the final dissolution of his own individual being? In other words, we ask if the poet is equipped to deal with death with integrity, candor, and sensitivity—not as an abstract reality, but as a fate that constitutes part of the common heritage of a people being systematically pushed back into the cave of disaster, into the womb of chaos.

There is very little doubt that Okigbo passes these exacting tests. His poetic sensibilities, refined and sharpened by each stimulus in the vast es-calating disaster of the Nigerian national crisis, imaginatively penetrate that intangible void, the abysmal and original chaos, from which creation grew. "Distances" reports this vision:

> . . . Beyond the archway
> like pentecostal orbs
> resplendent far distant
> in the intangible void

> an immense crucifix
> of phosphorescent mantles:
>
> *after we had formed*
> *then only the forms were formed*
> *and all the forms*
> *were formed after our forming . . .*
>
> . . . each step is the step of the mule in the abyss—
> the archway the oval the panel oblong
> to that sanctuary at the earth's molten bowel
> for the music woven into the funerary rose
> the water in the tunnel its effervescent laughter
> the open laughter of the grape or vine
> the question in the inkwell the answer on the monocle
> the unanswerable question in the tabernacle's silence—
> Censers, from the cradle,
> of a nameless religion:
> each sigh is time's stillness, in the abyss. . . .
>
> (57–58)

This quality of poetic perception, it must be insisted upon, distinguishes the poet of destiny from the ordinary lyricist, the songbird who warbles about the vicissitudes of life without necessarily partaking of their toil, or from the heroic poet who shares, often vicariously, in the glories and surface levels of a people's predicaments. The poet of destiny is not only a sharer of his people's aspirations, a prophet and spokesman for them in time and out of time, but a carrier of their burden in the last resort when they are overwhelmed by calamity and driven backward toward dissolution and chaos. The essential difference here is that the poet of destiny would be in the forefront of his people's celebrations; he would carry the cross in front of them as they tread the weary path to their calvary. He does not bring up the rear in their march to Golgotha, nor does he loiter behind to supply the footnotes after their crucifixion. His kind of poetry is not "an emotion recollected in tranquillity" but a red-hot cry, integral and definitive, of the very rhythm of the action that engenders it.

Okigbo's perception of the world around him acquires a critical focus in "Fragments Out of the Deluge." He sees this world as vitiated by insidious forces of oppression. All is destruction here, a solidification into stone and iron, reinforced by tombstone images, by deadness and insensitivity. A deliberate policy of emasculation and destruction of creativity is ushered in by colonialists and Christian missionaries. They are symbolized by "a fleet of eagles."

But the poet, as the keeper of the common seal, whose sensitivity, in spite of the efforts of these twin oppressive forces to destroy him, survives to tell the tale. He describes the disaster and attempts to rouse the people (already reduced to impotence) to fight for their heritage. It is the poet-protagonist versus the spoilers and emasculators of the people. The people, lulled into a false sense of well-being, are lost in their innocence: "And there was none thirsty among them". (29) "The chosen/mongrel breeds/with slogan in hand, of/won divination," the collaborators with the oppressors, join in despoiling the unsuspecting people. But the poet, as sunbird and natural champion of the traditional heritage, carries the battle deep into the enemy camp, and, by painting a most terrifying picture of the desolation that comes with the invasion, attempts to jolt the people out of their complacency into an awareness of the nature of the disaster that has overtaken them. Perhaps, in all African poetry, including that by the most aggressively negritude poets, no writer has created such a picture of the total destruction of the native tradition by the invasion of Europe, as recorded in Okigbo's "Limits XI."

> And the gods lie in State
> And the gods lie in state
> Without the long-drum.
>
> And the gods lie unsung,
> Veiled only with mould,
> Behind the shrine house.
>
> Gods grow out
> Abandoned;
> And so do they. . . .
>
> (34)

It is bad that gods should die at all; it is terrible that they should be denied the basic funeral rites ordinarily accorded to simple mortals. In European myths, the death of gods has evolved into the cyclic phenomenon of the seasons—the gods die with the coming of winter to be resurrected in spring. In other words, they are dead only in the figurative sense of a suspension of active natural life, followed inevitably by revival. In Africa, on the other hand, where people's consciousness is deeply informed by a sacred, metaphysical view of life, the undermining of traditional religion with its symbolic representations amounts to an unhinging of things that give stability and anchorage to life.

There is a warning in all this. When people allow the core of their culture to be destroyed and their sacred beliefs to be desecrated, they lose the cohesive aspects of their society and their psychological anchor and are ready to be enslaved by foreigners and converted to foreign ways. That is also why successful colonialism begins with an attack on its victims' religion, sacred myths, and cultural beliefs. The poet, as the guardian of the common heritage, has the duty to save the people, through his art and craft, from a disaster worse than death, a rout as total as the overthrow of the Titans. His uniqueness lies in his indestructibility; for, though the gods are as vulnerable and as fragile as the people who create them and the ends for which they make them, the poet escapes the net of the enemy's treachery and brutality by his activated imagination and creative intelligence, which thus become the final insurance against permanent enslavement of the people. Out of an encounter as gory as the scene depicted by Picasso in "Guernica," the poet, like the proverbial phoenix, rises to continue the task of leadership and inspiration, by carrying the burden of his people's destiny. His duty is to oppose the enemy's brutality and destructiveness with his constructive and creative humanism. His duty is to sing his admonishments to his people, to renew their fallen light, as Blake puts it in "The Bard."

In Okigbo's *Labyrinths*, this bardic role expands in "Lament of the Silent Sisters" (1962) and "Lament of the Drums" (1964). "Fragments out of the Deluge" (1961/62) treats the reader to a robust cultural nationalism in the wake of the heady celebration of formal independence; but "Laments" follows the eruption of post-independence crises in the former Belgian Congo and Nigeria, the emotional focal points being the assassination of Patrice Lumumba, the first prime minister of the Congo, and the imprisonment of Chief Obafemi Awolowo, the leader of the opposition party in the Nigerian Federal Parliament, followed by the death of his eldest son. What these events did was to sharpen the awareness that political independence brought with it unforeseen dangers more threatening than those predictable atrocities of colonialism. The unleashing of barbaric violence on little-suspecting people, and the cynical strategies of neocolonial imperialism to destroy real independence and replace it with puppetry, sounded the alarm that the great tragic drama that had opened with colonial incursions was about to reach its climax.

The mood deepens in "Lament of the Silent Sisters" and the tone becomes more tragic and somber. The structural organization of the poetry is more complex, while a more widely defined context replaces the lens through which the lyrical persona viewed events until now. The emotional pitch is raised by the use of movements in the verse, structured round the Crier and a chorus of anguished nuns, the point of reference being Gerald Manley Hopkins's "The Wreck of the Deutschland," a poem that recalls the drowning of several Franciscan nuns in a noncombatant ship torpedoed during the First World War.

The poet exercises great ingenuity in the use of two sequences to vary the angle of view and to reinforce one set of events with the help of the other set, harmonizing the feelings of despair that attend the two events. The hopelessness of a ship sinking in the ocean without chance of rescue is used to depict the hopelessness of the African situation when imperialist eagles and "Scavengers" descend with unparallel ferocity, bent on reestablishing themselves in the so-called independent states, "How does one say NO in thunder?" is a question that echoes through the void. There is no answering action.

The images are saturated with despair and impotence, golden eggs empty of albumen; compass and cross that fail to provide an escape; absence of anchorage, shank, or archways. In place of action, there are rhythms of silence, broken hidden feather-of-flight, hollow seascapes without memory, swan song, sense's stillness, and worlds that have failed. The dominance of sibilants and fricatives tends to underline the feeling of exhaustion and hopelessness. The paralyzing sense of futility and despond cannot be disguised; there is no lulling of the people into a false sense of well-being. All is fear and cowardice typified by "yellow images," "voices in the senses' stillness," "painted harmonies."

In contrast to the helplessness of the victims, the imperialists and their local collaborators ("the choir of inconstant dolphins") appear now as "a fleet of eagles" and now as steely, all-conquering phalanx with "cast-iron steps cascading down the valley all forged into thunder of tanks/and detonators cannoned into splintered flames." (40)

The poet laments the impotence of the people that invites the aggression of their oppressors. At this stage, there is no positive response except to "dip one's tongue in the ocean//(camp) with the choir of inconstant dolphins by shallow sand banks//sprinkled with memories//and to maintain a silence distilled in yellow melodies." (44) In other words, there is hardly anything viable to do to oppose the oppressors' massive violence other than to find outlet, at least temporarily, in "silence."

The mood of this first "Lament" is largely defeatist and an expression of hopelessness by sensitive Nigerians at the sudden and treacherous return of the imperialists with the active collaboration of some local politicians. This mood is reinforced by the involvement of a women's chorus, aptly, because mourning and lamentation are conventionally associated with women in several cultures. In many African societies, dirges and funeral lamentations are associated more with women than with men, and, even in pre-industrial Europe, as in the case of the dying King Arthur of the Round Table, women were charged with the task of lamentation and funeral wailing. The poet is therefore realistic in his use of the silent sisters to give emotional underpinning and reinforcement to the heart-rending destruction of the hopes and prospects of the independent states of Africa overwhelmed by a new, brutal oppression of imperialist Europe.

It is noteworthy that two years separate the first "Lament" from "Lament of the Drums." Those two years were critical in the unfolding chaos that was rapidly swallowing up the Nigerian nation. Violence had become endemic and the governments were proving unequal to the task of leading the people forward in a peaceful, harmonious atmosphere. The workers were growing restive, life was full of insecurities, and the absence of a national sense of direction created a favorable atmosphere for corruption to thrive in. The resources of the country were being stolen by public trustees or being fought over by those eager to get their fingers in the pie. It had become clear that the country had been plunged headlong into the abyss, and that the forces of disorder were propelling it toward its fatal destiny.

The texture of the poetry in the second "Lament" is finer; the voice of prophecy is firmer and more authoritative. Some of the earlier images reappear but in sharper focus. The cadence is slower, more evenly measured, almost leisurely. The worst is now known. We experience the effect of the calm that follows a great catastrophe and, in turn, prepares the way for an even greater catastrophe. Before the poet there stands the "chaliced vintage" that must be drunk.

The key evidence for this radicalization of crises and the willingness to confront it can be seen in the syntactical movement of the second "Lament" sequences. If we compare the opening movement of "Lament of the Silent Sisters" with the opening invocation in "Lament of the Drums," we are struck by the broken syntax of the former and the slow, steady, almost cheerful flow of the verse in the latter. In the first "Lament," the Crier opens with the fear-suffused lines:

> IS THERE . . . Is certainly there—
> For as in sea-fever globules of fresh anguish
> immense golden eggs empty of albumen
> sink into our balcony . . .

How does one say NO in thunder—.(39) [The element of confusion and uncertainty capped by terror is manifested in the broken syntax of the first line. We have a certain incompleteness in both the sentence structure and the structure of meaning in the lines following. In contrast, "Lament of the Drums" opens with fully rounded syntactical structures:

> LION-HEARTED cedar forest, gonads for our thunder,
>
> Even if you are very far away, we invoke you:
>
> Give us our hollow heads of long-drums . . .
>
> Antelopes for the cedar forest, swifter messengers
> Than flash-of-beacon-flame, we invoke you:
> Hide us; deliver us from our nakedness. . . .
>
> (45)

Here the syntactical control is not only firm, but even complex, with phrasal and clausal elaborations, and the powerful, highly accentuated, end-placed sentence, "we invoke you." The opening epithet, "lion-hearted," is obviously transferred from the poet or his persona to the "cedar forest." It is quite clear that what the earlier crises have achieved is to rouse a deep resolve in the poet to confront the dangerous issues threatening the security of all. There is no more room for illusions but a certain inevitability that the crises have intensified and that suffering is about to become the common heritage of those beguiled by the hope of redemption. The voice of prophecy is firm and unequivocal: there will be unparalleled suffering and death, and many will suffer martyrdom because "the robbers"—the imperialists and their internal collaborators—are on the offensive and bent on destroying all who stand in the way of wholesale spoliation of the so-called independent state. The poet proclaims the threat unequivocally:

> . . . We sense
> With dog-nose a Babylonian capture,
> The martyrdom
> Blended into that chaliced vintage.
>
> (46)

But the challenge of the robbers will not be adequately answered because those who should tackle it are themselves too deeply sunk in corruption to muster the will to resist:

> Nothing remains, only smoke after storm—
> Some strange Celaeno and harpy crew,
> Laden with night and their belly's excrement.
> Profane all things with hooked feet and foul teeth.
>
> (47)

The one man, Palinurus, capable of standing up to the robbers, has already been put away to rot in detention:

> Like palm oil fostered in an ancient clay bowl,
> A half-forgotten name; like a stifled sneeze. . . .
>
> (48)

But this failure to resist oppression does not bring reprieve; instead, it calls forth more intensive oppression and more widespread destruction. The prophecy that concludes this section of the "Laments" is fulfilled to an uncanny exactitude in a matter of months by the immense escalation of Nigerian political crises:

> *The wailing is for the fields of crop:*
>
> The drums' lament is:
> They grow not . . .
>
> *The wailing is for the fields of men*
>
> For the barren wedded ones;
> For perishing children . . .
>
> *The wailing is for the Great River:*
>
> Her pot-bellied watchers
> Despoil her. . . .
>
> (50)

But the crises and destructions of 1964 were to be far surpassed by those of 1965. From May 1965, Okigbo began the sequences of poems he called "Path of Thunder," which record the hallmarks of the tragic events that led up to the Nigerian civil war. Okigbo was greatly troubled by the further escalation of violence, lawlessness, and corruption that made sustaining a stable civil state increasingly difficult. He put his poetic integrity at the service of his battered country and allowed the full benefits of his poetical maturity to shine through in spite of the desperate nature of the situation. His poetical sensibilities, now sharpened to razor-edge, cut through the tangled mass of passionate complexities to grasp at the core of the deadly issues. The stakes had become too high to be dealt with through poetical disguises and far-fetched analogies. The very immediacy and magnitude of the dangers called for a certain directness of address and plain speaking somewhat at odds with the stances of his earlier poetry. Moreover, it had become obvious that the stages of oracular exposition had come to an end and the stage was set for plain-speaking, for a directness of address, which constitutes the acme of the apocalyptic tradition. All prophets, oracles, and diviners must, at crisis points of their vocations, lay aside their specialized medium to espouse the simplest and directest modes of address. The essential paradox here is that the profoundest truths are reserved for the simplest and most direct language structure. The masks are laid aside and the man speaks in his own voice:

> I have lived the sapling sprung from the bed of the old vegetation:
> Have shouldered my way through a mass of ancient nights to chlorophyll;
> I have lived the oracle dry on the cradle of a new generation.
>
> (64)

And elsewhere, later:

> If I don't learn to shut my mouth I'll soon go to hell.
> I, Okigbo, town-crier, together with my iron bell.
>
> (67)

Okigbo recognized the dangers of plain speaking at a time of immense passions and irrational violence, but here his poetic responsibility asserted itself: the stakes were just too high to allow for the fine consideration of personal safety. He assumed the full responsibility of a poet of destiny who would not stand aside from the cataclysmal waves threatening the survival of his people. He recognized the revolutionary nature of the events sweeping through the land, as well as the risks that formed part and parcel of such events; for, a revolution, like a boa, might destroy its own children in its fevered movement. A poet as self-conscious as Okigbo could hardly be expected to be ignorant of the deepest implications of the forces sweeping over the land or to ignore the vast opportunity which the situation constituted for the writer whose destiny was coterminous with that of his country and his people.

In "Come Thunder," which was written in December 1965, when the state of anomic violence had reached the peak of disaster, the poet made his final prophecy, which was to be fulfilled to the minutest detail by the events of the next four years. It deserves to be quoted in full because it constitutes the apex of Okigbo's poetry in its prophetic and apocalyptic grandeur:

> Now that the triumphant march has entered the last street corners,
> Remember, O dancers, the thunder among the clouds . . .
> Now that laughter, broken in two, hangs tremulous between the teeth,
> Remember, O dancers, the lightning beyond the earth . . .
> The smell of blood already floats in the lavender-mist of the afternoon
> The death sentence lies in ambush along the corridors of power;
> And a great fearful thing already tugs at the cables of the open air,
> A nebula immense and immeasurable, a night of deep waters
> An iron dream unnamed and unprintable, a path of stone
> The drowsy heads of the pods in barren farmlands witness it,
> The homesteads abandoned in this century's brush fire witness it;
> Magic birds with the miracle of lightning flash on their feathers . . .
> The myriad eyes of deserted corn cobs in burning barns, witness it;
> The arrows of God tremble at the gates of light,
> The drums of curfew pander to a dance of death;
> And the secret thing in its heaving
> Threatens with iron mask
> The last lighted torch of the century. . . .

(66)

The dancers referred to here were the politicians, the effete public servants, and the exploiting classes who made common cause with imperialism to snuff out the bright prospect of independence. These were too far gone in corruption and decadence to heed the urgent import of prophecy. Of course, such people never read any literature as exacting and exalting as poetry. The spiritual dimension informed by social justice was far away from their lives, and with the insensitivity of renowned comedians, they pushed their country over the precipice into abysmal violence and civic disorder.

In January 1966, Nigeria experienced a coup d'état that brought the army into power politics in the country. Okigbo, like most of his contemporaries, reflecting popular disenchantment with the misrule of the civilian politicians, welcomed the change with enthusiasm because that change, even if only for a brief while, called a halt to the anarchy which had immobilized the country. But he was also one of the first people to warn that popular enthusiasm was not enough, it could be, and is, as easily dissipated. The celebration of the coup in "Elegy for Slit-Drum" and written for "rattles accompaniment" is composed in jerky, elliptical syntax, embodying mixed sentiments of hopes and considerable foreboding:

> The cabinet has gone to hell
> the timbers are now on fire
> the cabinet that sold itself
> ministers are now in gaol—

condolences quivering before the iron throne of a new conqueror:
the mythmaker accompanies us (*the Egret had come and gone*)
Okigbo accompanies us the oracle enkindles us
the Hornbill is there again (*the Hornbill has had a bath*)
Okigbo accompanies us the rattles enlighten us—
condolences with the miracle of sunlight on our feathers—.

(68–69)

The rattles provide ideal musical punctuation for the jaunty minstrel rhythm that at this stage has become the dominant impulse in Okigbo's verse. Minstrelsy is musically versatile and highly inspired in sentiment, as well as providing many grants for social commentary. Musicality, which has from the very beginning become a major defining principle of Okigbo's verse, attains the highest flights in these last poems, mainly because the events themselves yield the greatest concentration of emotive response, which finds loftiest expression in outgoing musical celebrations. The simplicity and directness of the lyrical sentiments invite, with a certain inevitability, a musical approach that thoroughly utilizes the rhythmic advantages of caesuras, end-stoppages, accentuated lines, and repetitions.

The nature of the situation itself requires a lifting of the masks and the revelation of the true resonance of the natural voice. The lyrical persona whose self-conscious individuality up until now controlled the poetic inspiration is overridden by the social persona who absorbs the deeply felt fears and anxieties of a whole people. The "us," which increasingly supplants the "I" of the earlier sequences, symbolizes this acceptance of the destiny of the individual within the larger, inclusive destiny of the group. The poet's assertion in "Elegy of the Wind" that he had lived the oracle dry on the cradle of a new generation marks a significant, nearly total submergence of his individuality within the wider, collective interests of the entire people. The mythmaker Okigbo, whose outlook is objectified in the unique role of community poet, can no longer stand aside from the "us," the collectivity, now hemmed in by immense possibilities of both salvation and damnation. The poet is lost in the people. Okigbo, the poet, "accompanies" us, the people, and his rattle music unifies the emotional aspirations of the group. The mixture of dread and elation at these new developments is suggested by "the miracle of sunlight on our feathers" and the "quivering before the iron throne of a new conqueror."

The limited euphoria of the military coup was soon over. By May 1966, it had become clear that the forces of reaction had re-emerged and that the hopes for redemption of the nation were not to be realized. In "Elegy for Alto," Okigbo, now fully integrated into the collective consciousness of the people and sensing the imminence of the great terrible times ahead, wrote his final testimony, in which he bemoaned the death of a great dream. The country stood at the brink of war, and the reversion to chaos, only temporarily staved off, continued with accelerated speed. For a man who had stood at the center of the great dream of Nigerian nationhood, the alienation and sense of doom were most distressing and painful:

> For beyond the blare of sirened afternoons, beyond the motorcades;
> The voices and days, the echoing highways;
>   beyond the latescence
> Of our dissonant airs; through our curtained eyeballs,
>   through our shuttered sleep,
> Onto our forgotten selves, onto our broken images;
>   beyond the barricades
> Commandments and edicts, beyond the iron tables,
>   beyond the elephant's
> Legendary patience, beyond the inviolable bronze bust;
>   beyond our crumbling towers—
> Beyond the iron path careering along the same beaten track—
> The Glimpse of a dream lies smouldering in a cave, together with
>   the mortally wounded birds.
> Earth, unbind me; let me be the prodigal; let this be the ram's
>   ultimate prayer to the tether. . . .
>
> (72)

The signs of dissolution were unmistakable:

> —The Eagles are now in sight:
> Shadows in the horizon—
> The robbers are here in black sudden steps of showers, of caterpillars—
> . . . .
> The eagles descend on us.
> Bayonets and cannons—
> . . . .
> Politicians are here in this iron dance of mortars, of generators—.
>
> (71)

Nothing remained but to leave "the cave" of the wrecked dream and to seek shelter and safety in the open air of his nativity, to discard the large but unrealized dream for another destiny with a new sense of freedom:

So let the horn paw the air howling goodbye. . . . (71) Herein again, Okigbo, the oracle, the prophet, the town-crier, the sunbird, reaffirms for the last time the integrity of his individuality as a seer. Borrowing the profound words of the Spanish poet Serafén Alvarez Quintero, that in a time of immense upheavals in the lives of peoples and nations the great natural law of change and continuity remains the permanent and inviolable reality, Okigbo wrote:

> An old star departs, leaves us here on the shore
> Gazing heavenward for a new star approaching;
> The new star appears, foreshadows its going
> Before a going and coming that goes on forever. . . .
>
> (72)

In this masterly stroke of prophetic insight, he foretells not only his own going but the course of events that were to come and to affect the world whose humanistic values he had so vitally and singlemindedly and beautifully illuminated, and within which he had painstakingly sowed the seed of imperishable love and harmony against the wild, subversive passions of materialistically bound obsessions.

The crumbling of a great edifice is always a painful spectacle; so also is the dissolution of a great dream. But it is in the nature of things that the greatest dreamers are also the greatest despairers; the most refined and sensitive souls are the most tragical sufferers when great hopes dissolve. Thus, Wordsworth could write, in "Resolution and Independence":

> We poets in our youth, begin in gladness;
> But thereof come in the end despondency and madness.[15]

Christopher Okigbo, like most of his contemporaries, believed in the great dream of Nigerian nationhood. This dream, always assumed and implicit in his poetic exertions, formed one of the great impulses of his creativity. In this regard, he was like most of the creative artists of his generation—fine and plastic artists, musicians, novelists, dramatists, creative journalists, and so on, who were deeply animated by the stirring events affecting the evolving and potentially great nation. But, more than his contemporaries, Okigbo's imaginative integration with the hopes and aspirations of his people was so total, so close, that with the sudden collapse of the dream it also meant, of course, that he himself had come to the end of things. The poet of destiny cannot survive independently of the destiny of his people which he had taken up and made his own. Romantic poets, in spite of their dreams and idealism, almost surmounted the failure of their dreams: they managed to dream other dreams, because of their imaginatively detachable abilities. Only poets of destiny among them, because of the integrative nature of their commitment, their inextricable identification of their individual destinies with those of their people, find it hard to create new destinies and new dreams when those of the people have collapsed.

The special nature of the relationship of poets of destiny with their peoples and their people's aspirations makes it almost inevitable that the world can only have very few such poets at any given moment of history, but more so in this modern age. In antiquity, there was a greatly integrated world outlook, and many communities probably had their poets of destiny, their bards, who sounded their heartbeats and reflected their deepest yearnings. But in the modern age, with its consuming passion for egotistic self-definitions and self-fulfilments, the breed of such poets has dwindled to almost none. Christopher Okigbo and, undoubtedly, Pablo Neruda of Chile and Latin America, were perhaps, among the last of that breed. Neruda's commitment to his native Chile and his beloved Latin America was as total as Okigbo's to his people of Nigeria, and both poets, in the nature of things and of their peculiar commitments, were destined to meet a tragic end. The worldwide tributes that have been paid to these two poets offer incontestable testimony that their greatness transcended the narrow limits of poetic creativity.[16] They stood for those values of light and truth and love and freedom and compassion without which nations and peoples perish and generations go to perdition. Neruda summed up such unique commitment in two memorable lines of personal testament that conclude his poem "Do Not Ask Me," when he wrote:

> I have a pact of love with beauty:
> I have a pact of blood with my people.[17]

Such could also be Christopher Okigbo's testament.

NOTES

1. William Blake, "Song of Experience," *The Norton Anthology of Poetry*, 3d ed. (New York and London, 1983), 503.

2. Ibid.

3. William Wordsworth, "Resolution and Independence," *The Norton Anthology of Poetry* (New York and London, 1983), 547.

4. The present writer does not quite agree with those critics who say that Okigbo's poems suffer from an overromantic concern with the poet as hero. See, for example, Dan Izevbaye, "From Reality to Dream: The Poetry of Christopher Okigbo," in *The Critical Evaluation of African Literature*, ed. Edgar Wright (London, 1973), 148. The view here is that the poetical tasks undertaken by Okigbo and the seriousness of his statements require certain validation, including the unravelling of the processes of poetic maturation and the laying bare of the poet's own credentials. Notwithstanding the Eliot canon enjoining impersonality and a poet's detachment from his work, certain kinds of poetry gain considerably from the poet's personal distinctiveness. The assumption is that the poet's personality is deeply involved in the experience he is exploring; he is both subject and object. The presence of the poet or his persona(e) in the poetry is inseperable from the total effect of the poem. Accounts of childhood and adolescence often trace an individual's journey to consciousness through the struggle to understand oneself and the world one lives in. As someone has validly asserted, such accounts, in a good proportion of African and Afro-Caribbean writing, generally have the salutary effect of indicating the issues upon which the individual has focused his powerful imagination.

5. Christopher Okigbo, *Labyrinths with Path of Thunder* (London, 1971), 7. As if Okigbo anticipated that he would not survive the storm already gathering in Nigeria, he painstakingly revised and reorganized his poems before his death in July 1967. This volume was published posthumously by Heinemann in 1971.

Some commentators on his poetry have noted the nature and extent of these revisions. He not only altered the structure of the poem, but strenghtened its poetic voice. See, for example, Theo Vincent, "Okigbo's *Labyrinths*" in *Black Orpheus* 2, 7 (1972): 32. In the revision, Okigbo may have benefited from the more perceptive of his early critics by getting rid of weaknesses such as were noted by M. J. C. Echeruo in "Traditional and Borrowed Elements in Nigerian Poetry," *Nigeria Magazine* 89 (June 1966): 142–55. For the most comprehensive bibliographical study of Okigbo's poems and the critical commentaries on them, see Joseph C. Anafulu, "Christopher Okigbo, 1932–1967: A Bio-Bibliography," *Research in African Literatures* 9 (Spring 1978): 65–78.

6. Okigbo, *Labyrinths*, 14.

7. See Chinweizu, Onwuchekwa Jemie, and Ihechukwu Madubuike, *Towards the Decolonization of African Literature* (Washington, D.C., 1983), 174–83, 208–9. Chinweizu exempts Okigbo's last poetic sequence, "Path of Thunder," from the censure directed at the rest of his poetry for its "Euro-modernist" tendencies in "Prodigals, Come Home!" *Okike, An Africa Journal of New Writing* 12 (April 1978): 40–46.

8. T. S. Eliot, *Selected Essays* (London, 1969), 13.

9. Ibid., 14.

10. Interview with Marjory Whitelaw, *Journal of Commonwealth Literature* 9 (July 1970): 34–35.

11. Christopher Okigbo, *Labyrinths with the Path of Thunder* (London, 1971), 67. Subsequent page references for quoted material are given in the text.

12. See, for example, R. N. Egudu's "Okigbo's 'Distances': A Retreat from Christ to Idoto," *Conch* 5 (1973): 29–42. Christopher Okigbo's attitudes to Christianity and the traditional religion are clearly stated by him in the interview with Marjory Whitelaw referred to earlier. In his view, ". . . all these gods [of traditional religion] are the same as the Christian God. . . . They are different aspects of the same power, the same force." *Journal of Commonwealth Literature*, 30.

13. Interview by Robert Serumaga published in *Transition* 7, 33 (1965): 18.

14. The text of *Labyrinths with The Path of Thunder*, shorn of the crudities of the earlier versions, justifies the statements embodied here. The tantalizing allusions and diversionary images regarded by Paul Theroux and some other commentators as the sources of the so-called obscurity of Okigbo's poetry (see, Theroux, "Christopher Okigbo," in *Introduction to Nigerian Literature*, ed. Bruce King (Lagos and London, 1971), 135–51) in this collection have been either eliminated altogether or have been successfully assimilated to a new organic unity. A comparison of earlier and later versions of the poems will indicate the profound transformations Okigbo wrought in intentions, strategies, and meanings. Whereas his earlier poems, individually and, perhaps, collectively, failed to yield a consistently powerful and unified vision, the consciously edited, condensed, and organically structured final work achieves his vision in a way no other African poet has succeeded in doing to this day.

15. William Wordsworth, "Resolution and Independence," *Norton Anthology of Poetry*, 3d ed. (New York and London, 1983), 547.

16. See Chinua Achebe and Dubem Okafor, eds., *Don't Let Him Die: An Anthology of Memorial Poems for Christopher Okigbo, 1932–1967*. With a preface by Chinua Achebe (Enugu, 1978). Contributors were from Nigeria, Africa, and different parts of the world. Many of them had never met Okigbo in life, but were inspired by the

distinctiveness of his poetry and the vitality of his personality in his poetry. The poet of destiny may be of a nation or nationality, but the very uniqueness of his commitment transcends national boundaries and makes the poet a citizen of the world.

17. There is also a remarkable similarity between the personal history, creative career, and death of Garcia Lorca, the young Spanish poet who died in the Spanish Civil War on the side of the Republicans, and Okigbo who died in the Nigerian Civil War. Both men were driven by the logic of their peculiar commitments and destinies to pay the final price. Okigbo admired Lorca's poetry exceedingly.